STAR WARS®
REBELLION

volume 2 THE AHAKISTA GAMBIT

THE REBELLION (From the Battle of Yavin to five years after) Open resistance begins to spread across the galaxy in protest of the Empire's tyranny. Rebel groups unite, and the Galactic Civil War begins. This era begins with the Rebel victory that secured the Death Star plans, and ends a year after the death of the Emperor high over the forest moon of Endor. This is the era in which the events in *A New Hope, The Empire Strikes Back,* and *Return of the Jedi* take place. The events in this story take place approximately nine months after the Battle of Yavin.

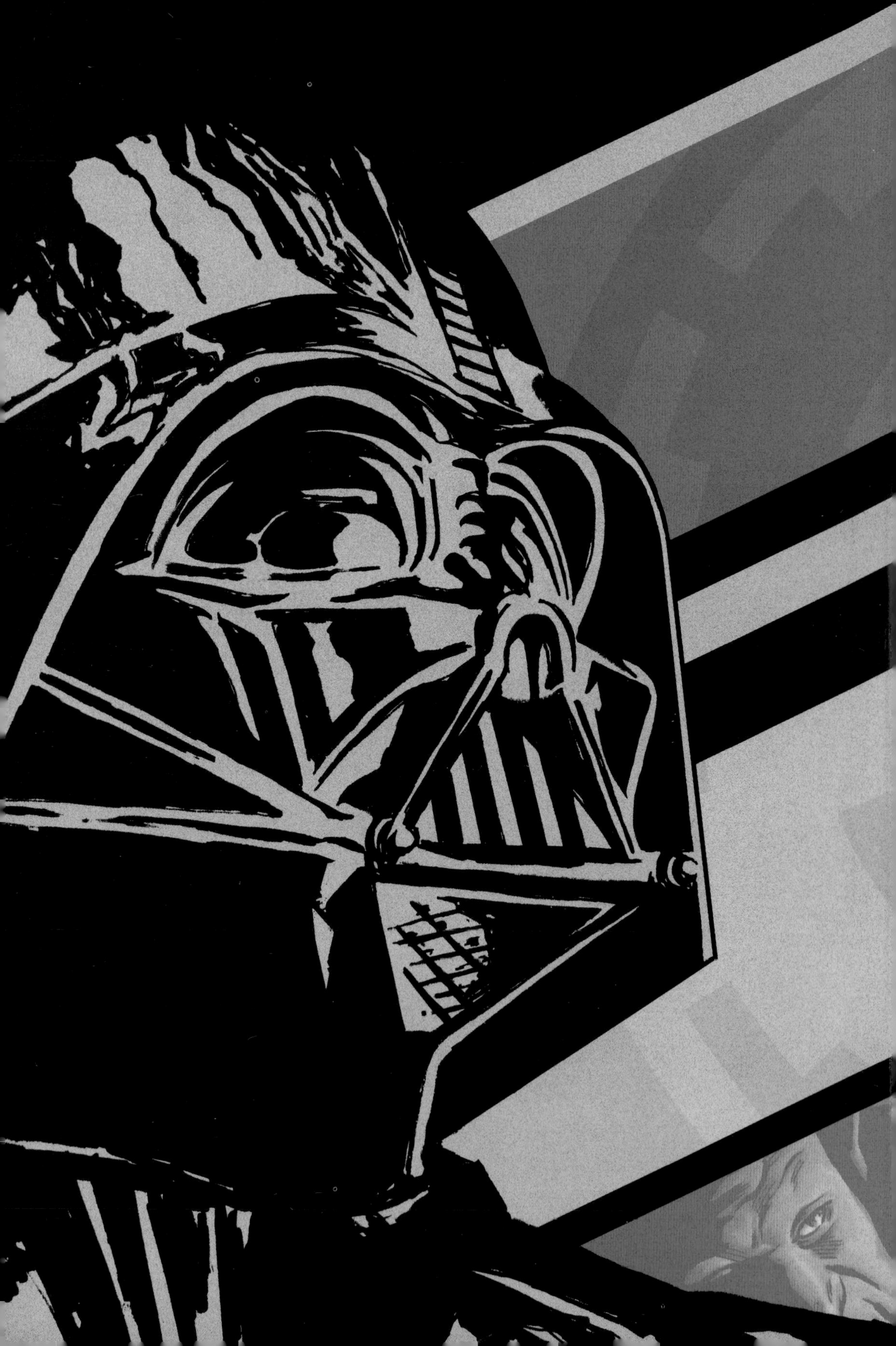

STAR·WARS®
REBELLION

volume 2

THE AHAKISTA GAMBIT

story BRANDON BADEAUX and ROB WILLIAMS

script ROB WILLIAMS

art MICHEL LACOMBE

colors WIL GLASS

lettering MICHAEL HEISLER

front cover art LUKE ROSS and WILL GLASS

back cover art RYAN SOOK

Dark Horse Books

publisher MIKE RICHARDSON

collection designer JOSHUA ELLIOTT

art director LIA RIBACCHI

assistant editor DAVE MARSHALL

editor JEREMY BARLOW

Special thanks to Elaine Mederer, Jann Moorhead, David Anderman, Leland Chee, Sue Rostoni, and Carol Roeder at Lucas Licensing

STAR WARS: REBELLION volume two

This volume collects issues six through ten of the Dark Horse comic-book series Star Wars: Rebellion.

Published by
Dark Horse Books
A division of Dark Horse Comics, Inc.
10956 SE Main Street
Milwaukie, OR 97222

darkhorse.com
starwars.com

To find a comics shop in your area, call the Comic Shop Locator Service toll-free at 1-888-266-4226

First edition: February 2008
ISBN: 978-1-59307-890-4

10 9 8 7 6 5 4 3 2 1

Printed in China

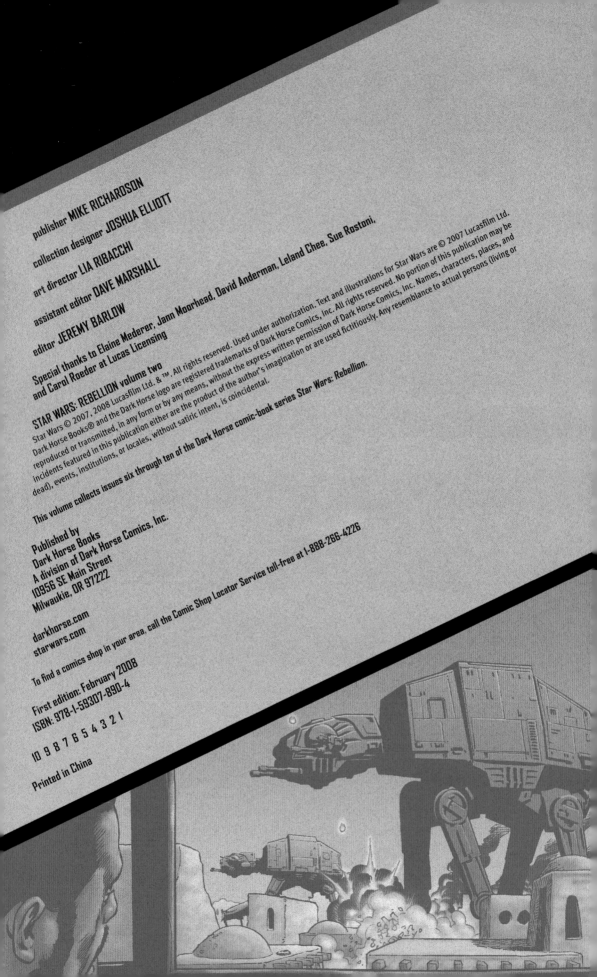

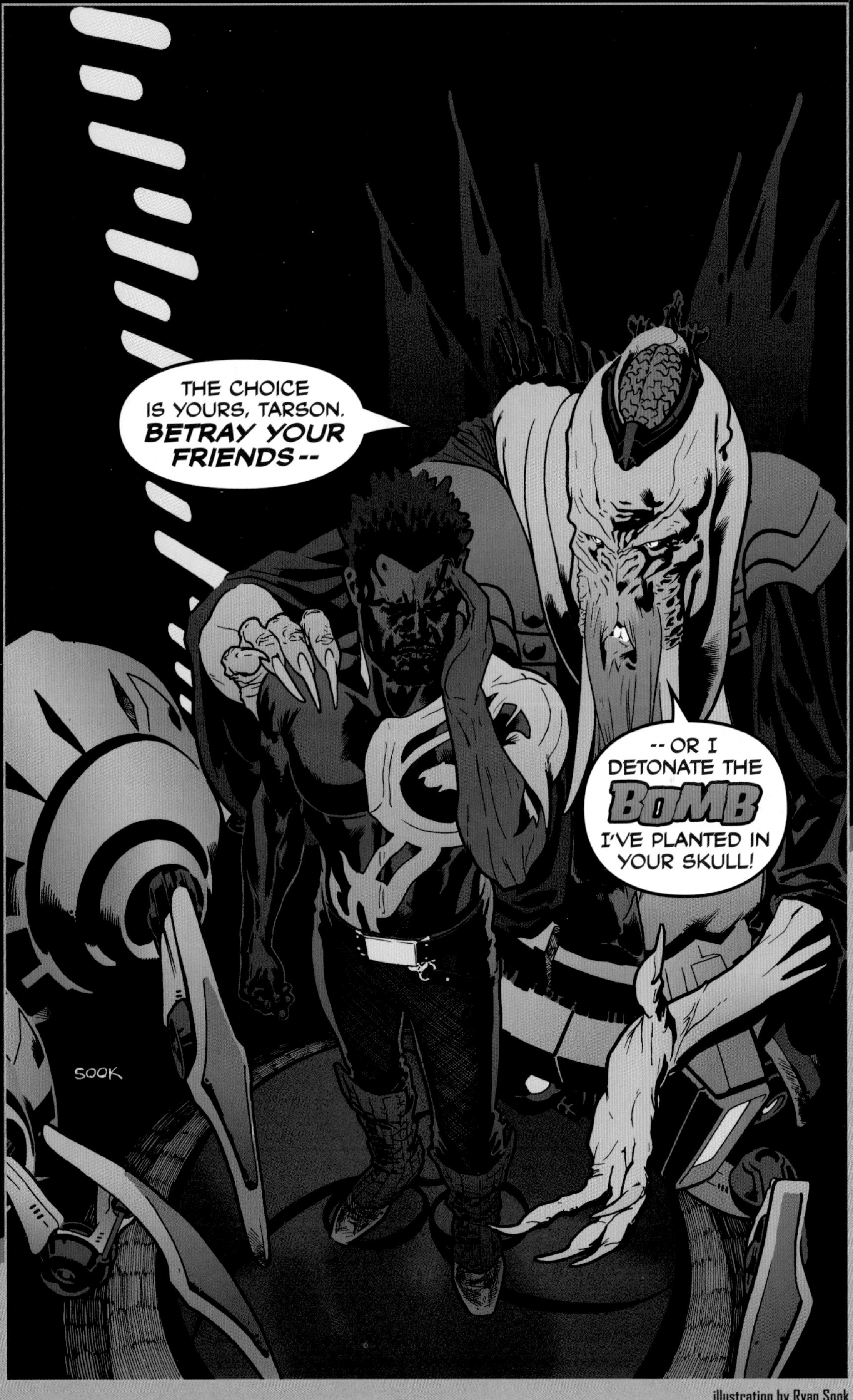
THE CHOICE IS YOURS, TARSON. BETRAY YOUR FRIENDS--
--OR I DETONATE THE BOMB I'VE PLANTED IN YOUR SKULL!
SOOK

illustration by Ryan Sook

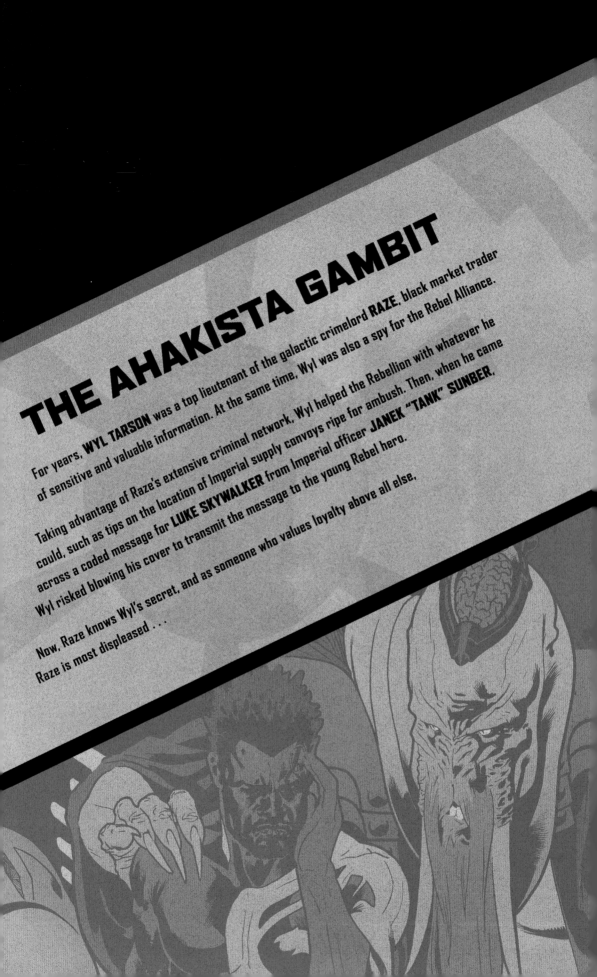

THE AHAKISTA GAMBIT

For years, **WYL TARSON** was a top lieutenant of the galactic crimelord **RAZE**, black market trader of sensitive and valuable information. At the same time, Wyl was also a spy for the Rebel Alliance.

Taking advantage of Raze's extensive criminal network, Wyl helped the Rebellion with whatever he could, such as tips on the location of Imperial supply convoys ripe for ambush. Then, when he came across a coded message for **LUKE SKYWALKER** from Imperial officer **JANEK "TANK" SUNBER**, Wyl risked blowing his cover to transmit the message to the young Rebel hero.

Now, Raze knows Wyl's secret, and as someone who values loyalty above all else, Raze is most displeased . . .

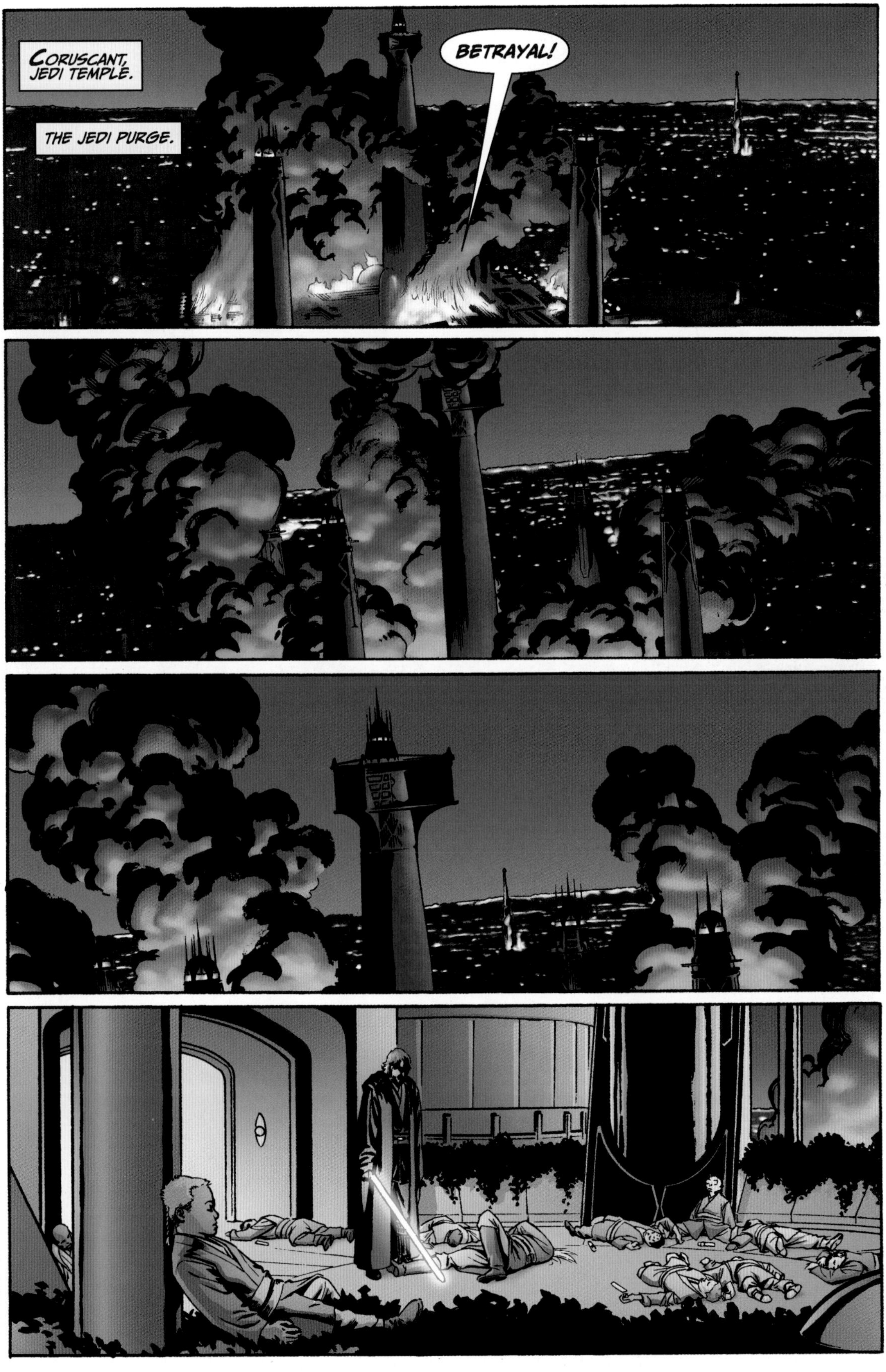
CORUSCANT, JEDI TEMPLE.
THE JEDI PURGE.
BETRAYAL!

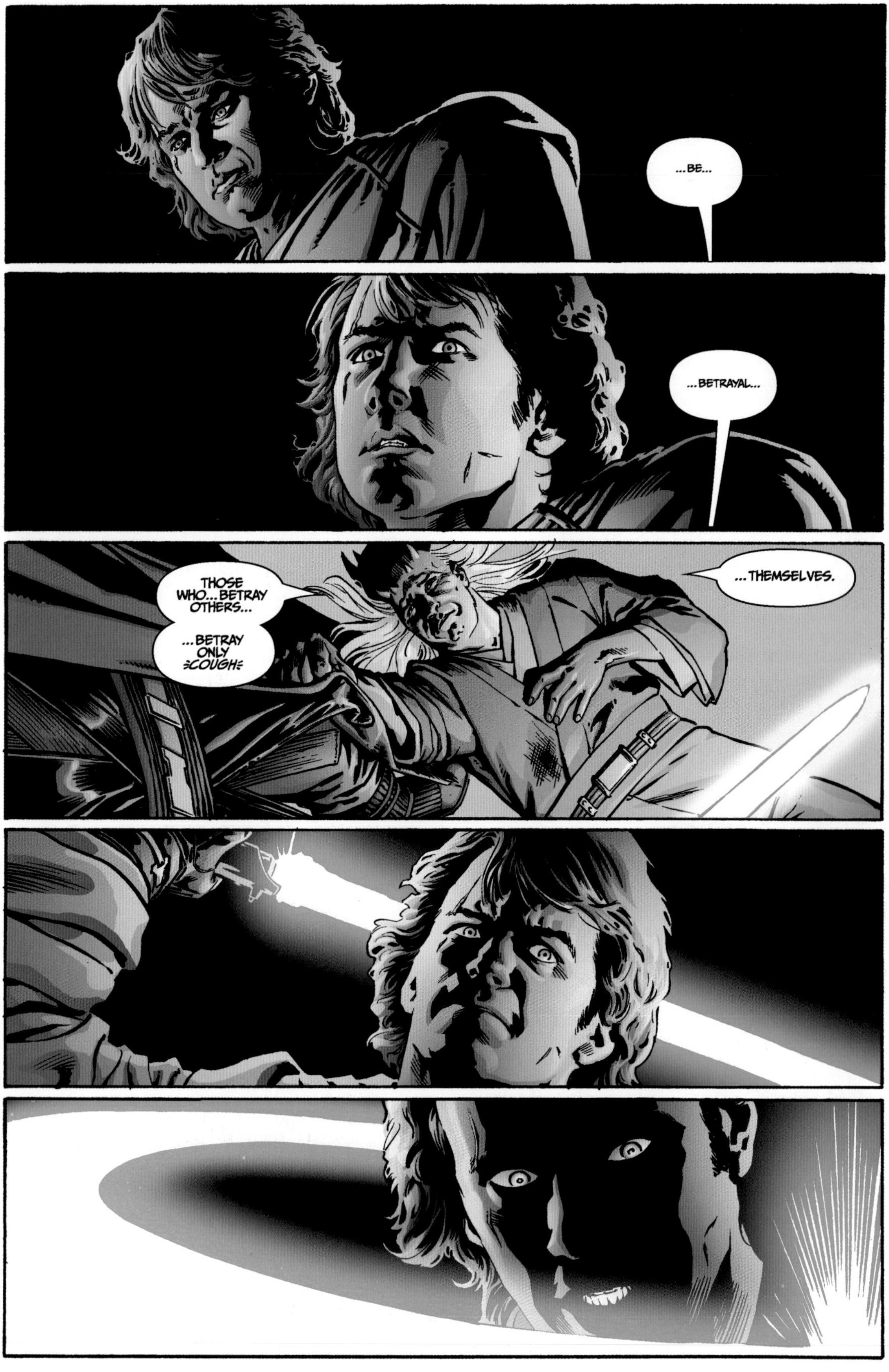
...BE...
...BETRAYAL...
THOSE WHO...BETRAY OTHERS...
...BETRAY ONLY *COUGH*
...THEMSELVES.

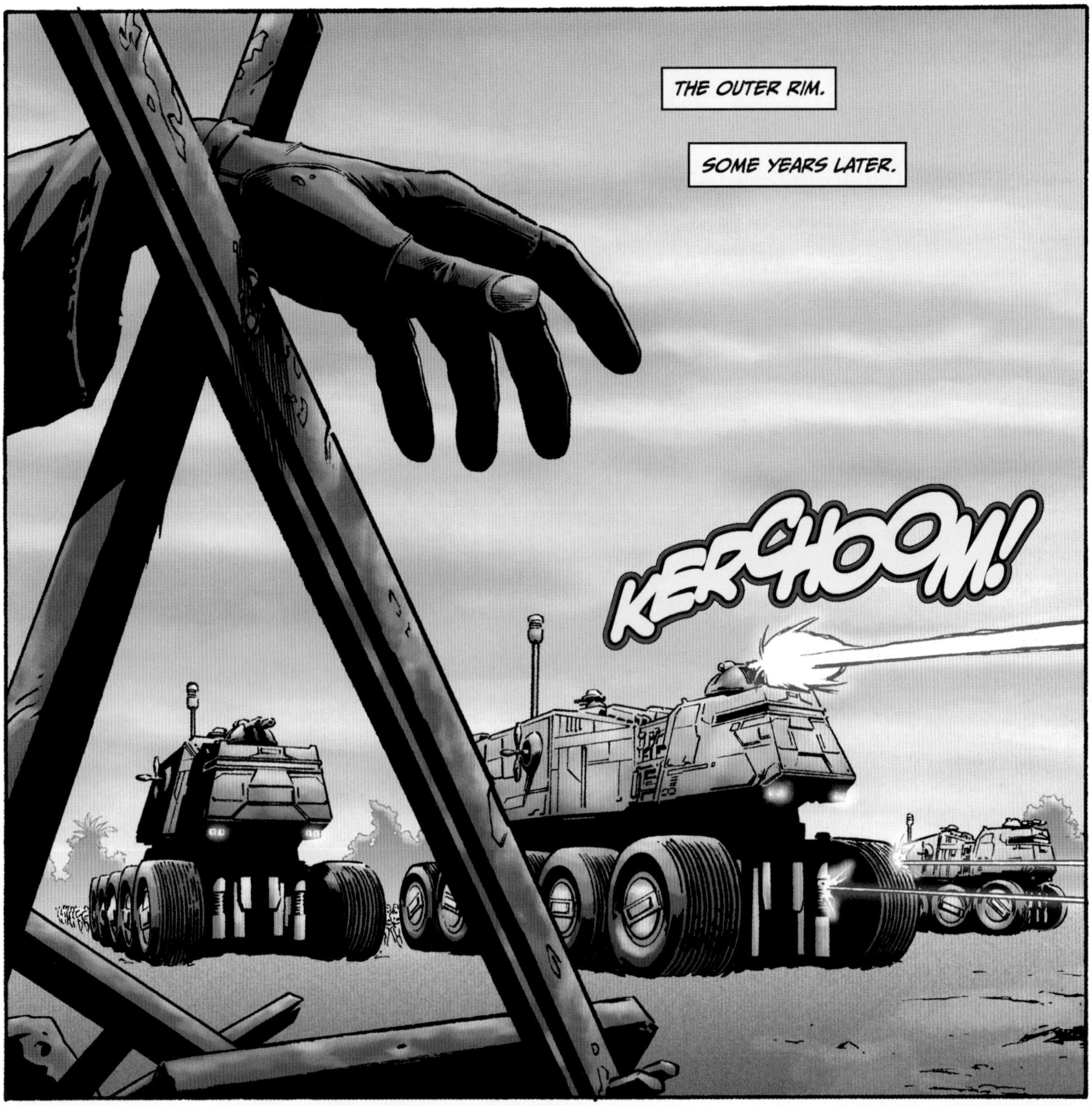
THE OUTER RIM.
SOME YEARS LATER.
KERCHOOM!

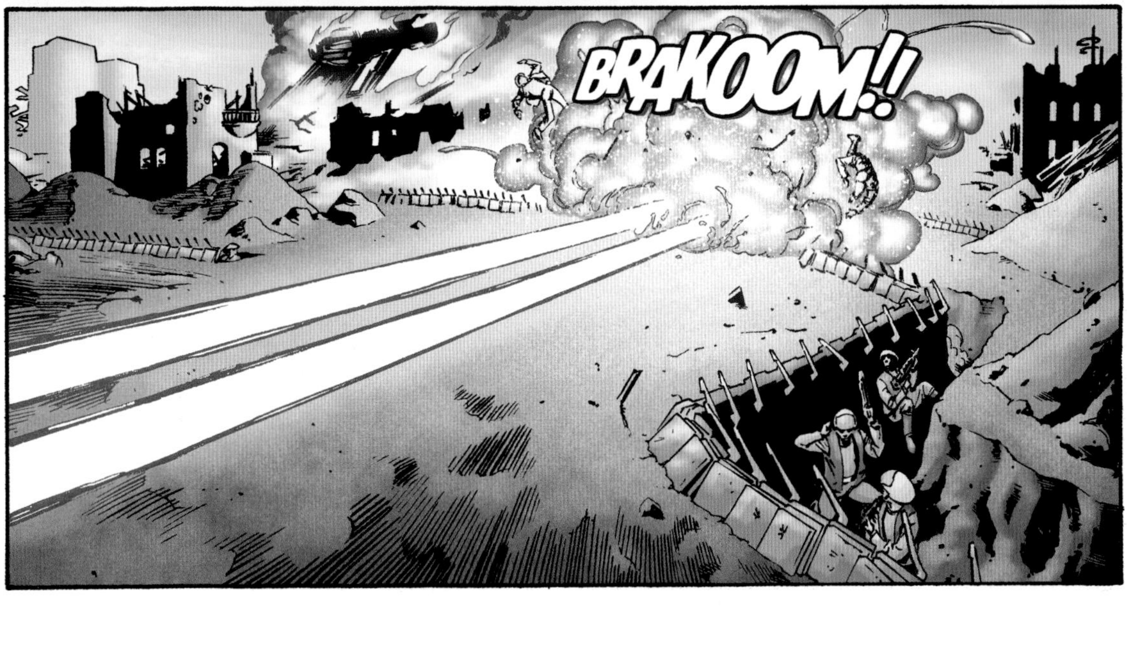
BRAKOOM!!

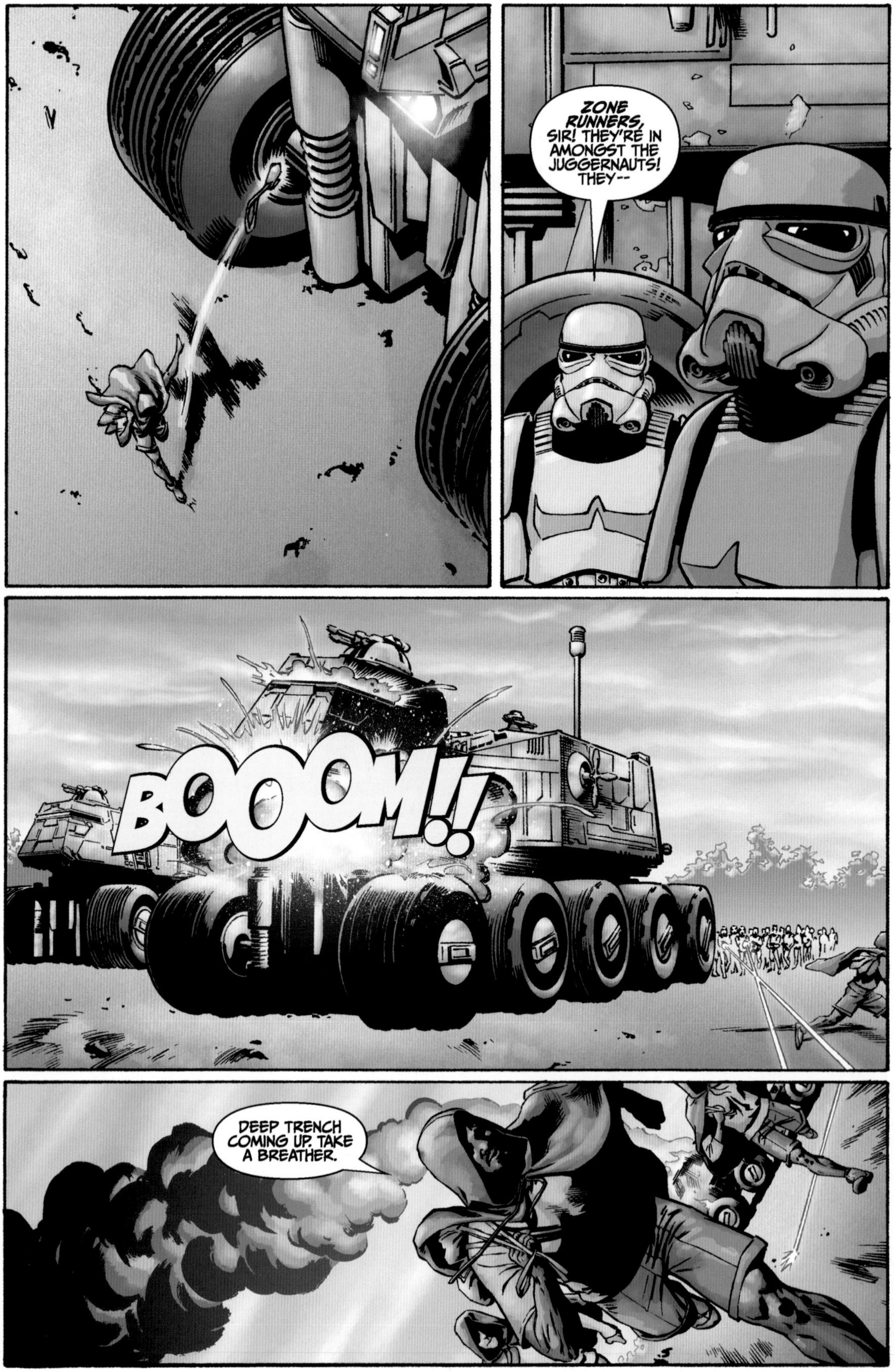
ZONE RUNNERS, SIR! THEY'RE IN AMONGST THE JUGGERNAUTS! THEY--
BOOOM!!
DEEP TRENCH COMING UP. TAKE A BREATHER.

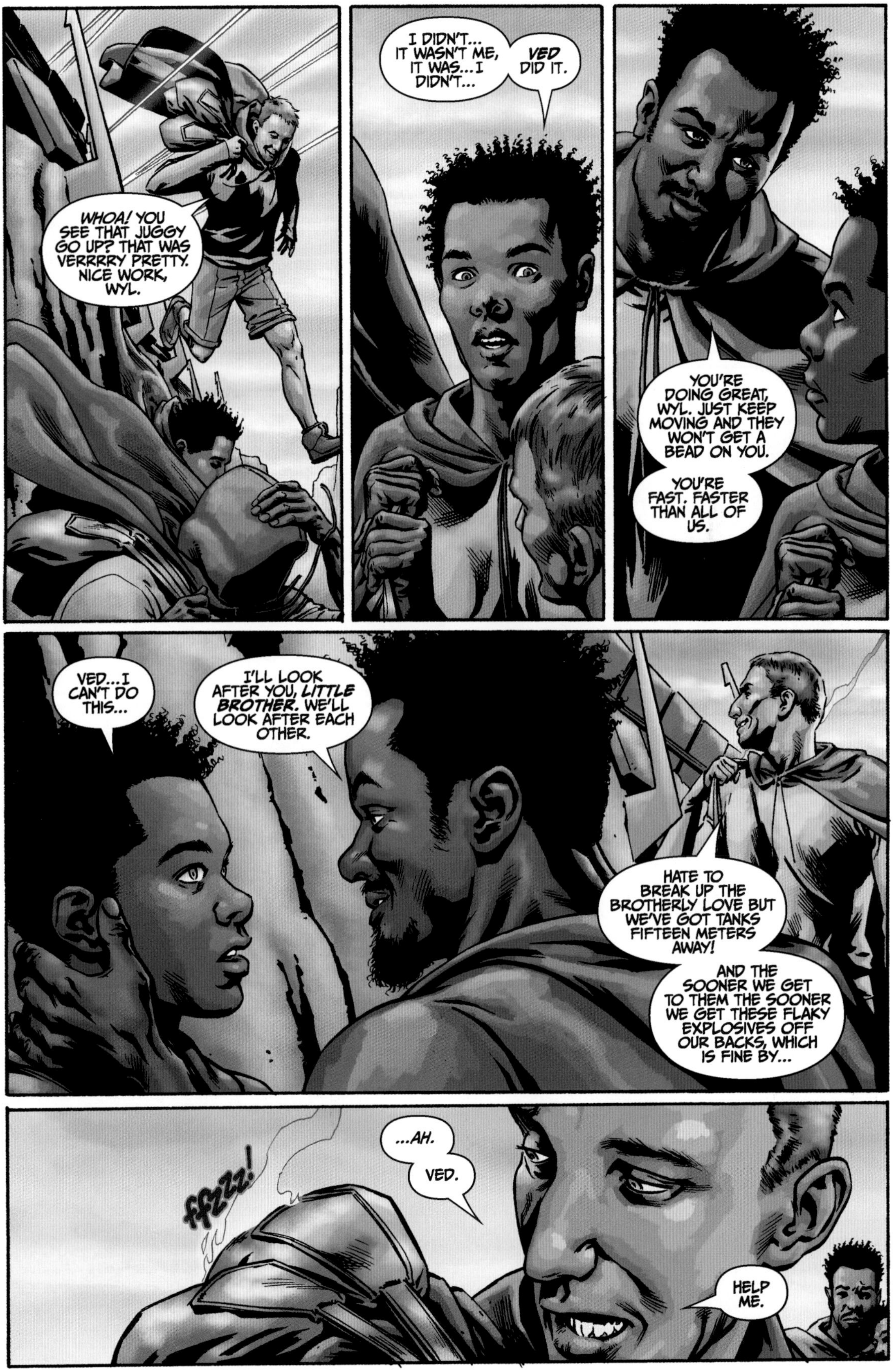
WHOA! YOU SEE THAT JUGGY GO UP? THAT WAS VERRRRY PRETTY. NICE WORK, WYL.
I DIDN'T... IT WASN'T ME, IT WAS...I DIDN'T...
VED DID IT.
YOU'RE DOING GREAT, WYL. JUST KEEP MOVING AND THEY WON'T GET A BEAD ON YOU.
YOU'RE FAST. FASTER THAN ALL OF US.
VED...I CAN'T DO THIS...
I'LL LOOK AFTER YOU, LITTLE BROTHER. WE'LL LOOK AFTER EACH OTHER.
HATE TO BREAK UP THE BROTHERLY LOVE BUT WE'VE GOT TANKS FIFTEEN METERS AWAY!
AND THE SOONER WE GET TO THEM THE SOONER WE GET THESE FLAKY EXPLOSIVES OFF OUR BACKS, WHICH IS FINE BY...
FFZZZ!
...AH.
VED.
HELP ME.

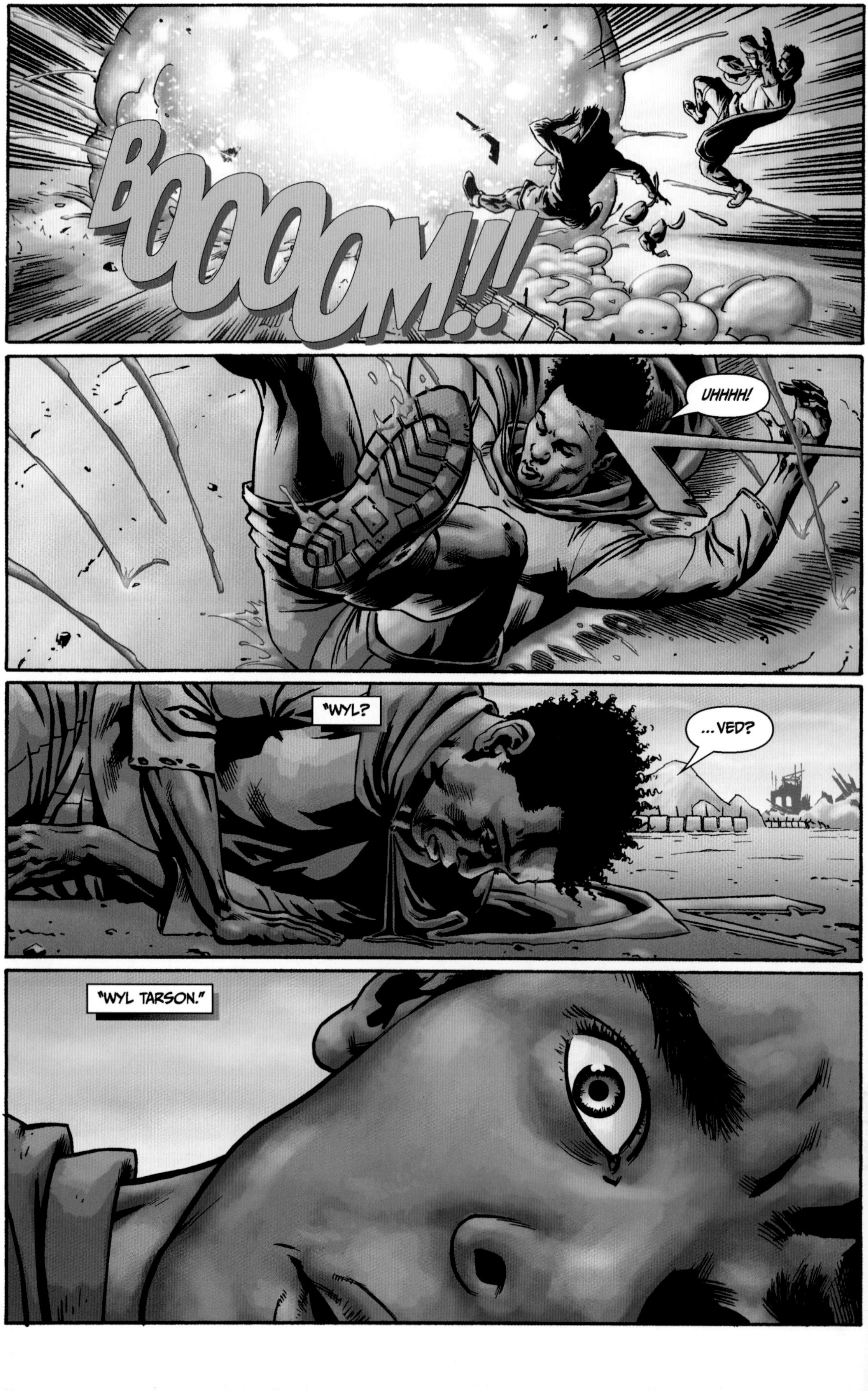
BOOOOM!!
UHHHH!
"WYL?
...VED?
"WYL TARSON."

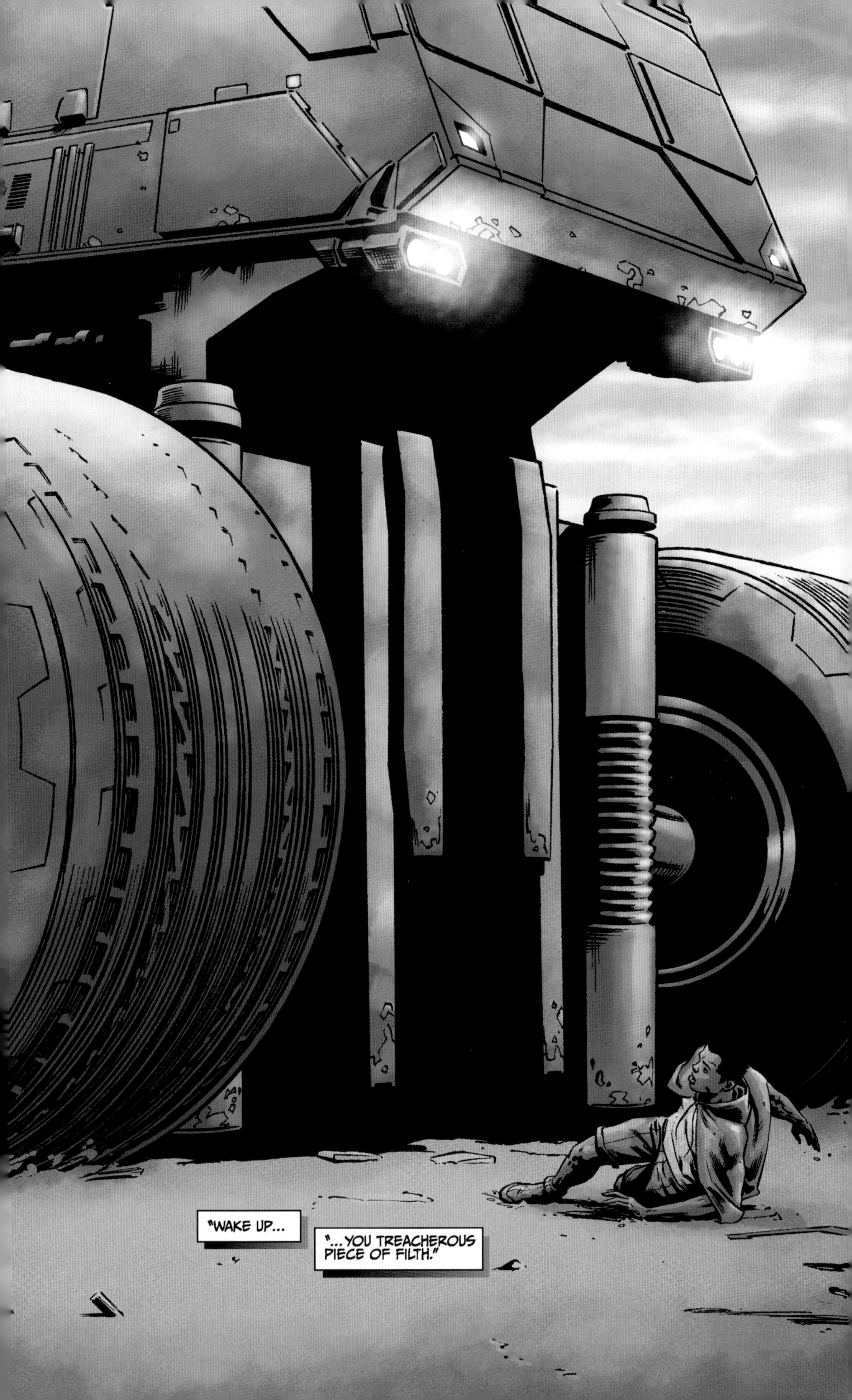
"WAKE UP...
"...YOU TREACHEROUS PIECE OF FILTH."

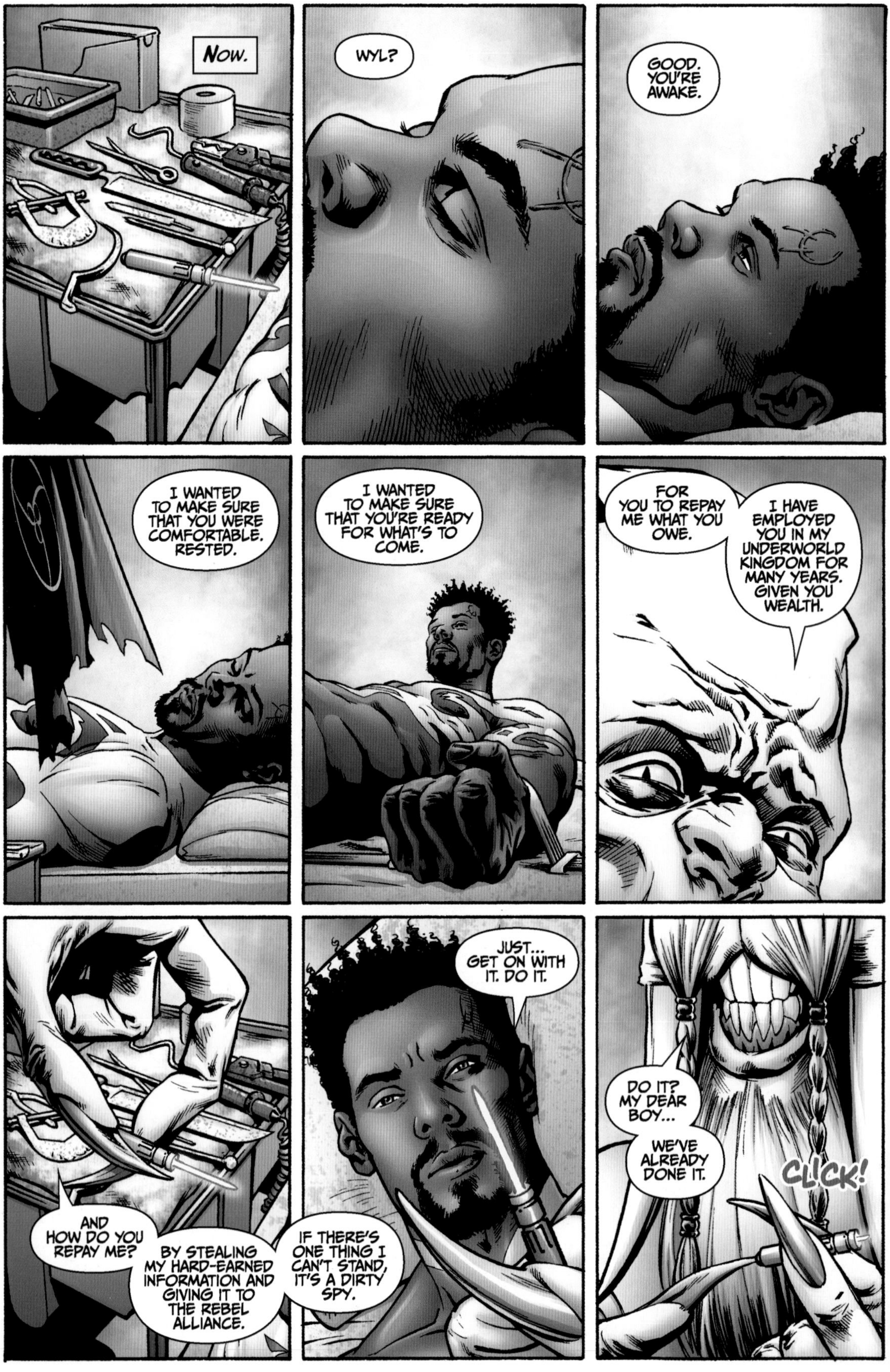
NOW.
WYL?
GOOD. YOU'RE AWAKE.
I WANTED TO MAKE SURE THAT YOU WERE COMFORTABLE. RESTED.
I WANTED TO MAKE SURE THAT YOU'RE READY FOR WHAT'S TO COME.
FOR YOU TO REPAY ME WHAT YOU OWE.
I HAVE EMPLOYED YOU IN MY UNDERWORLD KINGDOM FOR MANY YEARS. GIVEN YOU WEALTH.
AND HOW DO YOU REPAY ME?
BY STEALING MY HARD-EARNED INFORMATION AND GIVING IT TO THE REBEL ALLIANCE.
IF THERE'S ONE THING I CAN'T STAND, IT'S A DIRTY SPY.
JUST... GET ON WITH IT. DO IT.
DO IT? MY DEAR BOY...
WE'VE ALREADY DONE IT.
CLICK!

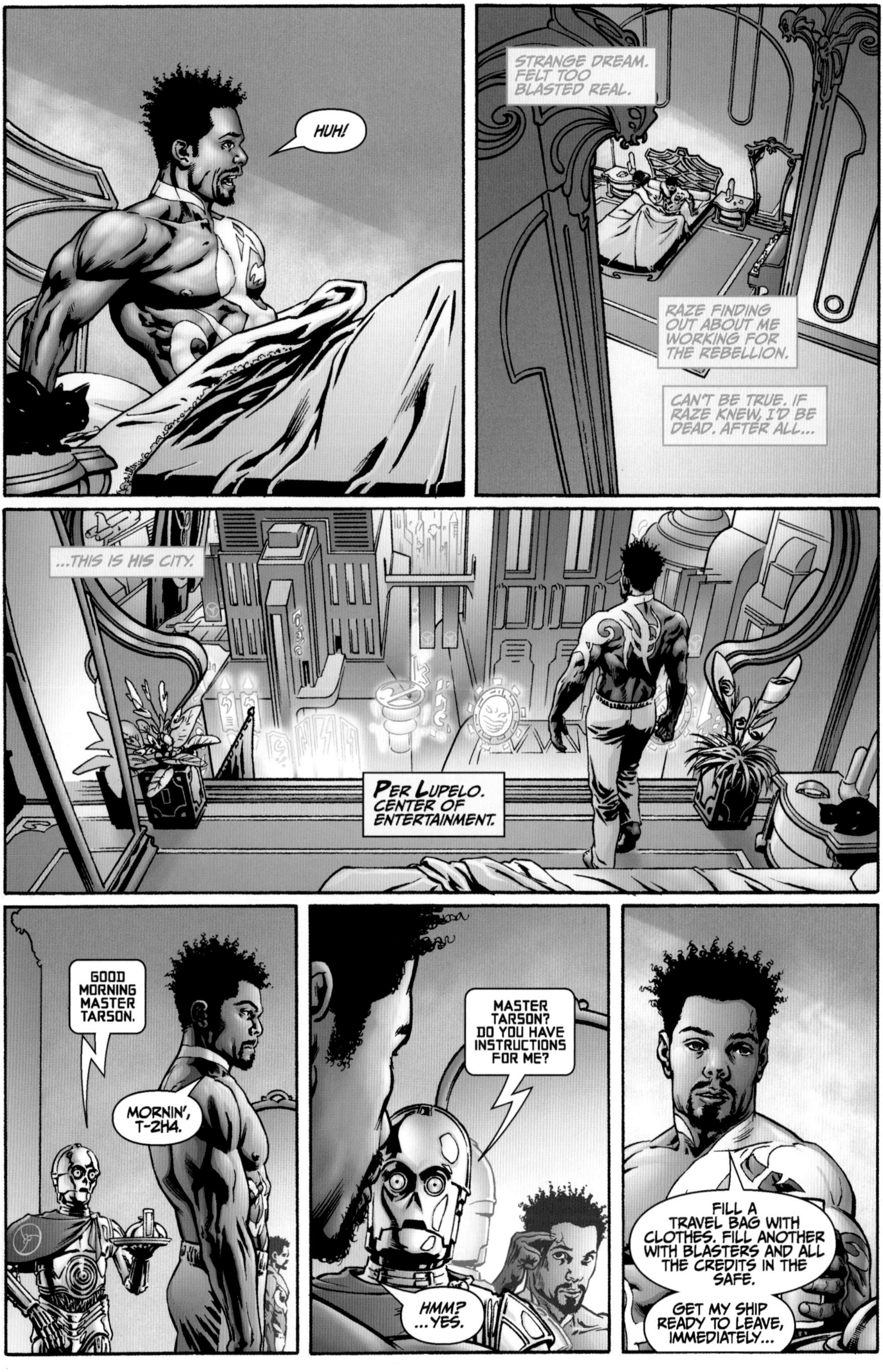
HUH!
STRANGE DREAM. FELT TOO BLASTED REAL.
RAZE FINDING OUT ABOUT ME WORKING FOR THE REBELLION.
CAN'T BE TRUE. IF RAZE KNEW, I'D BE DEAD. AFTER ALL...
...THIS IS HIS CITY.
PER LUPELO. CENTER OF ENTERTAINMENT.
GOOD MORNING MASTER TARSON.
MORNIN', T-2H4.
MASTER TARSON? DO YOU HAVE INSTRUCTIONS FOR ME?
HMM? ...YES.
FILL A TRAVEL BAG WITH CLOTHES. FILL ANOTHER WITH BLASTERS AND ALL THE CREDITS IN THE SAFE.
GET MY SHIP READY TO LEAVE, IMMEDIATELY...

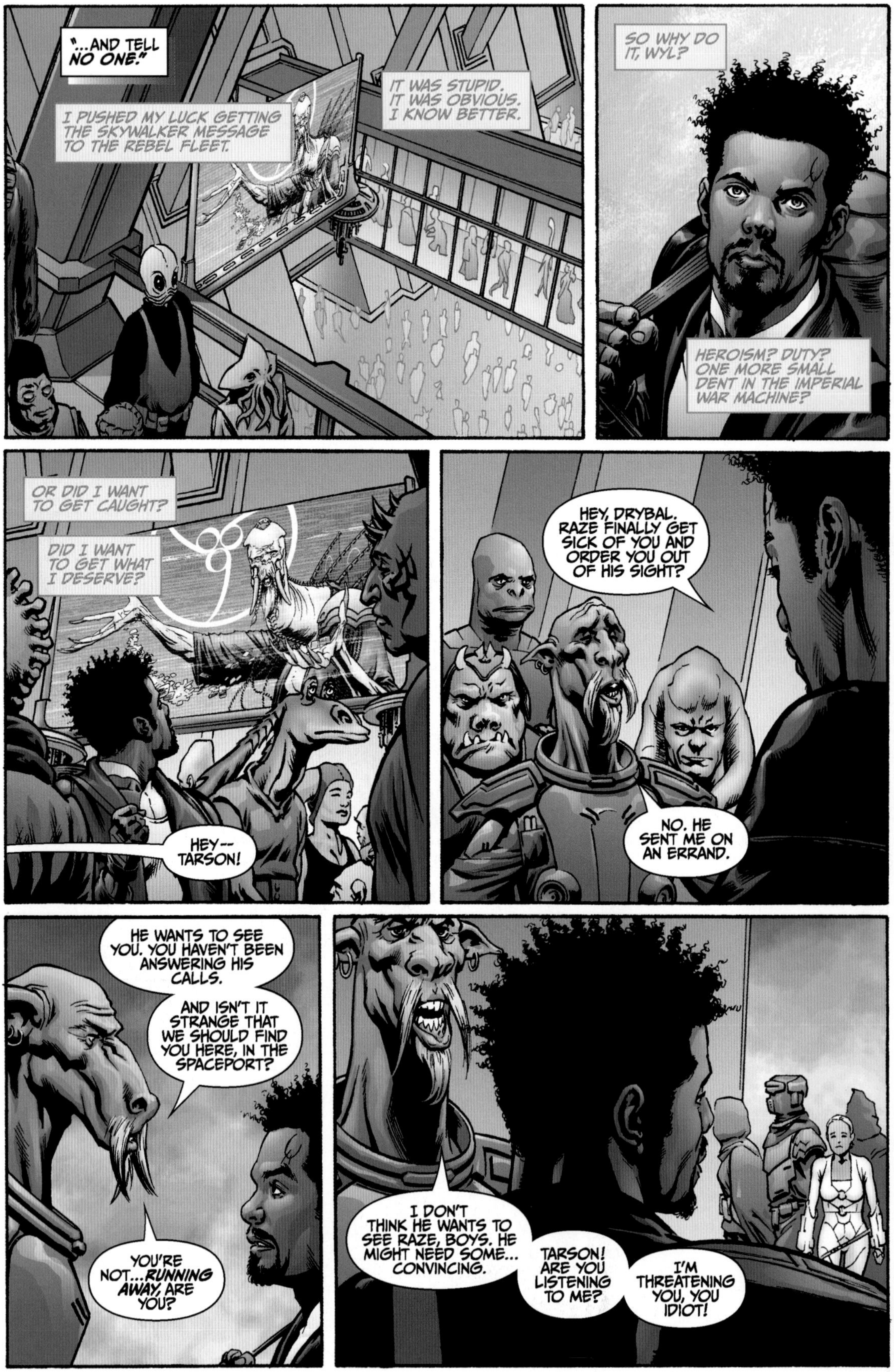
"...AND TELL NO ONE."
I PUSHED MY LUCK GETTING THE SKYWALKER MESSAGE TO THE REBEL FLEET.
IT WAS STUPID. IT WAS OBVIOUS. I KNOW BETTER.
SO WHY DO IT, WYL?
HEROISM? DUTY? ONE MORE SMALL DENT IN THE IMPERIAL WAR MACHINE?
OR DID I WANT TO GET CAUGHT?
DID I WANT TO GET WHAT I DESERVE?
HEY--TARSON!
HEY, DRYBAL. RAZE FINALLY GET SICK OF YOU AND ORDER YOU OUT OF HIS SIGHT?
NO. HE SENT ME ON AN ERRAND.
HE WANTS TO SEE YOU. YOU HAVEN'T BEEN ANSWERING HIS CALLS.
AND ISN'T IT STRANGE THAT WE SHOULD FIND YOU HERE, IN THE SPACEPORT?
YOU'RE NOT...RUNNING AWAY, ARE YOU?
I DON'T THINK HE WANTS TO SEE RAZE, BOYS. HE MIGHT NEED SOME... CONVINCING.
TARSON! ARE YOU LISTENING TO ME?
I'M THREATENING YOU, YOU IDIOT!

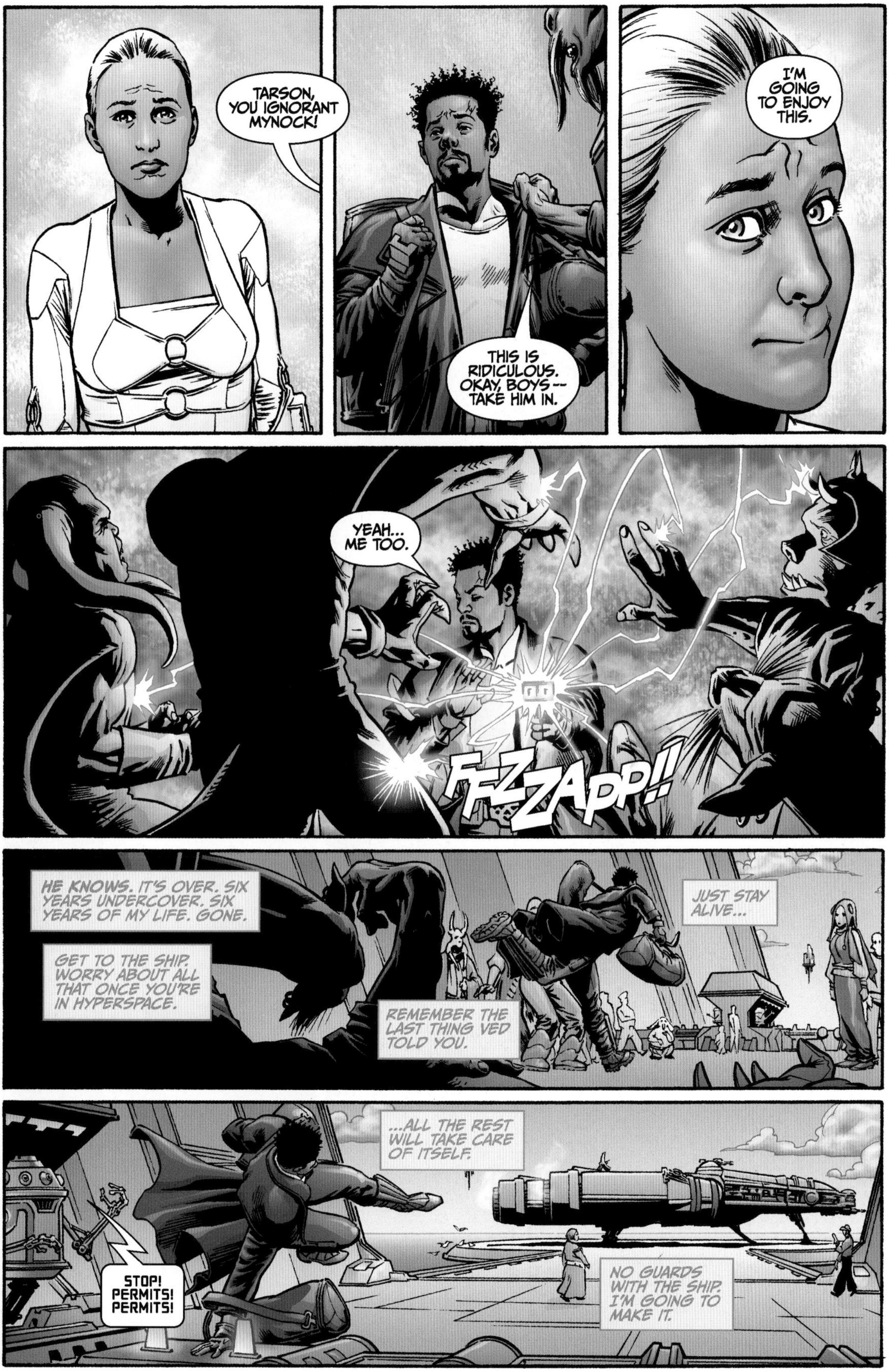
TARSON, YOU IGNORANT MYNOCK!
THIS IS RIDICULOUS. OKAY, BOYS-- TAKE HIM IN.
I'M GOING TO ENJOY THIS.
YEAH... ME TOO.
FFZZAPP!!
HE KNOWS. IT'S OVER. SIX YEARS UNDERCOVER. SIX YEARS OF MY LIFE. GONE.
GET TO THE SHIP. WORRY ABOUT ALL THAT ONCE YOU'RE IN HYPERSPACE.
REMEMBER THE LAST THING VED TOLD YOU.
JUST STAY ALIVE...
...ALL THE REST WILL TAKE CARE OF ITSELF.
STOP! PERMITS! PERMITS!
NO GUARDS WITH THE SHIP. I'M GOING TO MAKE IT.

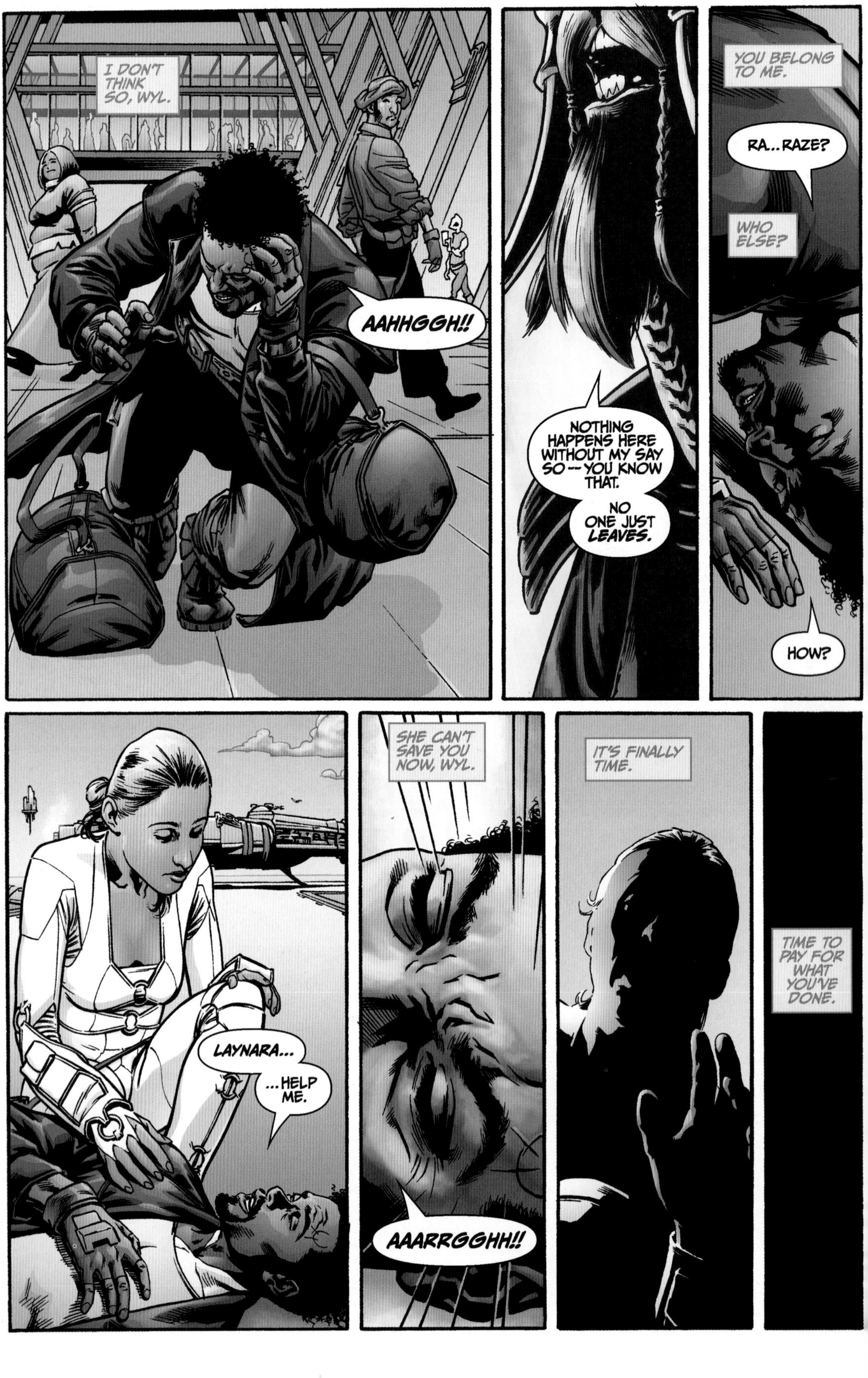
I DON'T THINK SO, WYL.
AAHHGGH!!
NOTHING HAPPENS HERE WITHOUT MY SAY SO--YOU KNOW THAT.
NO ONE JUST LEAVES.
YOU BELONG TO ME.
RA...RAZE?
WHO ELSE?
HOW?
LAYNARA...
...HELP ME.
SHE CAN'T SAVE YOU NOW, WYL.
AAARRGGHH!!
IT'S FINALLY TIME.
TIME TO PAY FOR WHAT YOU'VE DONE.

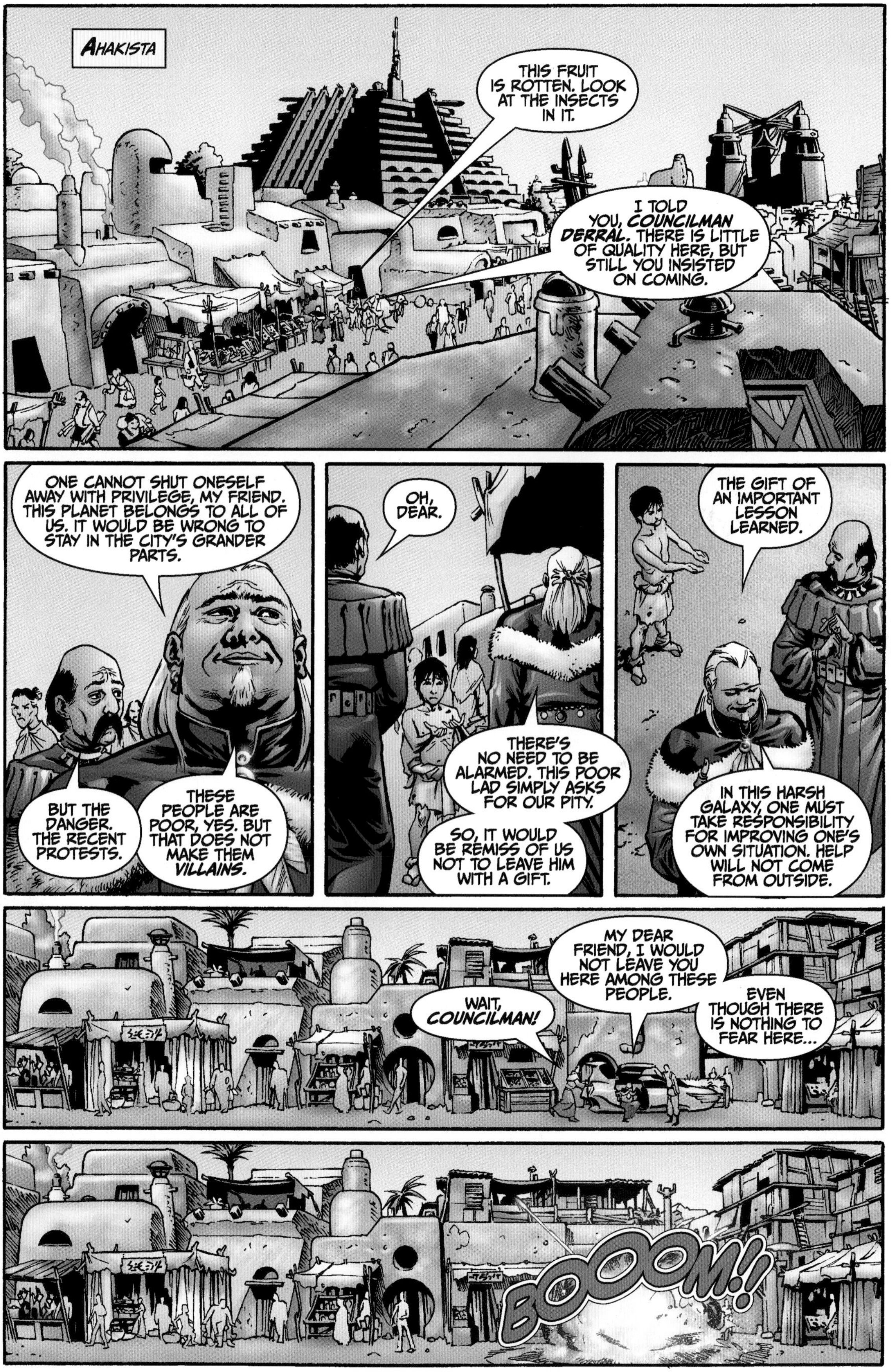
AHAKISTA
THIS FRUIT IS ROTTEN. LOOK AT THE INSECTS IN IT.
I TOLD YOU, COUNCILMAN DERRAL. THERE IS LITTLE OF QUALITY HERE, BUT STILL YOU INSISTED ON COMING.
ONE CANNOT SHUT ONESELF AWAY WITH PRIVILEGE, MY FRIEND. THIS PLANET BELONGS TO ALL OF US. IT WOULD BE WRONG TO STAY IN THE CITY'S GRANDER PARTS.
BUT THE DANGER. THE RECENT PROTESTS.
THESE PEOPLE ARE POOR, YES. BUT THAT DOES NOT MAKE THEM VILLAINS.
OH, DEAR.
THERE'S NO NEED TO BE ALARMED. THIS POOR LAD SIMPLY ASKS FOR OUR PITY.
SO, IT WOULD BE REMISS OF US NOT TO LEAVE HIM WITH A GIFT.
THE GIFT OF AN IMPORTANT LESSON LEARNED.
IN THIS HARSH GALAXY, ONE MUST TAKE RESPONSIBILITY FOR IMPROVING ONE'S OWN SITUATION. HELP WILL NOT COME FROM OUTSIDE.
WAIT, COUNCILMAN!
MY DEAR FRIEND, I WOULD NOT LEAVE YOU HERE AMONG THESE PEOPLE.
EVEN THOUGH THERE IS NOTHING TO FEAR HERE...
BOOOOM!!

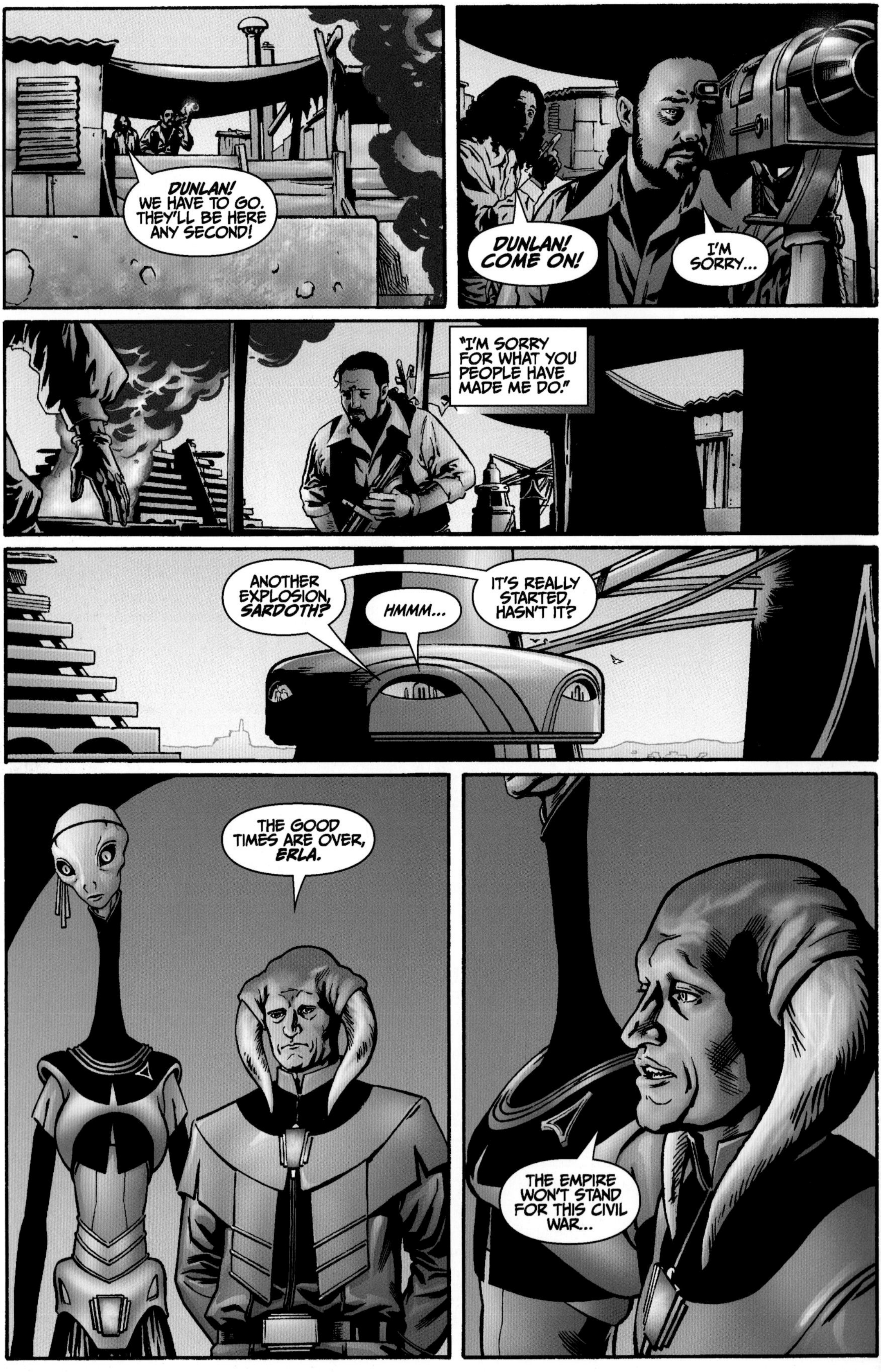
DUNLAN! WE HAVE TO GO. THEY'LL BE HERE ANY SECOND!
DUNLAN! COME ON!
I'M SORRY...
"I'M SORRY FOR WHAT YOU PEOPLE HAVE MADE ME DO."
ANOTHER EXPLOSION, SARDOTH?
HMMM...
IT'S REALLY STARTED, HASN'T IT?
THE GOOD TIMES ARE OVER, ERLA.
THE EMPIRE WON'T STAND FOR THIS CIVIL WAR...

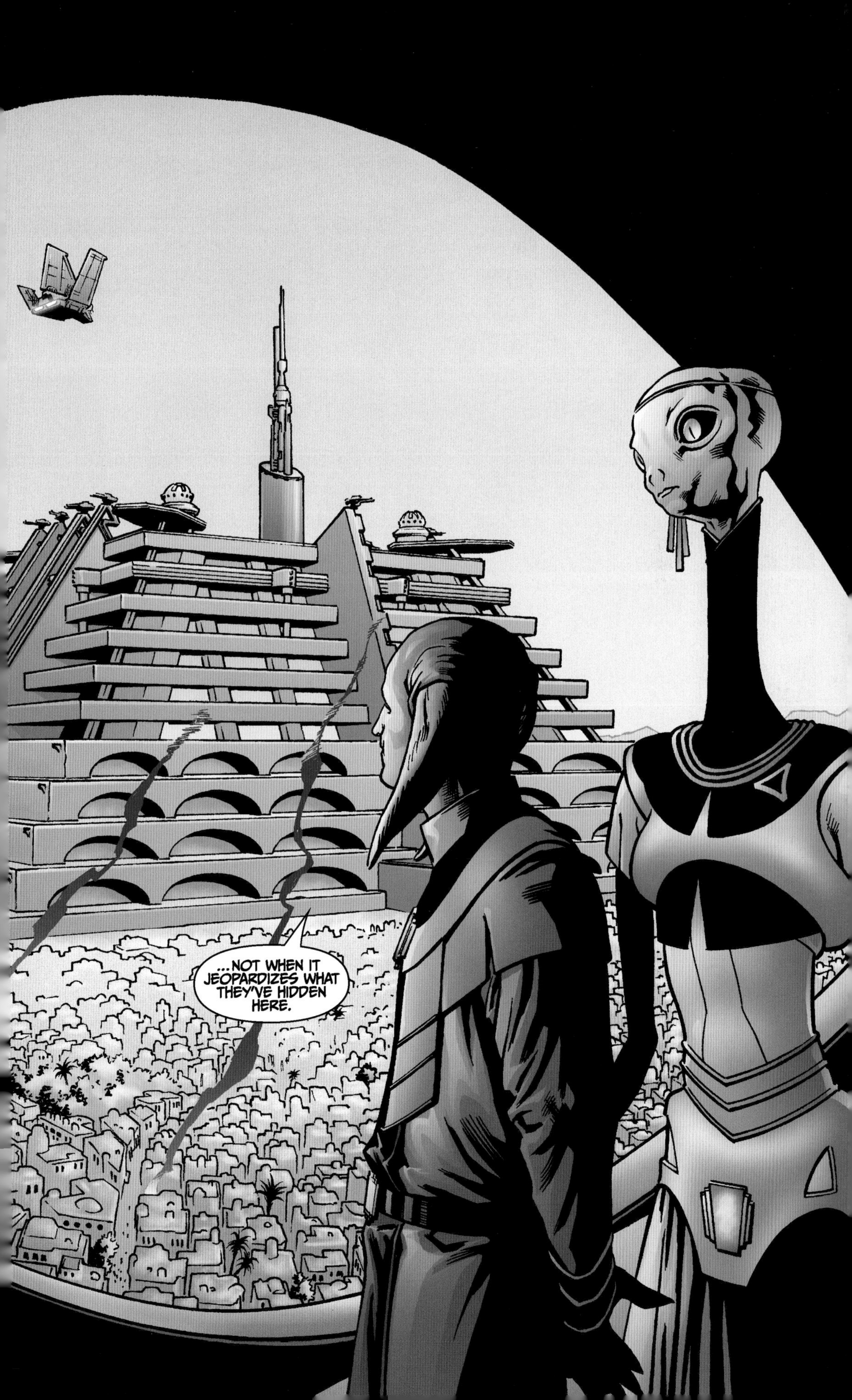
...NOT WHEN IT JEOPARDIZES WHAT THEY'VE HIDDEN HERE.

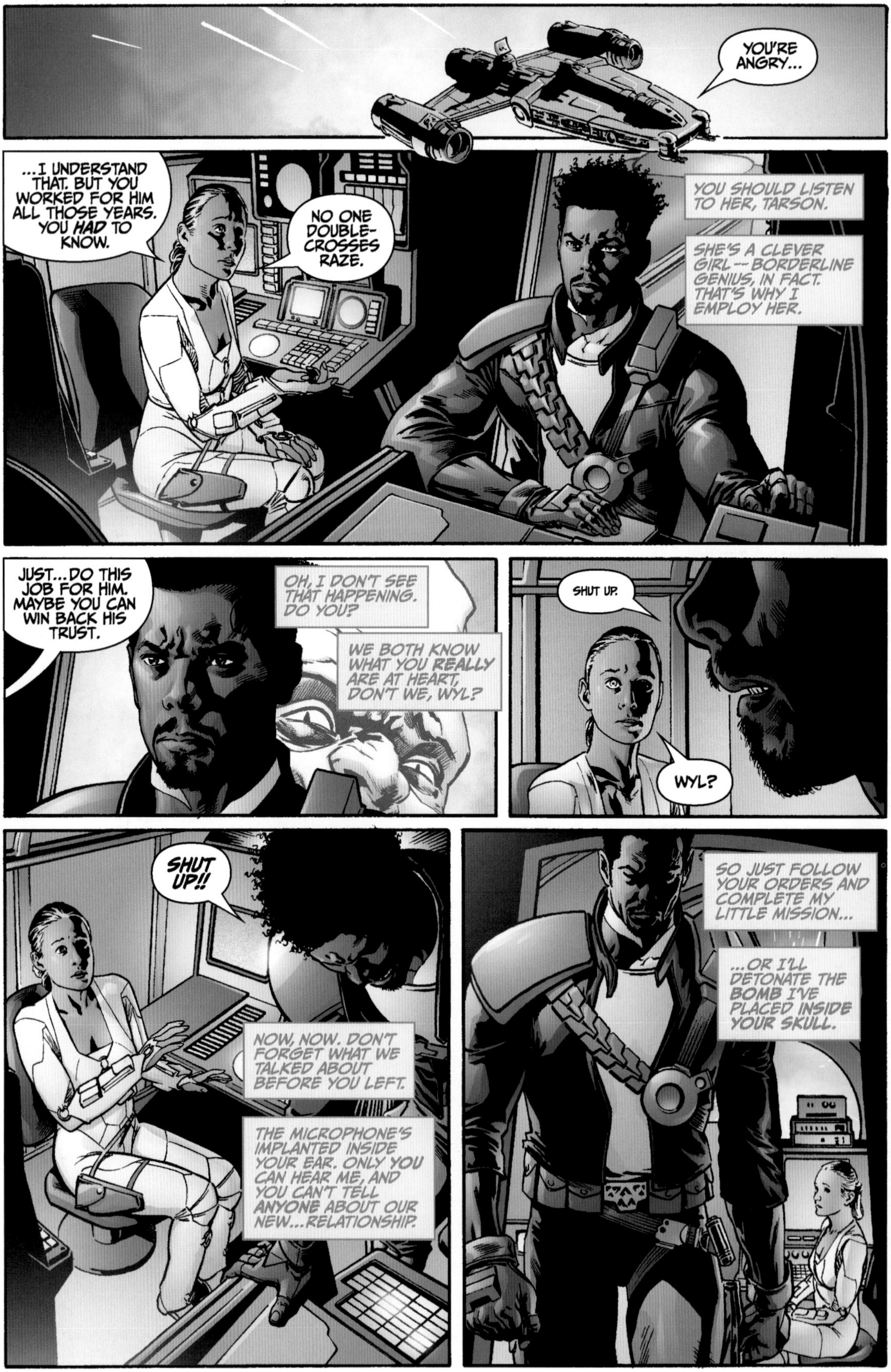
YOU'RE ANGRY...
...I UNDERSTAND THAT. BUT YOU WORKED FOR HIM ALL THOSE YEARS. YOU *HAD* TO KNOW.
NO ONE DOUBLE-CROSSES RAZE.
YOU SHOULD LISTEN TO HER, TARSON.
SHE'S A CLEVER GIRL--BORDERLINE GENIUS, IN FACT. THAT'S WHY I EMPLOY HER.
JUST...DO THIS JOB FOR HIM. MAYBE YOU CAN WIN BACK HIS TRUST.
OH, I DON'T SEE THAT HAPPENING. DO YOU?
WE BOTH KNOW WHAT YOU *REALLY* ARE AT HEART, DON'T WE, WYL?
SHUT UP.
WYL?
SHUT UP!!
NOW, NOW. DON'T FORGET WHAT WE TALKED ABOUT BEFORE YOU LEFT.
THE MICROPHONE'S IMPLANTED INSIDE YOUR EAR. ONLY YOU CAN HEAR ME, AND YOU CAN'T TELL **ANYONE** ABOUT OUR NEW...RELATIONSHIP.
SO JUST FOLLOW YOUR ORDERS AND COMPLETE MY LITTLE MISSION...
...OR I'LL DETONATE THE **BOMB** I'VE PLACED INSIDE YOUR **SKULL**.

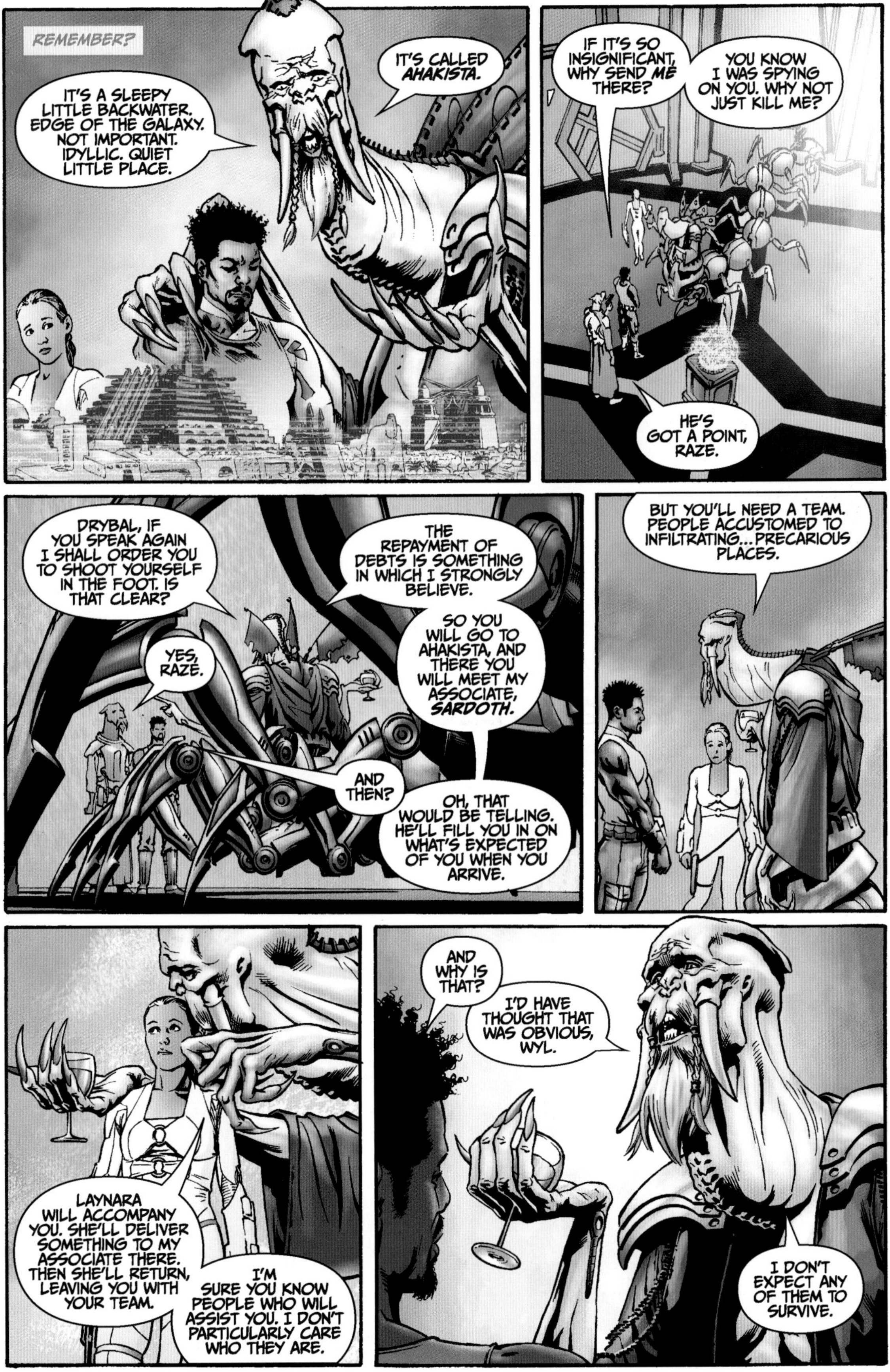
REMEMBER?
IT'S A SLEEPY LITTLE BACKWATER. EDGE OF THE GALAXY. NOT IMPORTANT. IDYLLIC. QUIET LITTLE PLACE.
IT'S CALLED AHAKISTA.
IF IT'S SO INSIGNIFICANT, WHY SEND ME THERE?
YOU KNOW I WAS SPYING ON YOU. WHY NOT JUST KILL ME?
HE'S GOT A POINT, RAZE.
DRYBAL, IF YOU SPEAK AGAIN I SHALL ORDER YOU TO SHOOT YOURSELF IN THE FOOT. IS THAT CLEAR?
YES, RAZE.
THE REPAYMENT OF DEBTS IS SOMETHING IN WHICH I STRONGLY BELIEVE.
SO YOU WILL GO TO AHAKISTA, AND THERE YOU WILL MEET MY ASSOCIATE, SARDOTH.
AND THEN?
OH, THAT WOULD BE TELLING. HE'LL FILL YOU IN ON WHAT'S EXPECTED OF YOU WHEN YOU ARRIVE.
BUT YOU'LL NEED A TEAM. PEOPLE ACCUSTOMED TO INFILTRATING... PRECARIOUS PLACES.
LAYNARA WILL ACCOMPANY YOU. SHE'LL DELIVER SOMETHING TO MY ASSOCIATE THERE. THEN SHE'LL RETURN, LEAVING YOU WITH YOUR TEAM.
I'M SURE YOU KNOW PEOPLE WHO WILL ASSIST YOU. I DON'T PARTICULARLY CARE WHO THEY ARE.
AND WHY IS THAT?
I'D HAVE THOUGHT THAT WAS OBVIOUS, WYL.
I DON'T EXPECT ANY OF THEM TO SURVIVE.

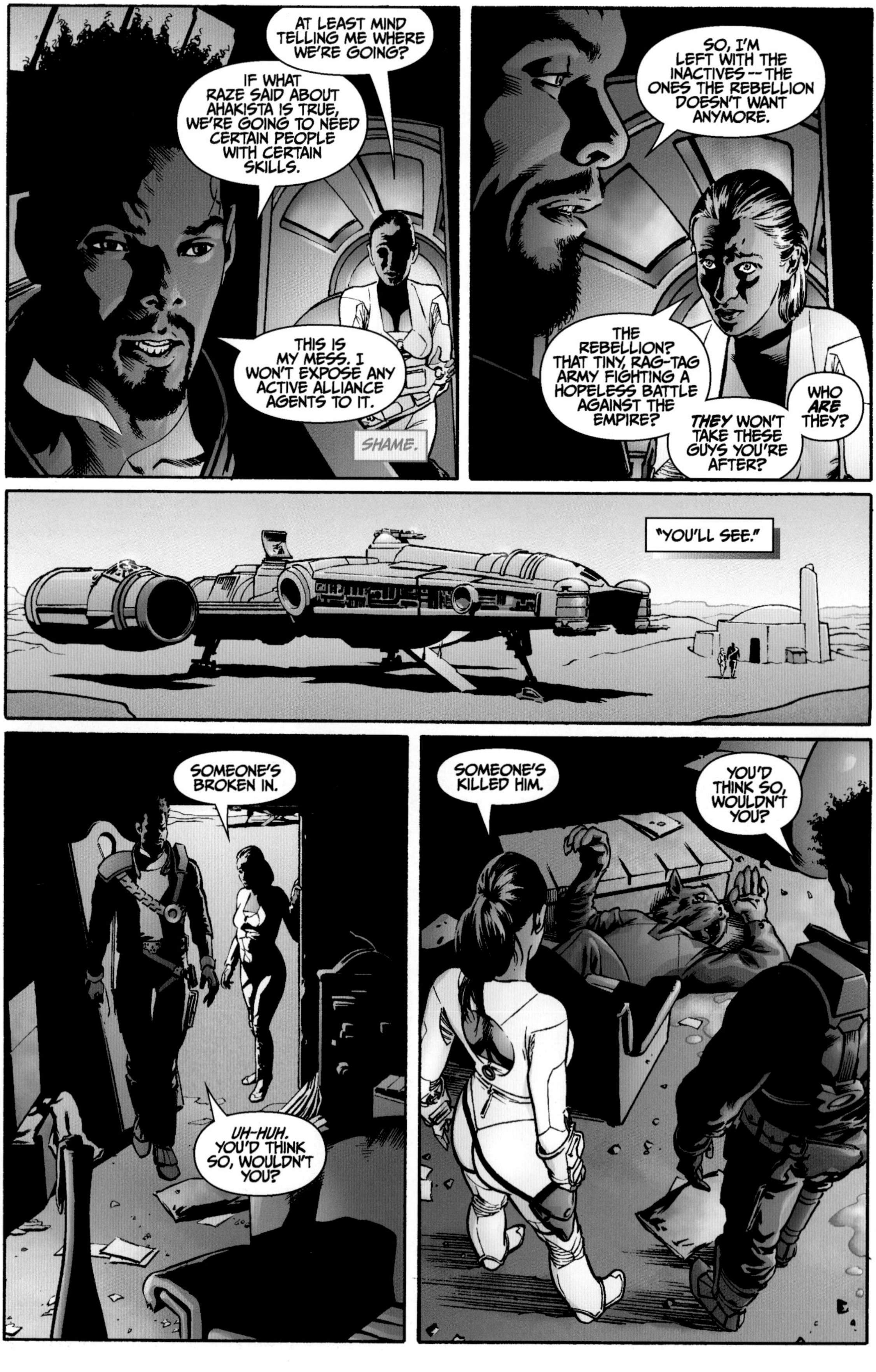
AT LEAST MIND TELLING ME WHERE WE'RE GOING?
IF WHAT RAZE SAID ABOUT AHAKISTA IS TRUE, WE'RE GOING TO NEED CERTAIN PEOPLE WITH CERTAIN SKILLS.
THIS IS MY MESS. I WON'T EXPOSE ANY ACTIVE ALLIANCE AGENTS TO IT.
SHAME.
SO, I'M LEFT WITH THE INACTIVES -- THE ONES THE REBELLION DOESN'T WANT ANYMORE.
THE REBELLION? THAT TINY, RAG-TAG ARMY FIGHTING A HOPELESS BATTLE AGAINST THE EMPIRE?
WHO ARE THEY?
THEY WON'T TAKE THESE GUYS YOU'RE AFTER?
"YOU'LL SEE."
SOMEONE'S BROKEN IN.
UH-HUH. YOU'D THINK SO, WOULDN'T YOU?
SOMEONE'S KILLED HIM.
YOU'D THINK SO, WOULDN'T YOU?

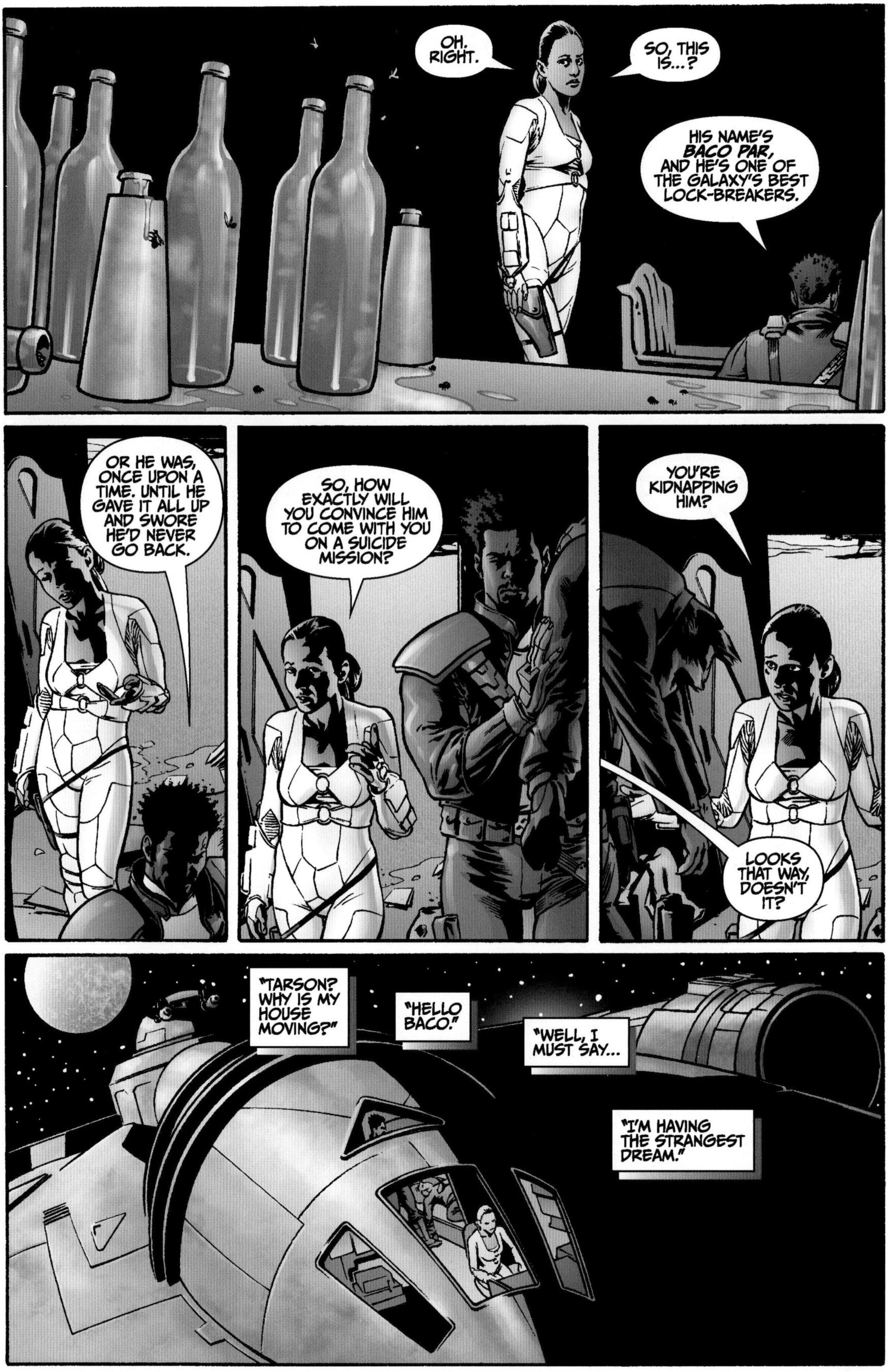
OH. RIGHT.
SO, THIS IS...?
HIS NAME'S BACO PAR, AND HE'S ONE OF THE GALAXY'S BEST LOCK-BREAKERS.
OR HE WAS, ONCE UPON A TIME. UNTIL HE GAVE IT ALL UP AND SWORE HE'D NEVER GO BACK.
SO, HOW EXACTLY WILL YOU CONVINCE HIM TO COME WITH YOU ON A SUICIDE MISSION?
YOU'RE KIDNAPPING HIM?
LOOKS THAT WAY, DOESN'T IT?
"TARSON? WHY IS MY HOUSE MOVING?"
"HELLO BACO."
"WELL, I MUST SAY...
"I'M HAVING THE STRANGEST DREAM."

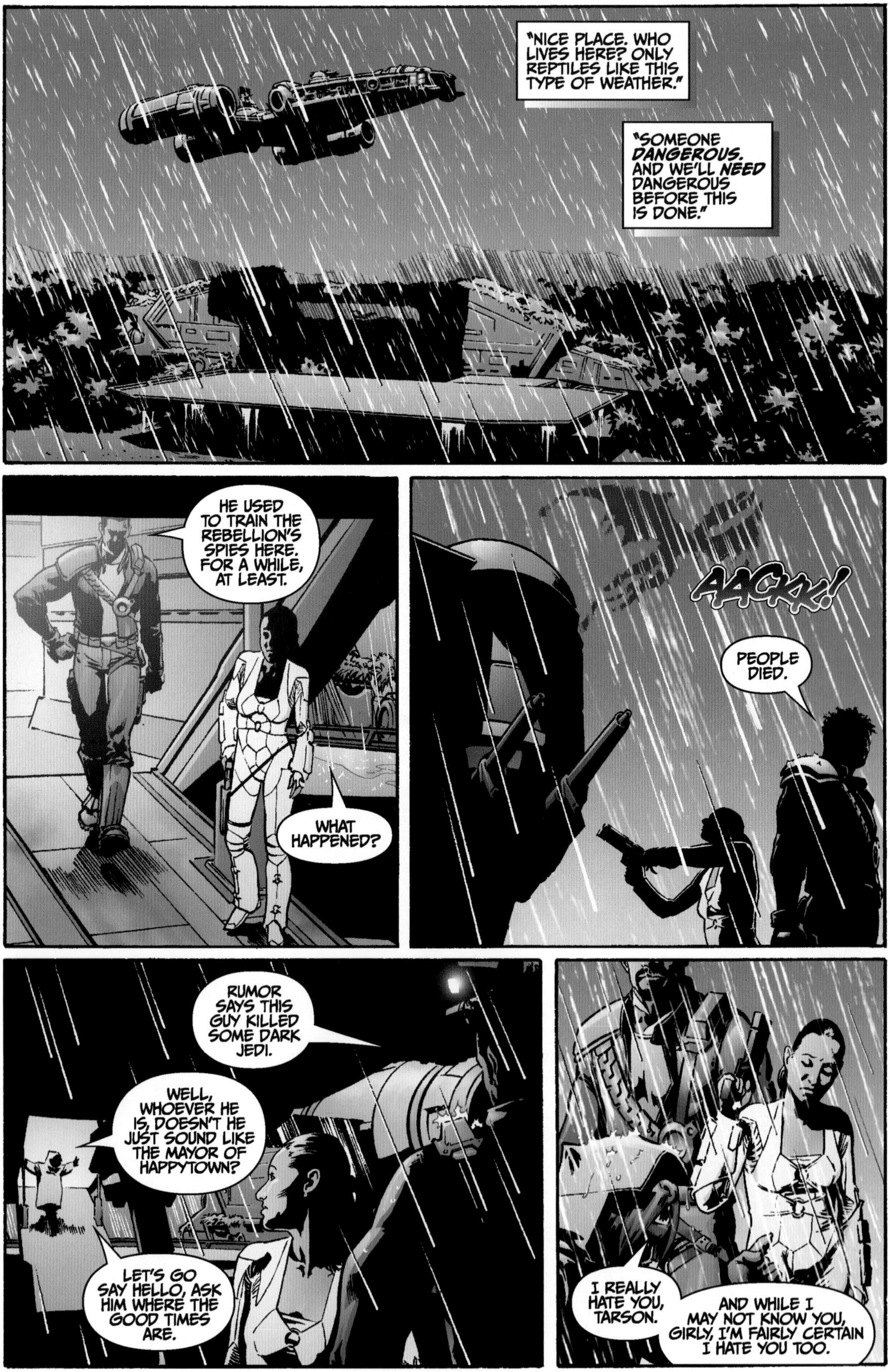
"NICE PLACE. WHO LIVES HERE? ONLY REPTILES LIKE THIS TYPE OF WEATHER."
"SOMEONE DANGEROUS. AND WE'LL NEED DANGEROUS BEFORE THIS IS DONE."
HE USED TO TRAIN THE REBELLION'S SPIES HERE. FOR A WHILE, AT LEAST.
WHAT HAPPENED?
AACKK!
PEOPLE DIED.
RUMOR SAYS THIS GUY KILLED SOME DARK JEDI.
WELL, WHOEVER HE IS, DOESN'T HE JUST SOUND LIKE THE MAYOR OF HAPPYTOWN?
LET'S GO SAY HELLO, ASK HIM WHERE THE GOOD TIMES ARE.
I REALLY HATE YOU, TARSON.
AND WHILE I MAY NOT KNOW YOU, GIRLY, I'M FAIRLY CERTAIN I HATE YOU TOO.

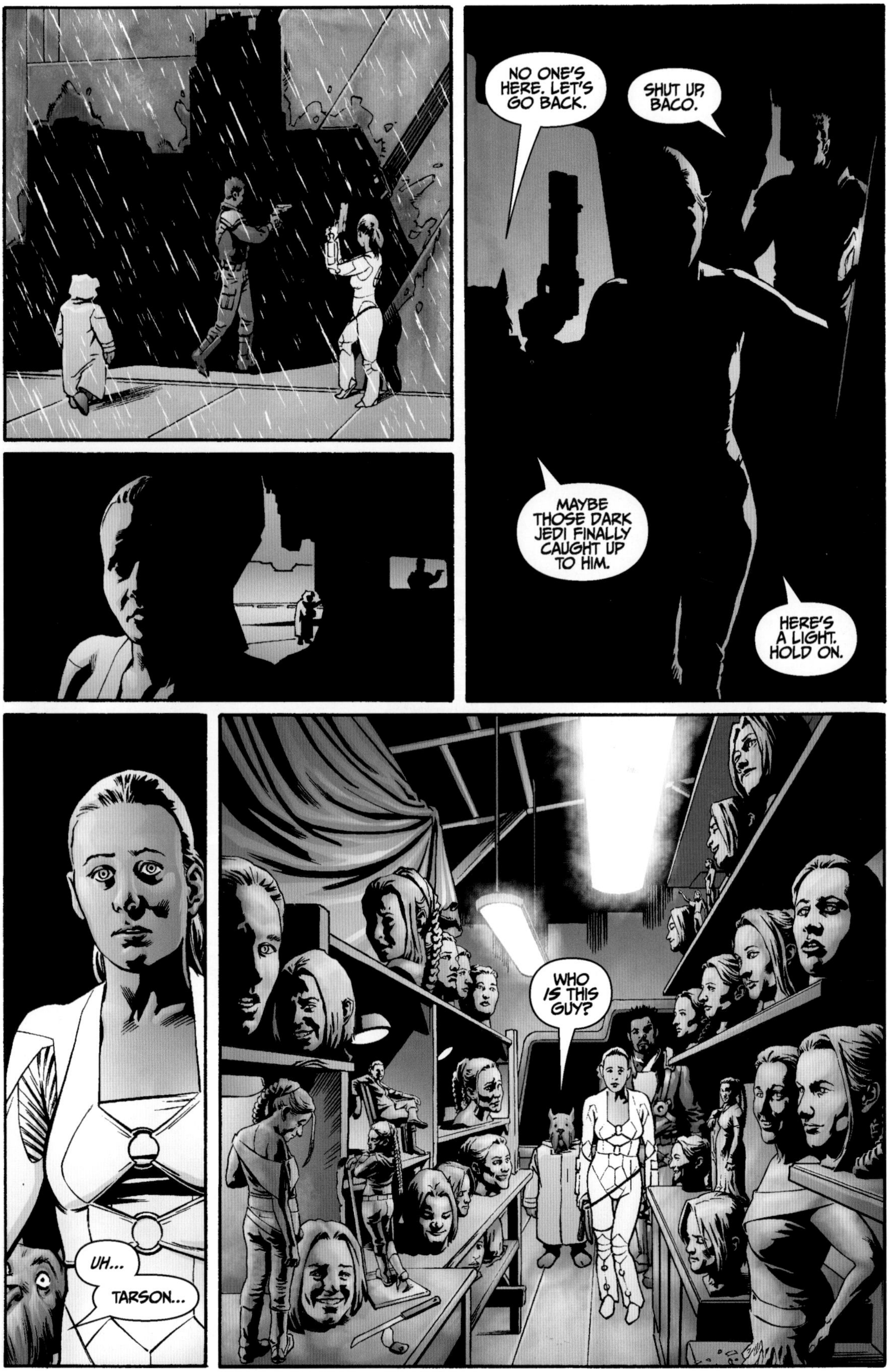
NO ONE'S HERE. LET'S GO BACK.
SHUT UP, BACO.
MAYBE THOSE DARK JEDI FINALLY CAUGHT UP TO HIM.
HERE'S A LIGHT. HOLD ON.
UH...
TARSON...
WHO *IS* THIS GUY?

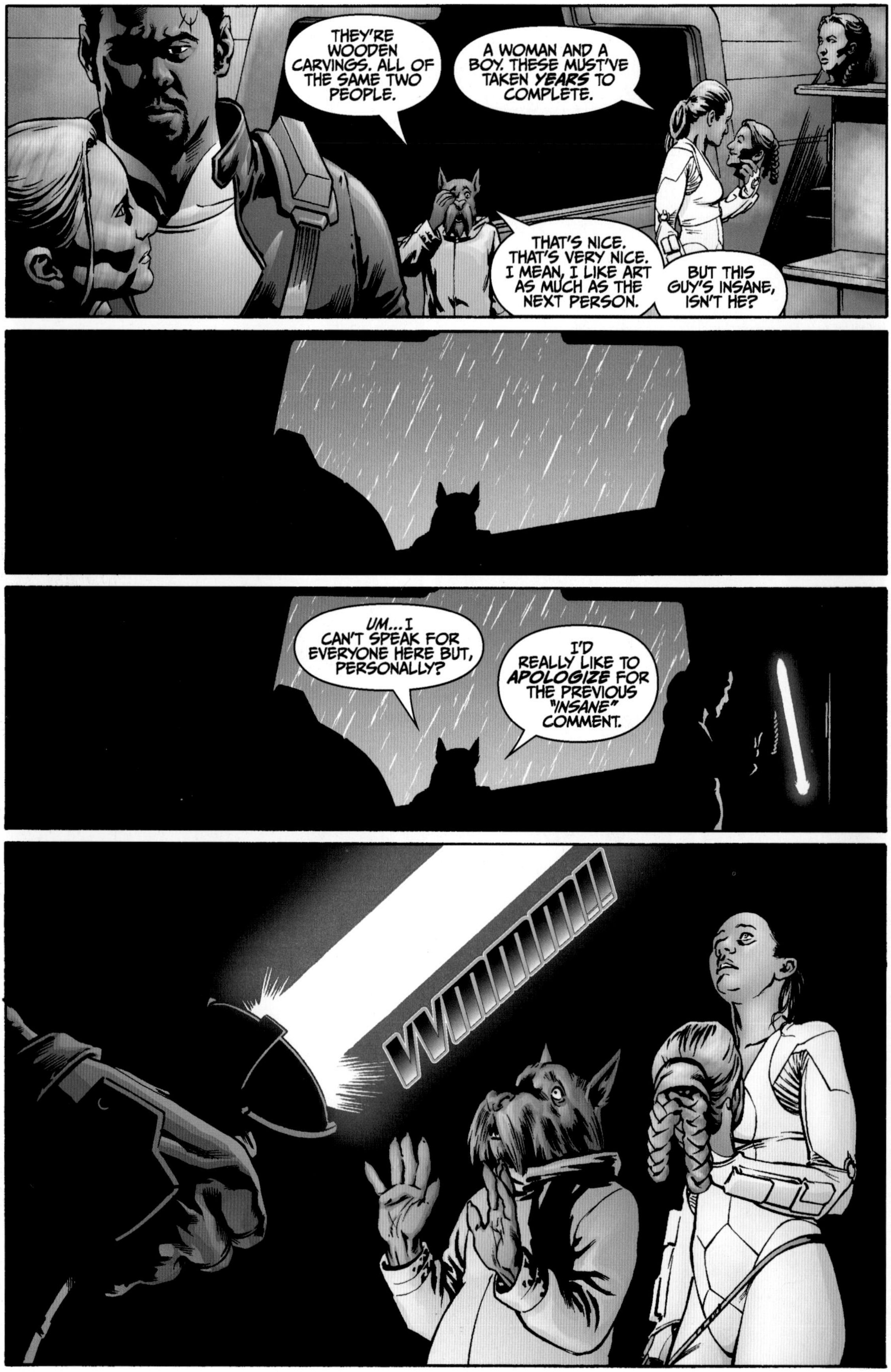
THEY'RE WOODEN CARVINGS. ALL OF THE SAME TWO PEOPLE.
A WOMAN AND A BOY. THESE MUST'VE TAKEN YEARS TO COMPLETE.
THAT'S NICE. THAT'S VERY NICE. I MEAN, I LIKE ART AS MUCH AS THE NEXT PERSON.
BUT THIS GUY'S INSANE, ISN'T HE?
UM... I CAN'T SPEAK FOR EVERYONE HERE BUT, PERSONALLY?
I'D REALLY LIKE TO APOLOGIZE FOR THE PREVIOUS "INSANE" COMMENT.
VVMMMM!!

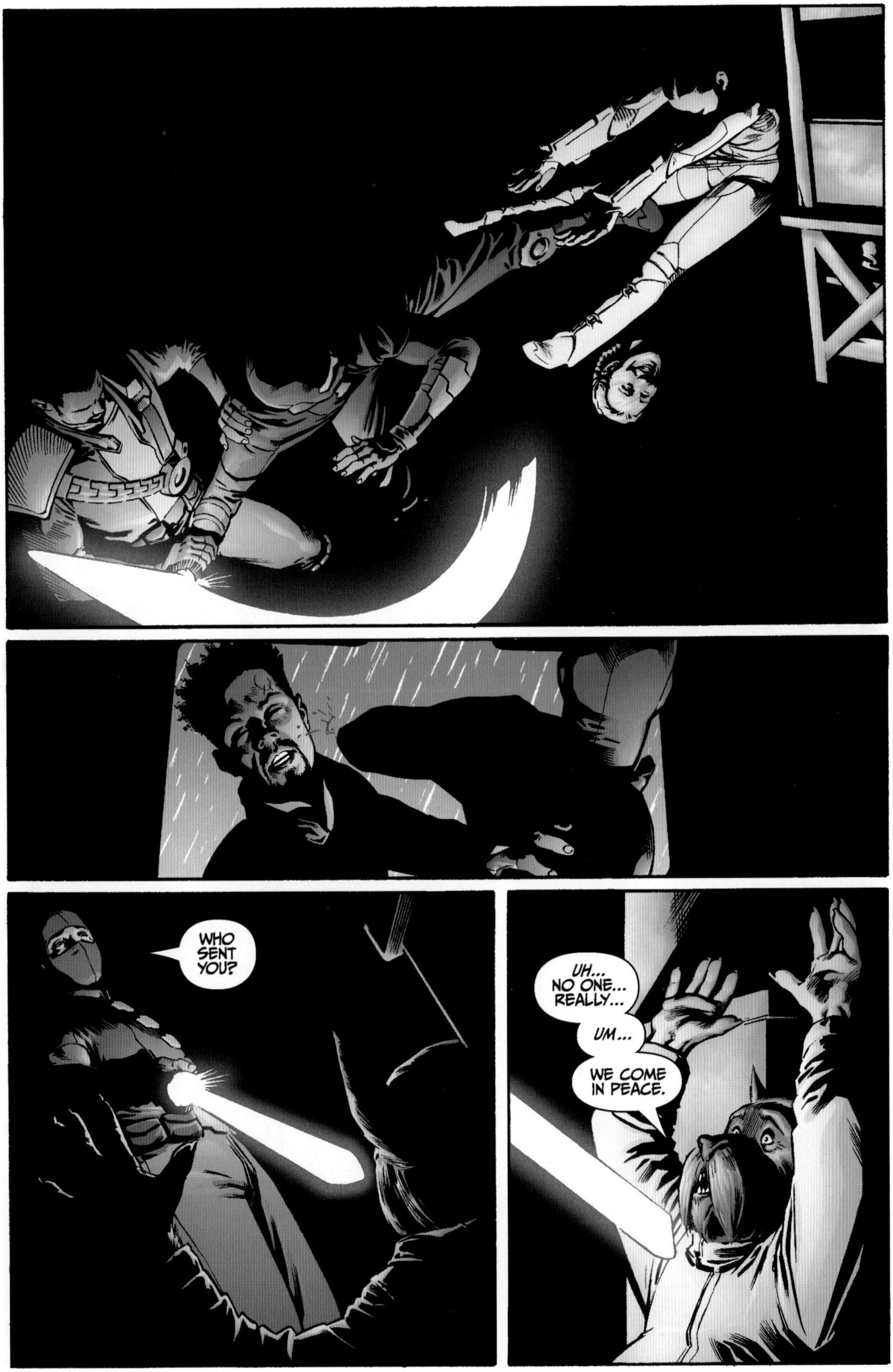
WHO SENT YOU?
UH... NO ONE... REALLY...
UM...
WE COME IN PEACE.

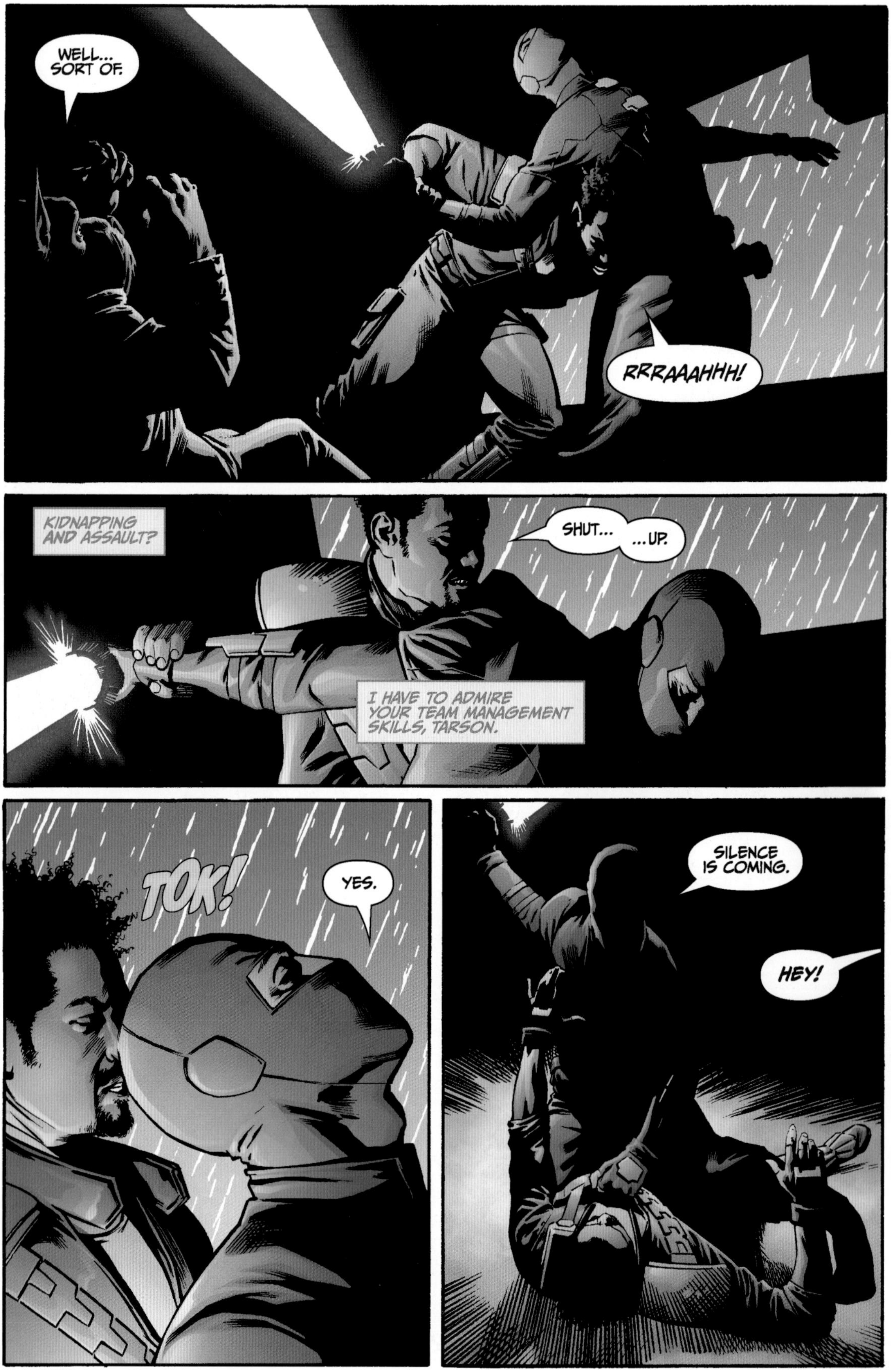
WELL... SORT OF.
RRRAAAHHH!
KIDNAPPING AND ASSAULT?
SHUT...
...UP.
I HAVE TO ADMIRE YOUR TEAM MANAGEMENT SKILLS, TARSON.
TOK!
YES.
SILENCE IS COMING.
HEY!

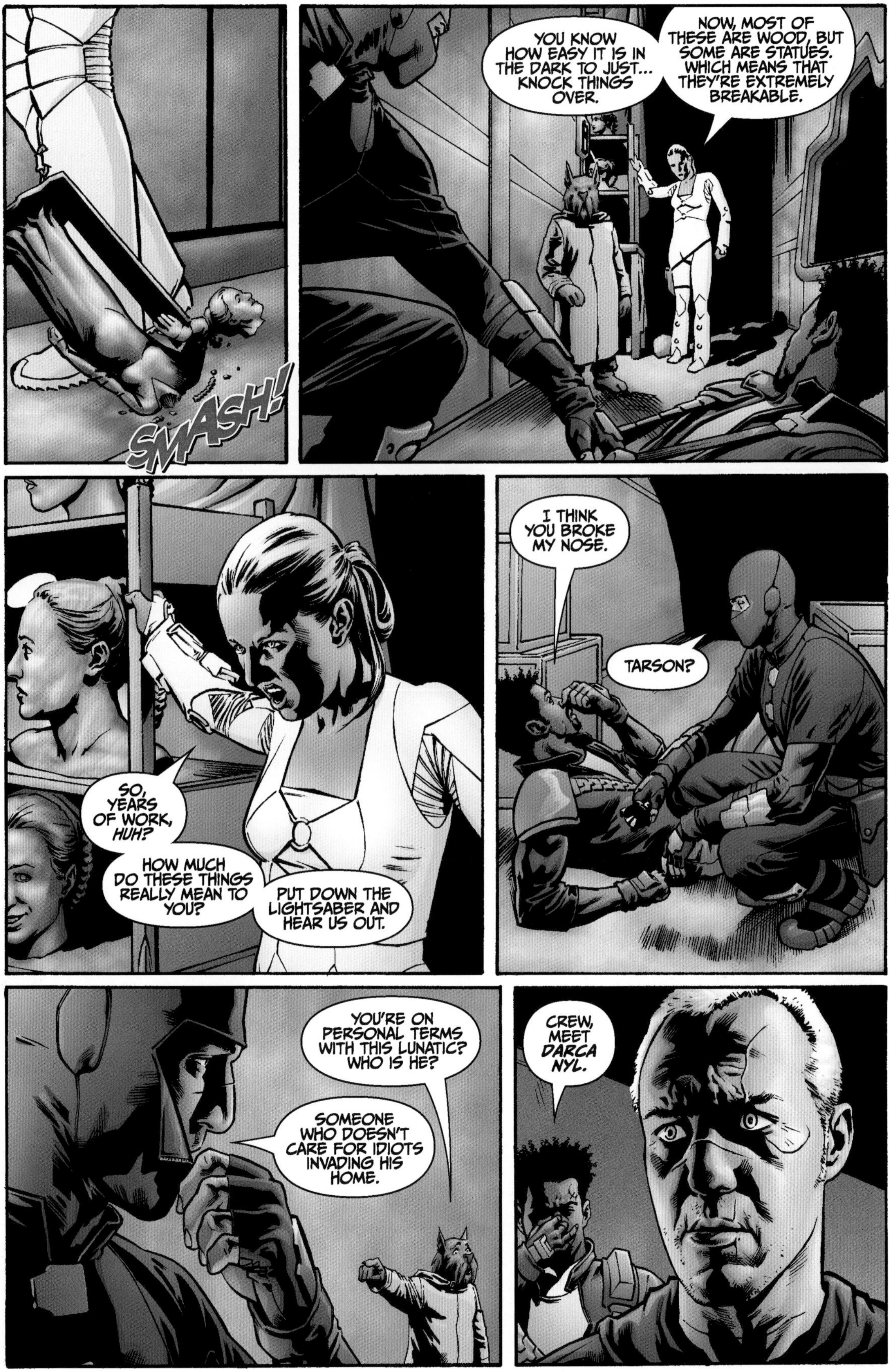
SMASH!
YOU KNOW HOW EASY IT IS IN THE DARK TO JUST... KNOCK THINGS OVER.
NOW, MOST OF THESE ARE WOOD, BUT SOME ARE STATUES. WHICH MEANS THAT THEY'RE EXTREMELY BREAKABLE.
SO, YEARS OF WORK, HUH?
HOW MUCH DO THESE THINGS REALLY MEAN TO YOU?
PUT DOWN THE LIGHTSABER AND HEAR US OUT.
I THINK YOU BROKE MY NOSE.
TARSON?
YOU'RE ON PERSONAL TERMS WITH THIS LUNATIC? WHO IS HE?
SOMEONE WHO DOESN'T CARE FOR IDIOTS INVADING HIS HOME.
CREW, MEET DARCA NYL.

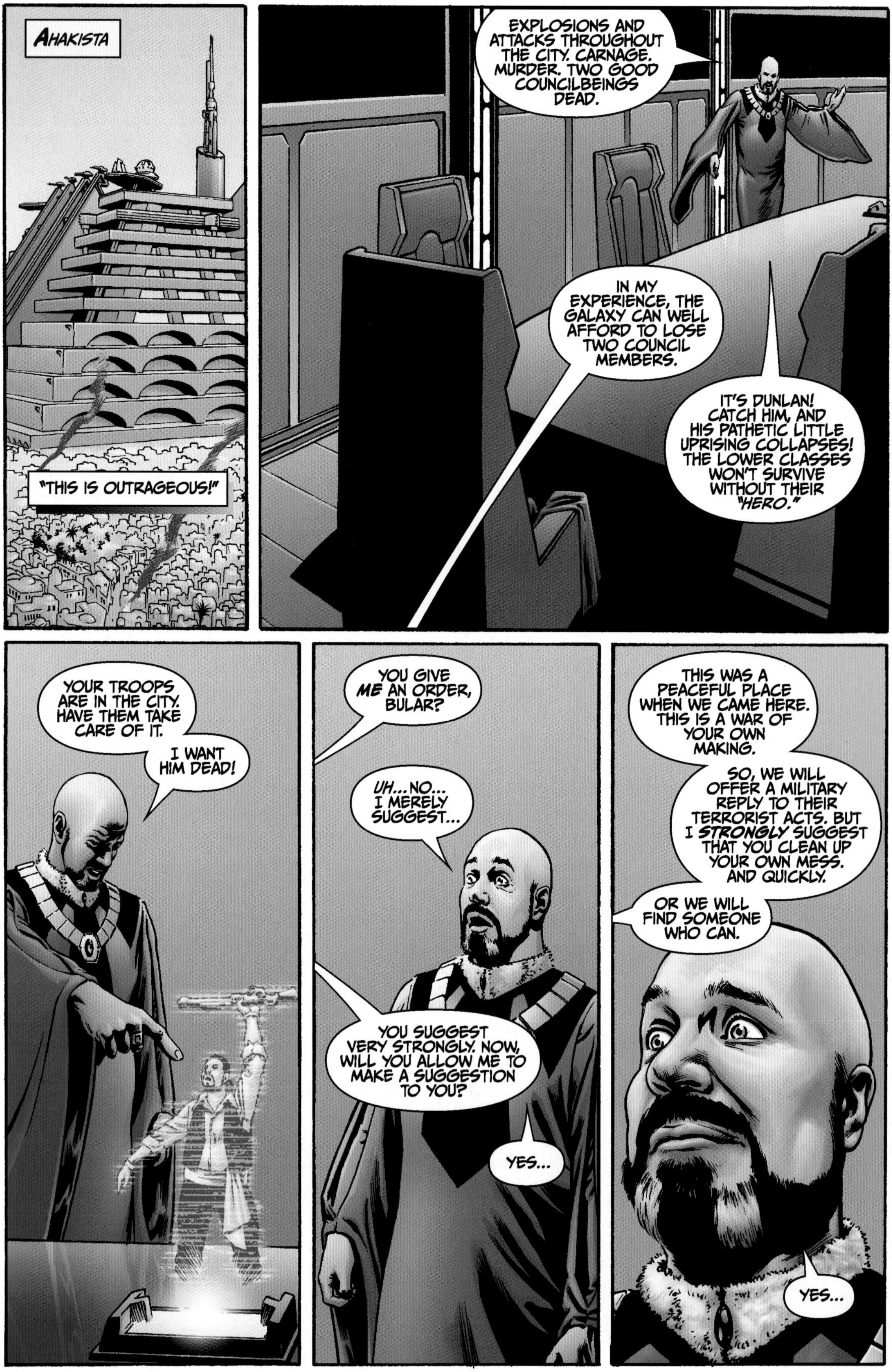
AHAKISTA
"THIS IS OUTRAGEOUS!"
EXPLOSIONS AND ATTACKS THROUGHOUT THE CITY. CARNAGE. MURDER. TWO GOOD COUNCILBEINGS DEAD.
IN MY EXPERIENCE, THE GALAXY CAN WELL AFFORD TO LOSE TWO COUNCIL MEMBERS.
IT'S DUNLAN! CATCH HIM, AND HIS PATHETIC LITTLE UPRISING COLLAPSES! THE LOWER CLASSES WON'T SURVIVE WITHOUT THEIR "HERO."
YOUR TROOPS ARE IN THE CITY. HAVE THEM TAKE CARE OF IT.
I WANT HIM DEAD!
YOU GIVE ME AN ORDER, BULAR?
UH...NO... I MERELY SUGGEST...
YOU SUGGEST VERY STRONGLY. NOW, WILL YOU ALLOW ME TO MAKE A SUGGESTION TO YOU?
YES...
THIS WAS A PEACEFUL PLACE WHEN WE CAME HERE. THIS IS A WAR OF YOUR OWN MAKING.
SO, WE WILL OFFER A MILITARY REPLY TO THEIR TERRORIST ACTS. BUT I STRONGLY SUGGEST THAT YOU CLEAN UP YOUR OWN MESS. AND QUICKLY.
OR WE WILL FIND SOMEONE WHO CAN.
YES...

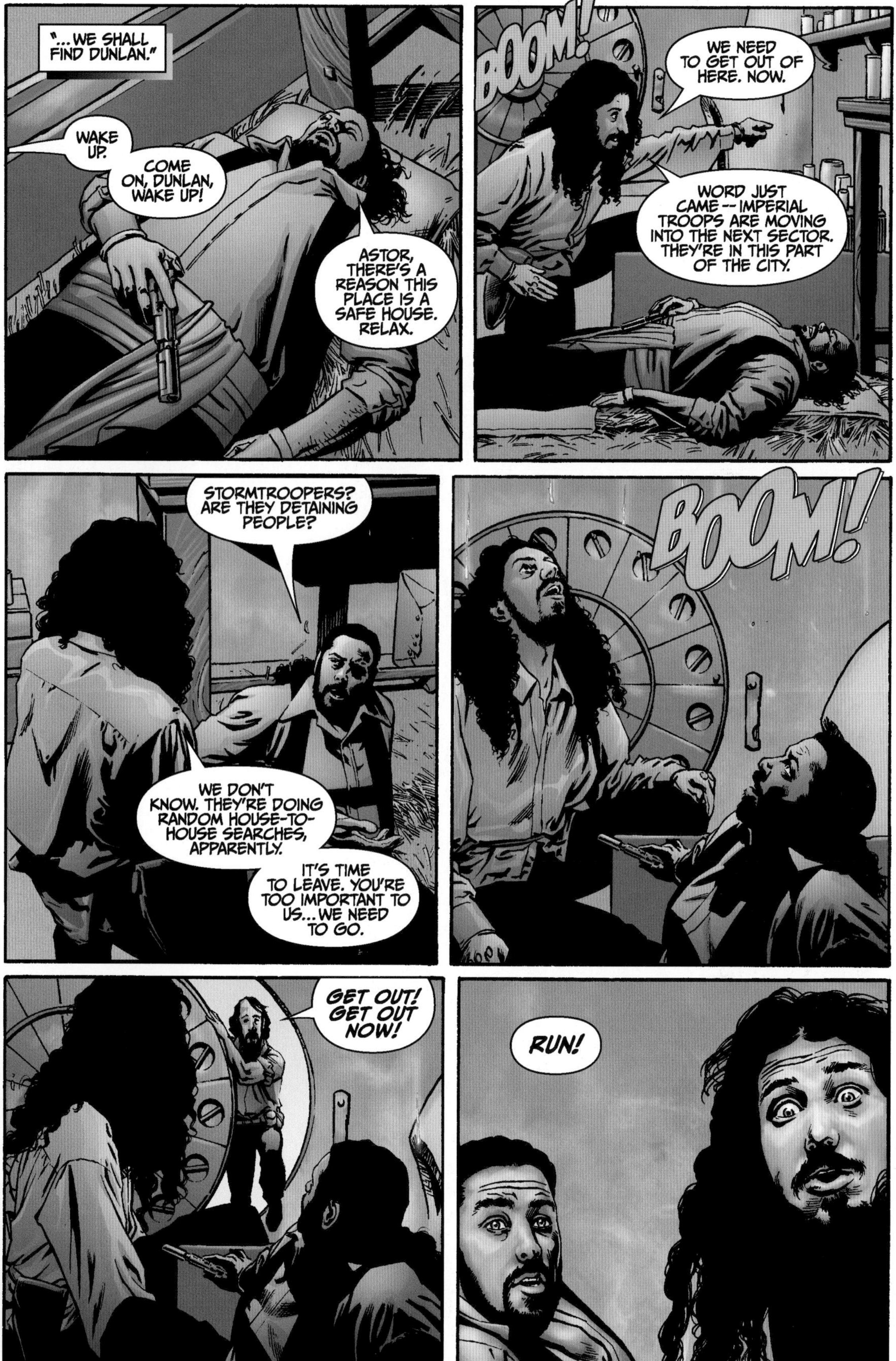
"...WE SHALL FIND DUNLAN."
WAKE UP.
COME ON, DUNLAN, WAKE UP!
ASTOR, THERE'S A REASON THIS PLACE IS A SAFE HOUSE. RELAX.
BOOM!
WE NEED TO GET OUT OF HERE. NOW.
WORD JUST CAME -- IMPERIAL TROOPS ARE MOVING INTO THE NEXT SECTOR. THEY'RE IN THIS PART OF THE CITY.
STORMTROOPERS? ARE THEY DETAINING PEOPLE?
WE DON'T KNOW. THEY'RE DOING RANDOM HOUSE-TO-HOUSE SEARCHES, APPARENTLY.
IT'S TIME TO LEAVE. YOU'RE TOO IMPORTANT TO US...WE NEED TO GO.
BOOM!
GET OUT! GET OUT NOW!
RUN!

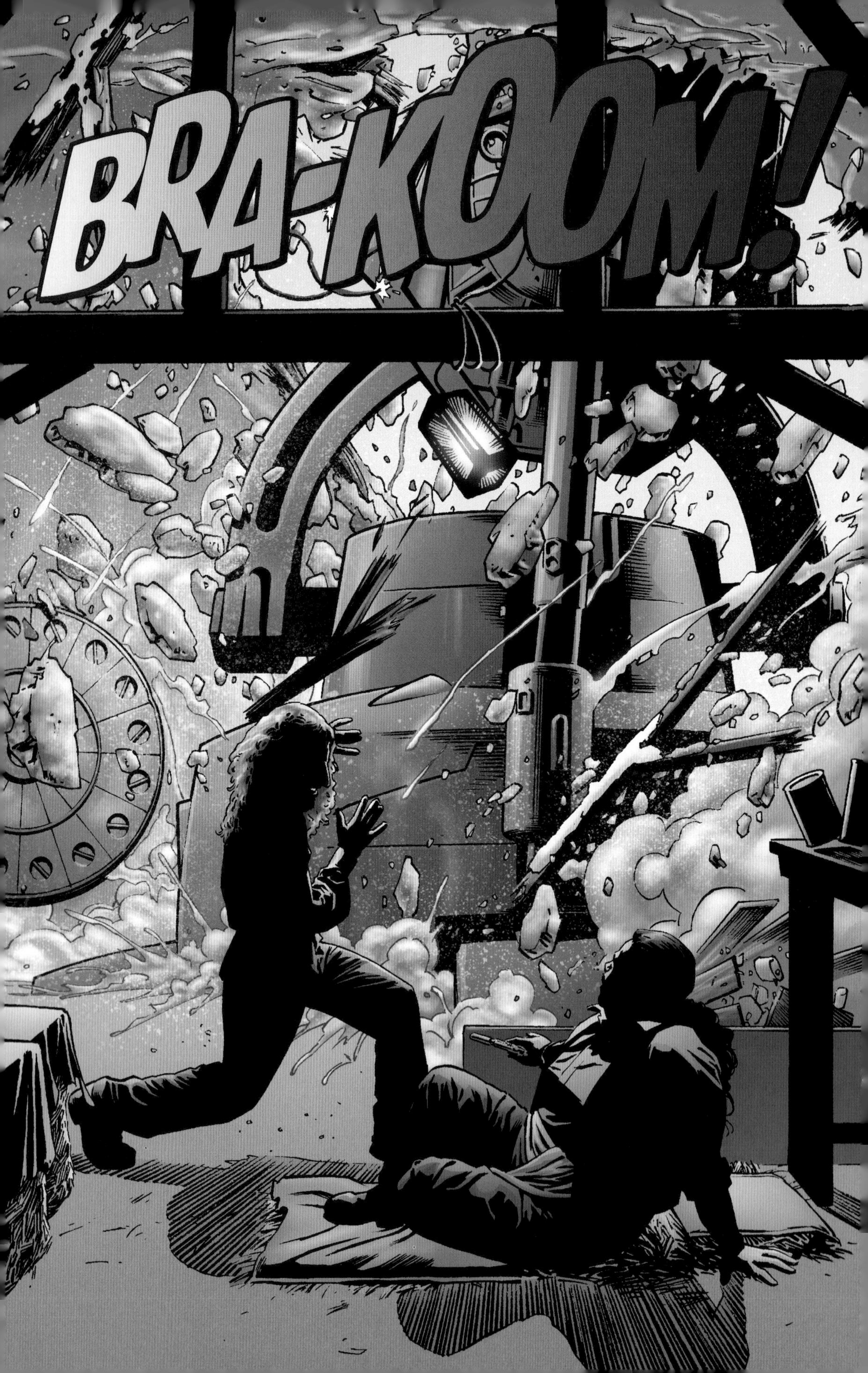
BRA-KOOM!

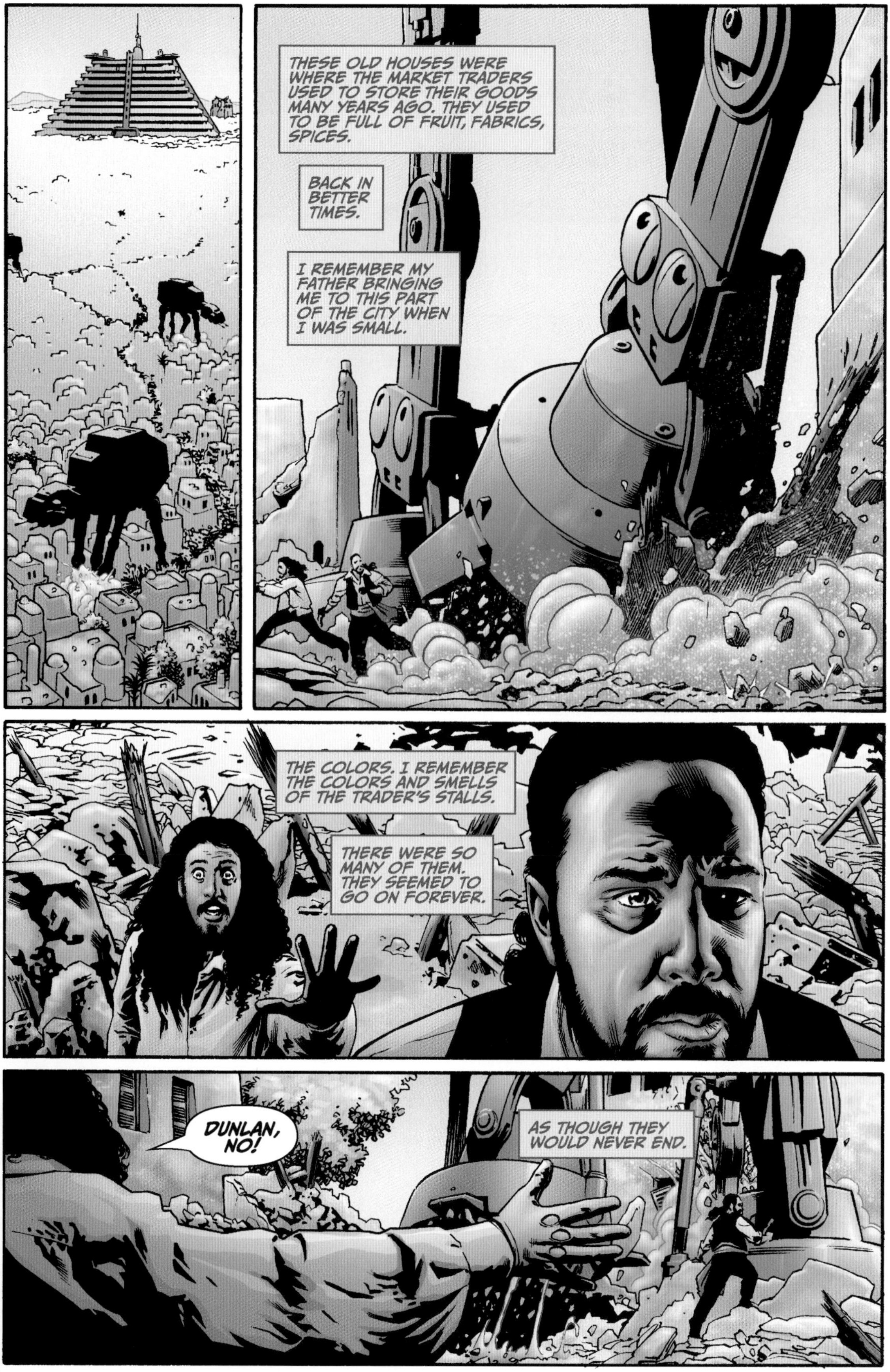
THESE OLD HOUSES WERE WHERE THE MARKET TRADERS USED TO STORE THEIR GOODS MANY YEARS AGO. THEY USED TO BE FULL OF FRUIT, FABRICS, SPICES.
BACK IN BETTER TIMES.
I REMEMBER MY FATHER BRINGING ME TO THIS PART OF THE CITY WHEN I WAS SMALL.
THE COLORS. I REMEMBER THE COLORS AND SMELLS OF THE TRADER'S STALLS.
THERE WERE SO MANY OF THEM. THEY SEEMED TO GO ON FOREVER.
DUNLAN, NO!
AS THOUGH THEY WOULD NEVER END.

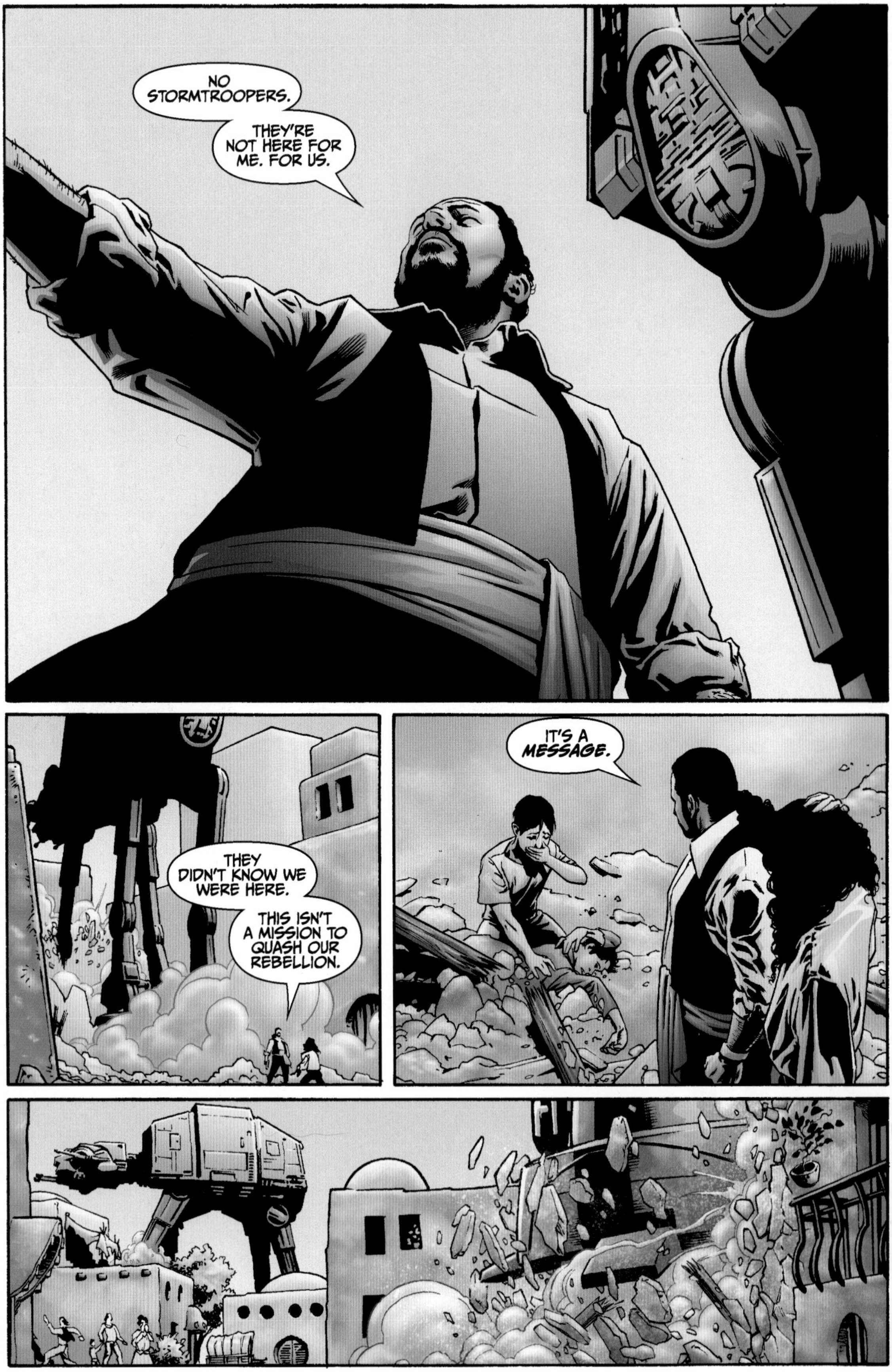
NO STORMTROOPERS.
THEY'RE NOT HERE FOR ME. FOR US.
THEY DIDN'T KNOW WE WERE HERE.
THIS ISN'T A MISSION TO QUASH OUR REBELLION.
IT'S A MESSAGE.

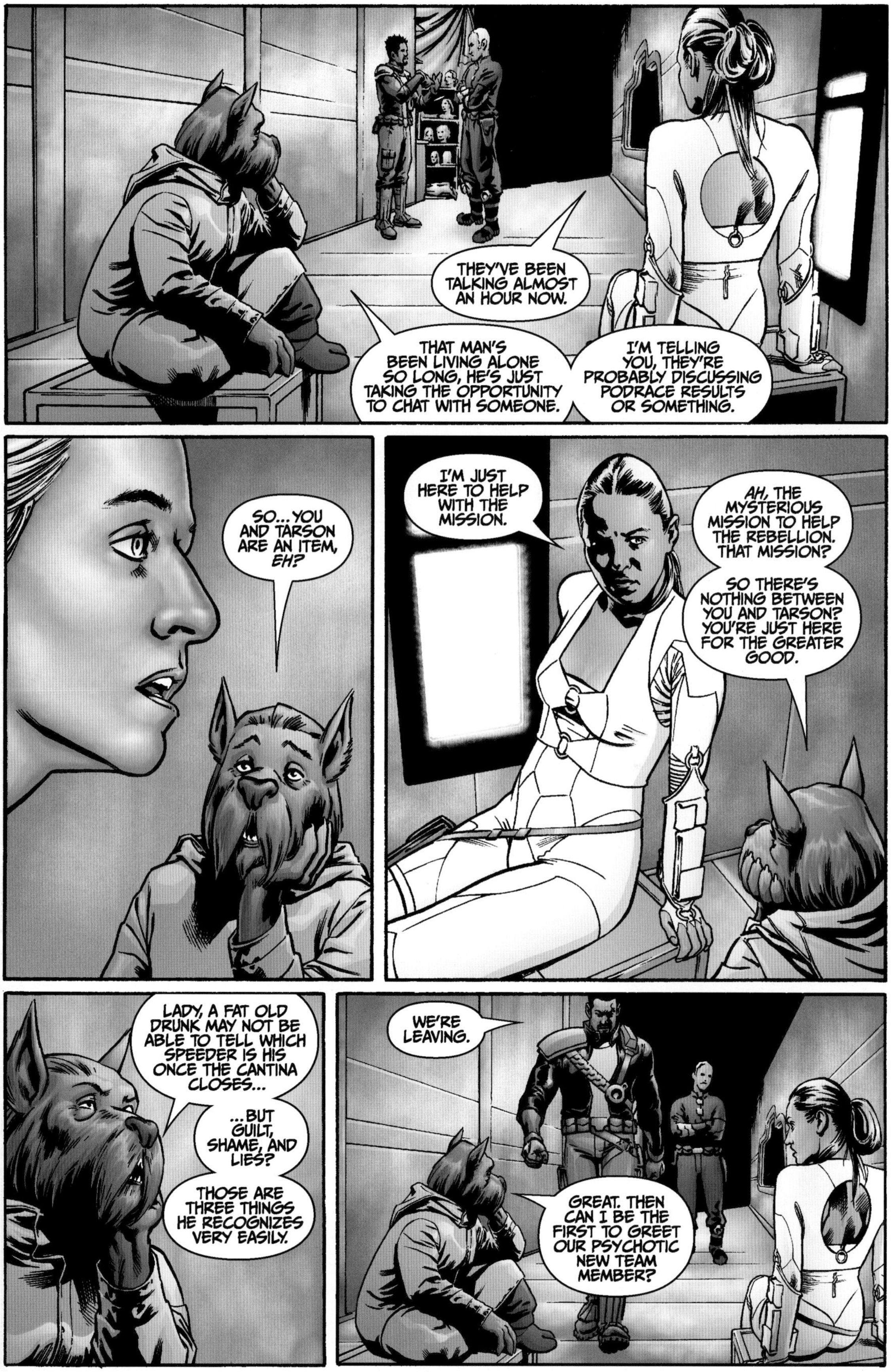
THEY'VE BEEN TALKING ALMOST AN HOUR NOW.
THAT MAN'S BEEN LIVING ALONE SO LONG, HE'S JUST TAKING THE OPPORTUNITY TO CHAT WITH SOMEONE.
I'M TELLING YOU, THEY'RE PROBABLY DISCUSSING PODRACE RESULTS OR SOMETHING.
SO...YOU AND TARSON ARE AN ITEM, *EH?*
I'M JUST HERE TO HELP WITH THE MISSION.
AH, THE MYSTERIOUS MISSION TO HELP THE REBELLION. THAT MISSION?
SO THERE'S NOTHING BETWEEN YOU AND TARSON? YOU'RE JUST HERE FOR THE GREATER GOOD.
LADY, A FAT OLD DRUNK MAY NOT BE ABLE TO TELL WHICH SPEEDER IS HIS ONCE THE CANTINA CLOSES...
...BUT GUILT, SHAME, AND LIES?
THOSE ARE THREE THINGS HE RECOGNIZES VERY EASILY.
WE'RE LEAVING.
GREAT. THEN CAN I BE THE FIRST TO GREET OUR PSYCHOTIC NEW TEAM MEMBER?

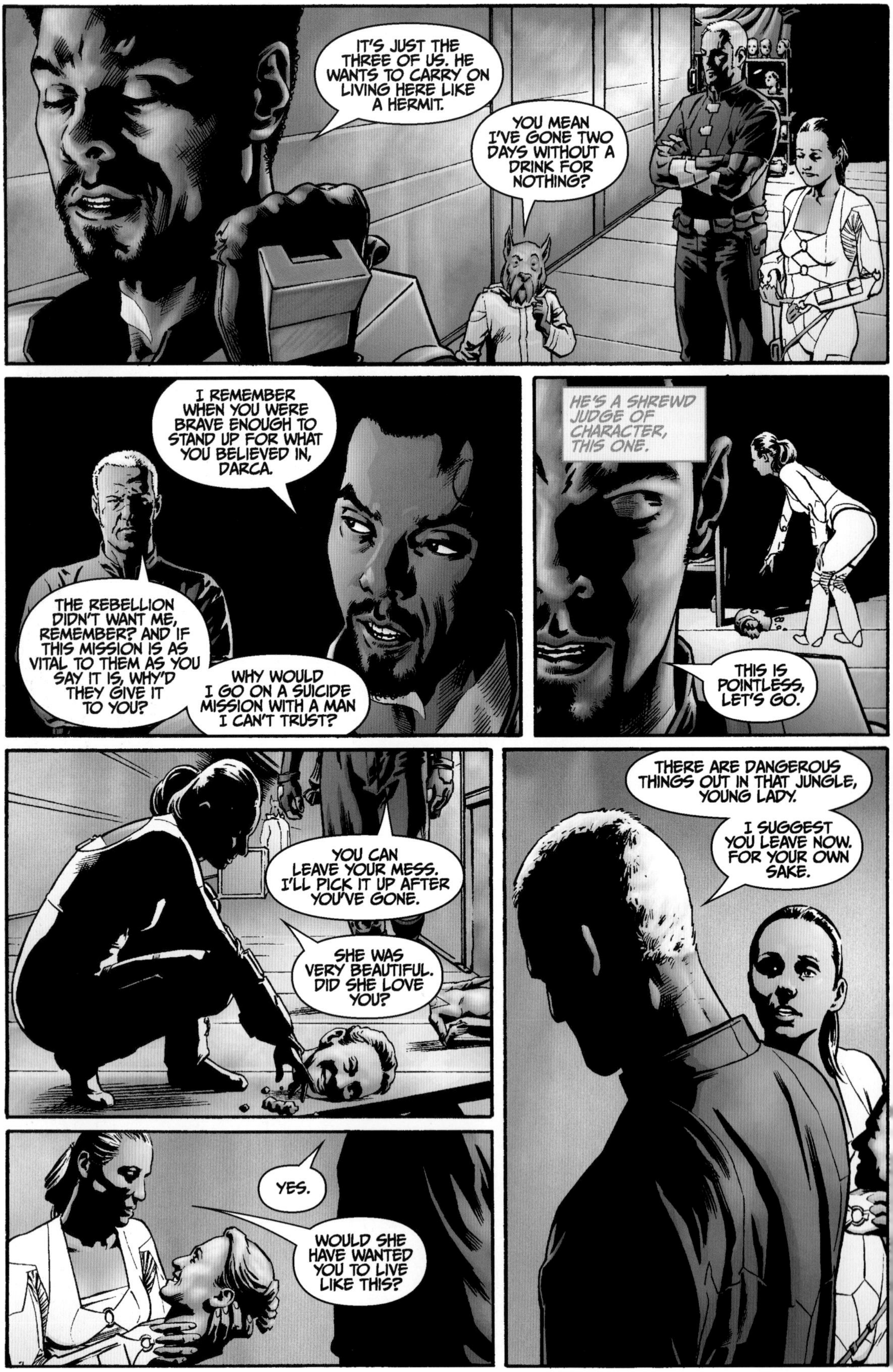
IT'S JUST THE THREE OF US. HE WANTS TO CARRY ON LIVING HERE LIKE A HERMIT.
YOU MEAN I'VE GONE TWO DAYS WITHOUT A DRINK FOR NOTHING?
I REMEMBER WHEN YOU WERE BRAVE ENOUGH TO STAND UP FOR WHAT YOU BELIEVED IN, DARCA.
THE REBELLION DIDN'T WANT ME, REMEMBER? AND IF THIS MISSION IS AS VITAL TO THEM AS YOU SAY IT IS, WHY'D THEY GIVE IT TO YOU?
WHY WOULD I GO ON A SUICIDE MISSION WITH A MAN I CAN'T TRUST?
HE'S A SHREWD JUDGE OF CHARACTER, THIS ONE.
THIS IS POINTLESS, LET'S GO.
YOU CAN LEAVE YOUR MESS. I'LL PICK IT UP AFTER YOU'VE GONE.
SHE WAS VERY BEAUTIFUL. DID SHE LOVE YOU?
YES.
WOULD SHE HAVE WANTED YOU TO LIVE LIKE THIS?
THERE ARE DANGEROUS THINGS OUT IN THAT JUNGLE, YOUNG LADY.
I SUGGEST YOU LEAVE NOW. FOR YOUR OWN SAKE.

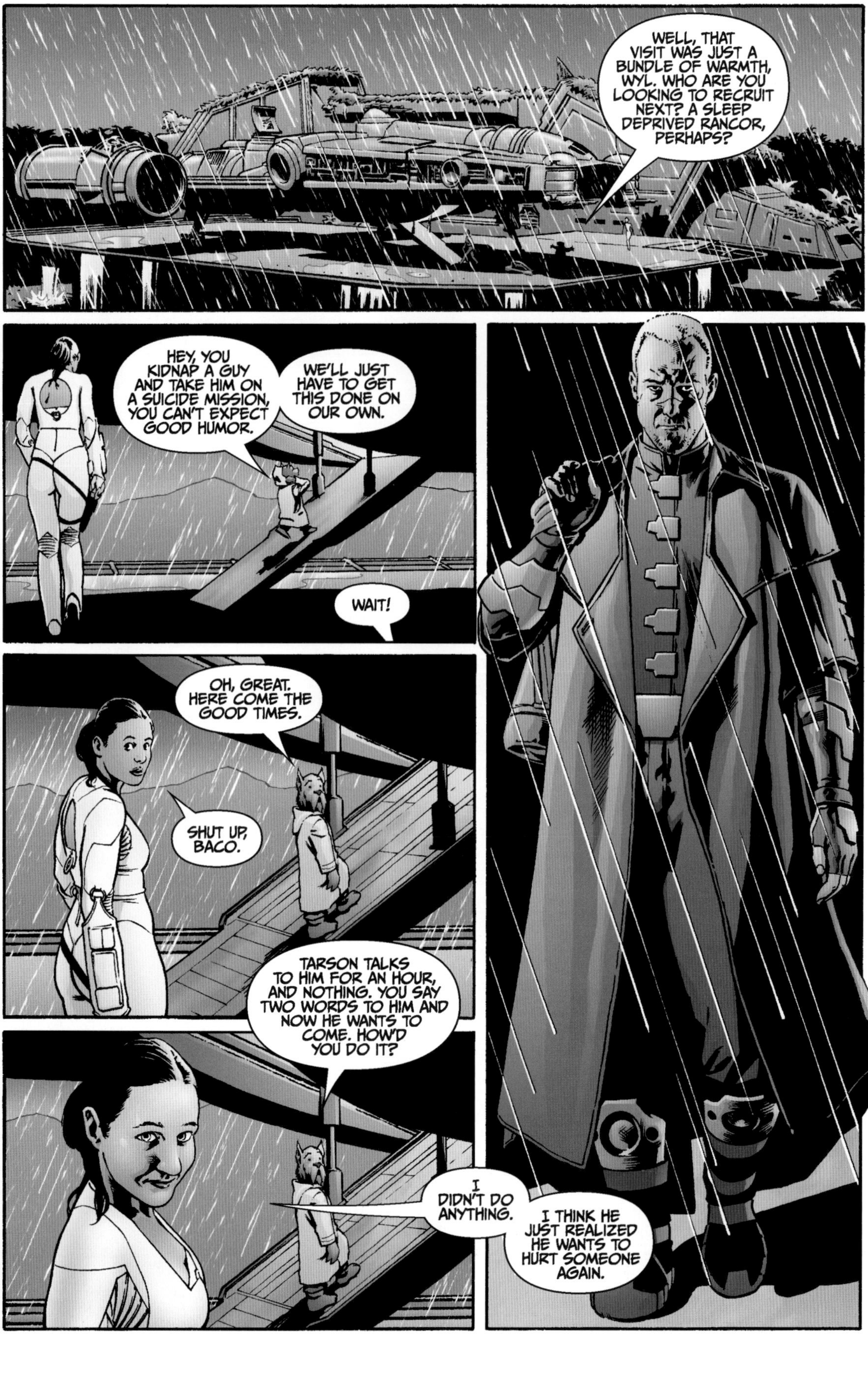
WELL, THAT VISIT WAS JUST A BUNDLE OF WARMTH, WYL. WHO ARE YOU LOOKING TO RECRUIT NEXT? A SLEEP DEPRIVED RANCOR, PERHAPS?
HEY, YOU KIDNAP A GUY AND TAKE HIM ON A SUICIDE MISSION, YOU CAN'T EXPECT GOOD HUMOR.
WE'LL JUST HAVE TO GET THIS DONE ON OUR OWN.
WAIT!
OH, GREAT. HERE COME THE GOOD TIMES.
SHUT UP, BACO.
TARSON TALKS TO HIM FOR AN HOUR, AND NOTHING. YOU SAY TWO WORDS TO HIM AND NOW HE WANTS TO COME. HOW'D YOU DO IT?
I DIDN'T DO ANYTHING.
I THINK HE JUST REALIZED HE WANTS TO HURT SOMEONE AGAIN.

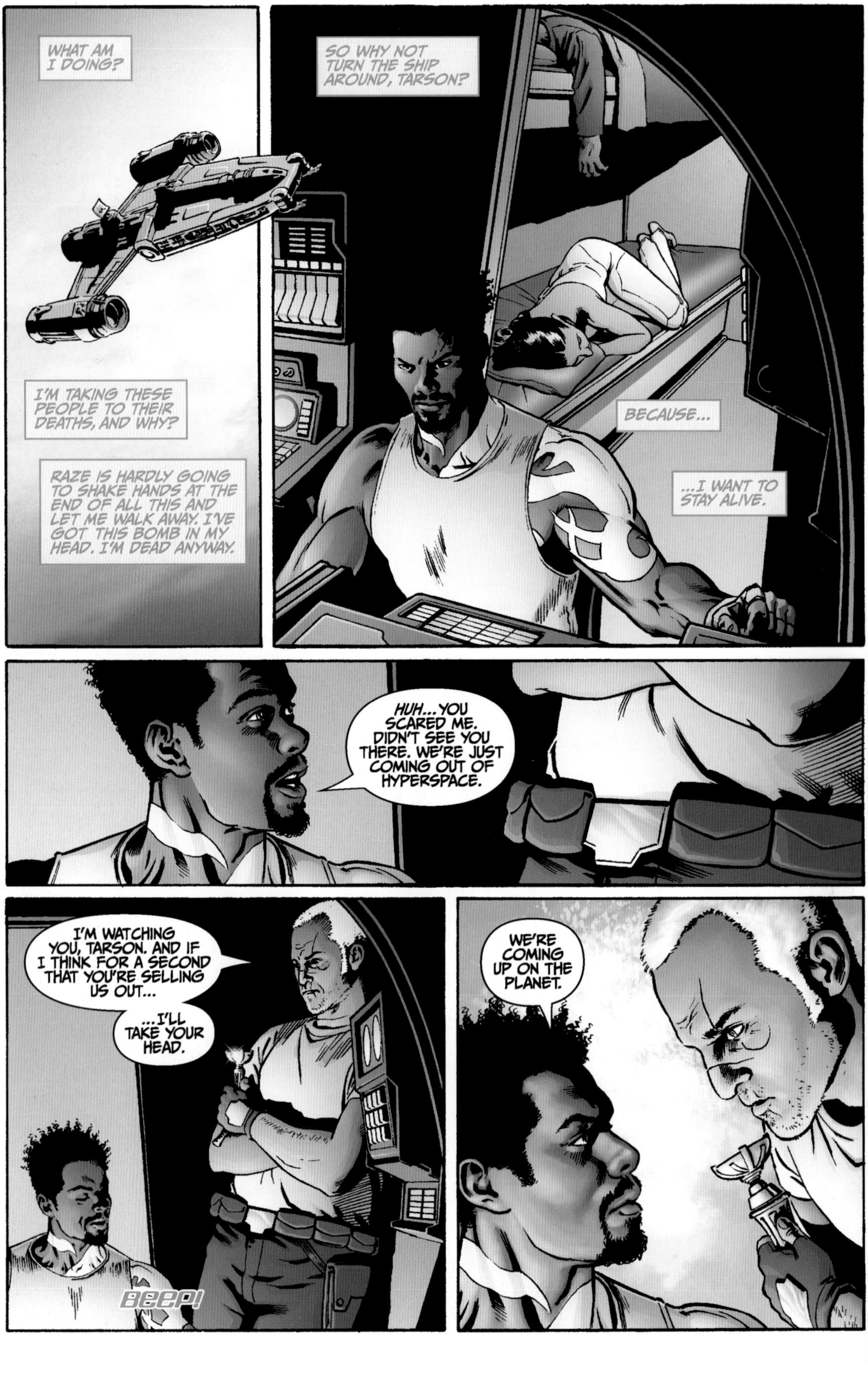
WHAT AM I DOING?
I'M TAKING THESE PEOPLE TO THEIR DEATHS, AND WHY?
RAZE IS HARDLY GOING TO SHAKE HANDS AT THE END OF ALL THIS AND LET ME WALK AWAY. I'VE GOT THIS BOMB IN MY HEAD. I'M DEAD ANYWAY.
SO WHY NOT TURN THE SHIP AROUND, TARSON?
BECAUSE...
...I WANT TO STAY ALIVE.
HUH...YOU SCARED ME. DIDN'T SEE YOU THERE. WE'RE JUST COMING OUT OF HYPERSPACE.
I'M WATCHING YOU, TARSON. AND IF I THINK FOR A SECOND THAT YOU'RE SELLING US OUT...
...I'LL TAKE YOUR HEAD.
BEEP!
WE'RE COMING UP ON THE PLANET.

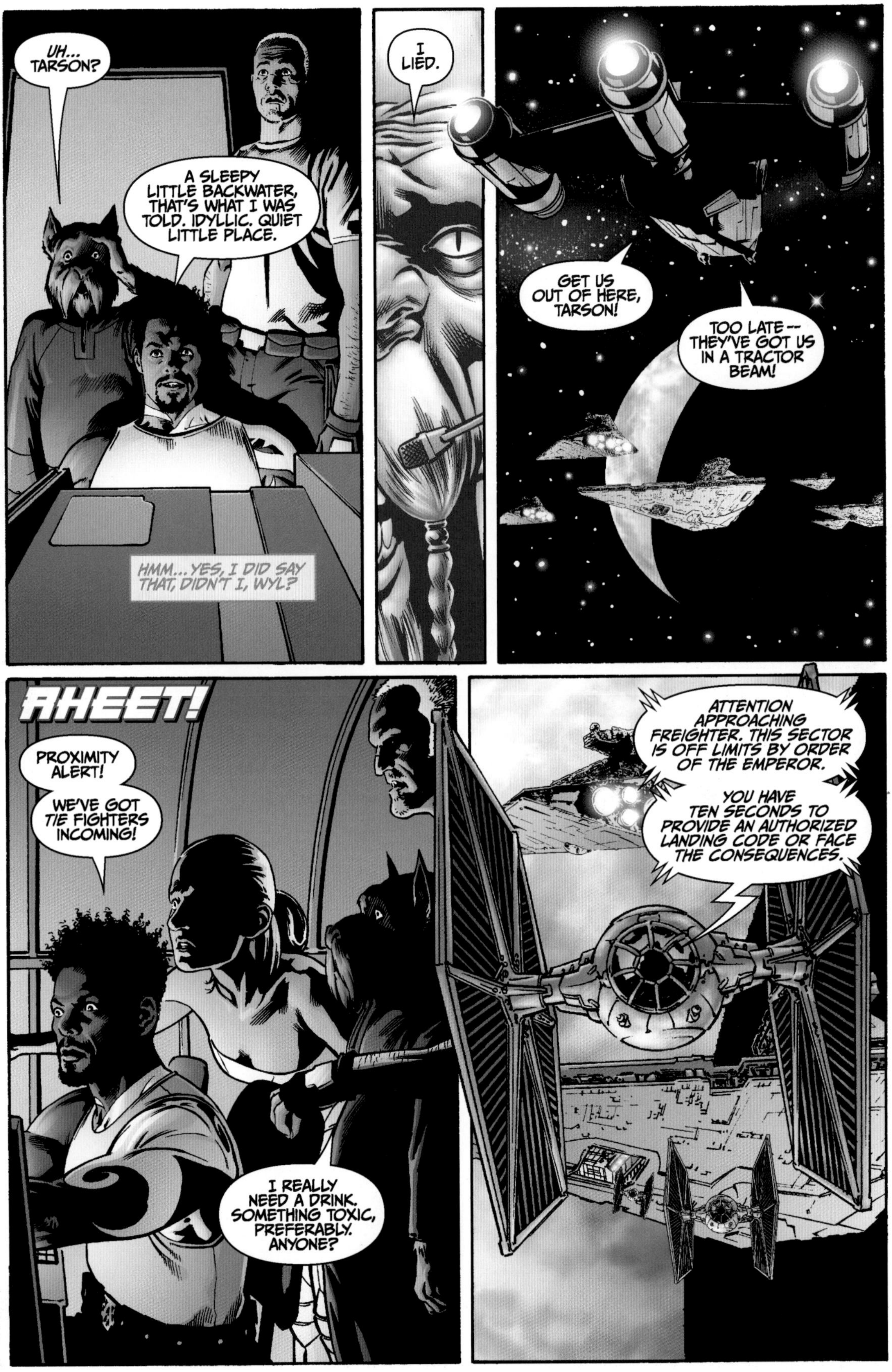
UH... TARSON?
A SLEEPY LITTLE BACKWATER, THAT'S WHAT I WAS TOLD. IDYLLIC. QUIET LITTLE PLACE.
HMM... YES, I DID SAY THAT, DIDN'T I, WYL?
I LIED.
GET US OUT OF HERE, TARSON!
TOO LATE-- THEY'VE GOT US IN A TRACTOR BEAM!
AHEET!
PROXIMITY ALERT!
WE'VE GOT TIE FIGHTERS INCOMING!
I REALLY NEED A DRINK. SOMETHING TOXIC, PREFERABLY. ANYONE?
ATTENTION APPROACHING FREIGHTER. THIS SECTOR IS OFF LIMITS BY ORDER OF THE EMPEROR.
YOU HAVE TEN SECONDS TO PROVIDE AN AUTHORIZED LANDING CODE OR FACE THE CONSEQUENCES.

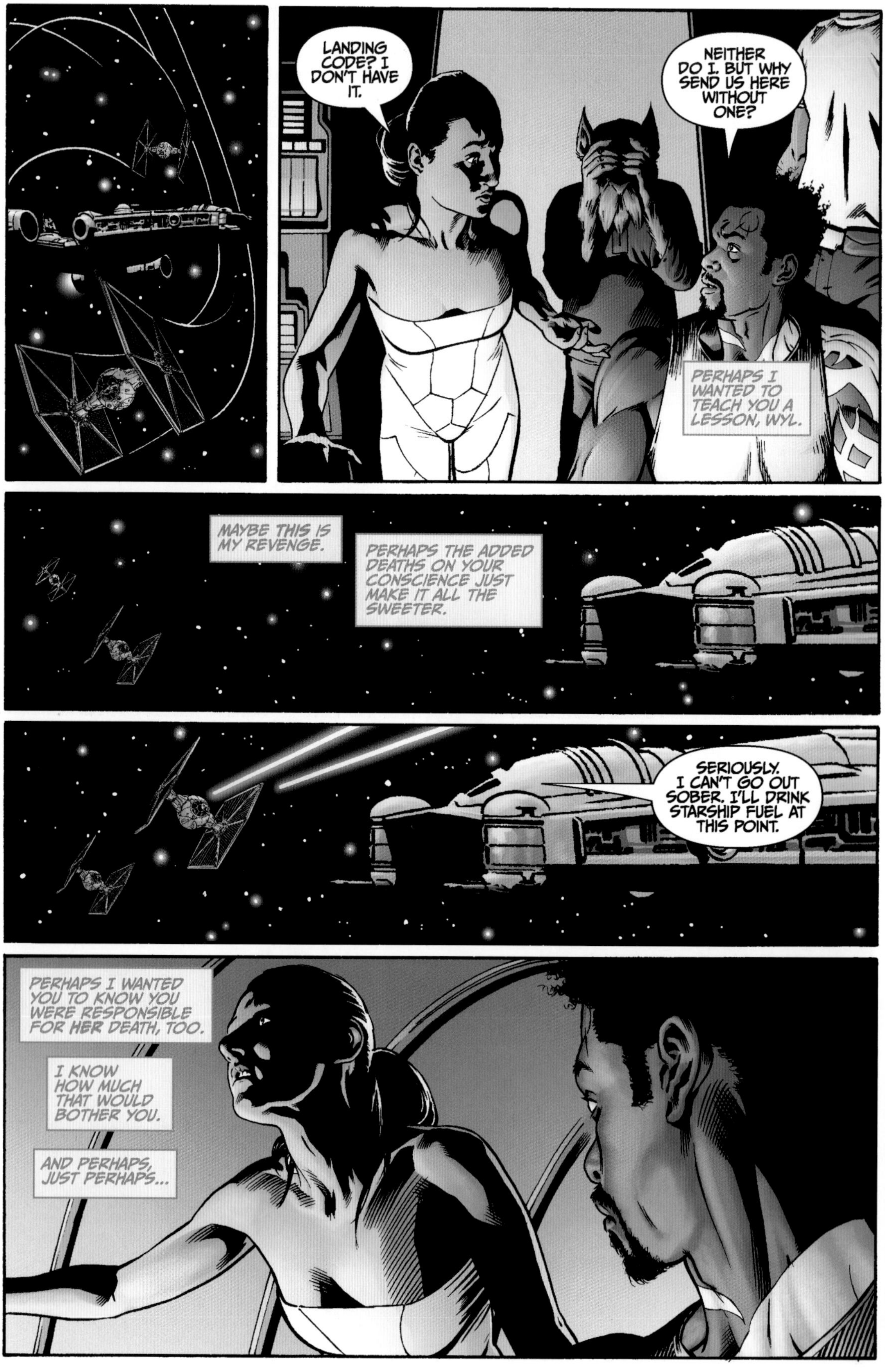
LANDING CODE? I DON'T HAVE IT.
NEITHER DO I. BUT WHY SEND US HERE WITHOUT ONE?
PERHAPS I WANTED TO TEACH YOU A LESSON, WYL.
MAYBE THIS IS MY REVENGE.
PERHAPS THE ADDED DEATHS ON YOUR CONSCIENCE JUST MAKE IT ALL THE SWEETER.
SERIOUSLY. I CAN'T GO OUT SOBER. I'LL DRINK STARSHIP FUEL AT THIS POINT.
PERHAPS I WANTED YOU TO KNOW YOU WERE RESPONSIBLE FOR HER DEATH, TOO.
I KNOW HOW MUCH THAT WOULD BOTHER YOU.
AND PERHAPS, JUST PERHAPS...

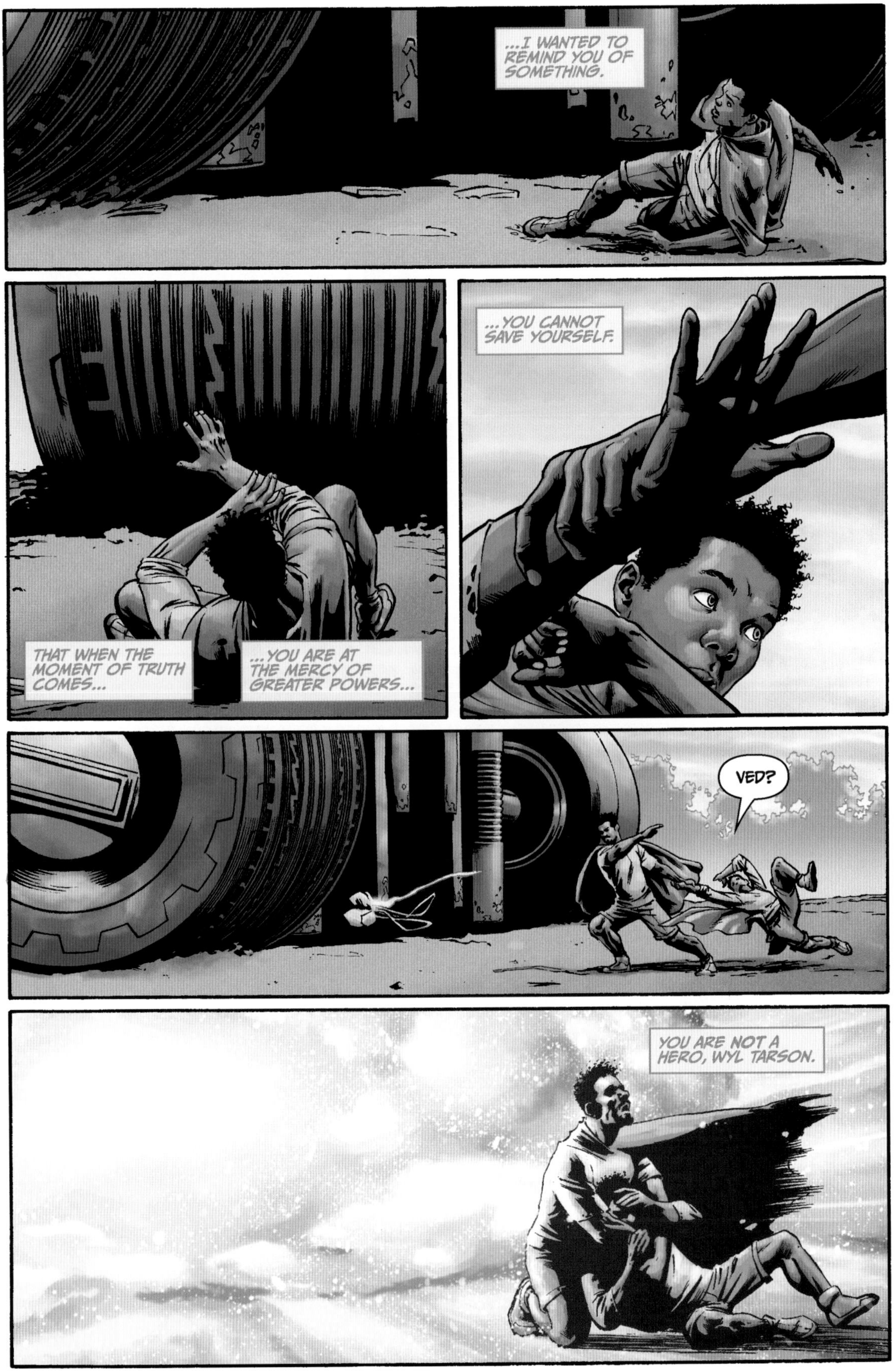
...I WANTED TO REMIND YOU OF SOMETHING.
THAT WHEN THE MOMENT OF TRUTH COMES...
...YOU ARE AT THE MERCY OF GREATER POWERS...
...YOU CANNOT SAVE YOURSELF.
VED?
YOU ARE NOT A HERO, WYL TARSON.

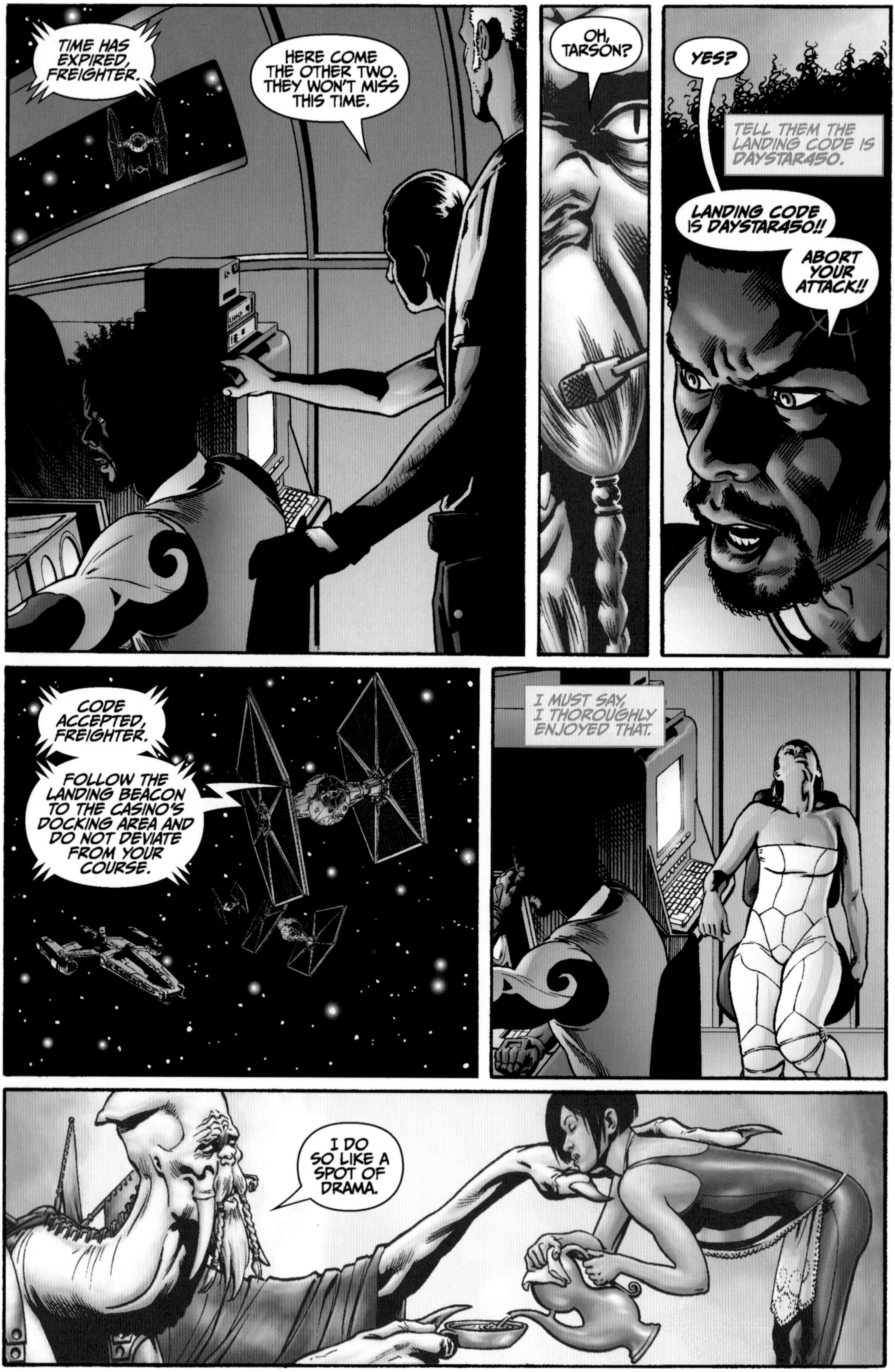
TIME HAS EXPIRED, FREIGHTER.
HERE COME THE OTHER TWO. THEY WON'T MISS THIS TIME.
OH, TARSON?
YES?
TELL THEM THE LANDING CODE IS DAYSTAR450.
LANDING CODE IS DAYSTAR450!!
ABORT YOUR ATTACK!!
CODE ACCEPTED, FREIGHTER.
FOLLOW THE LANDING BEACON TO THE CASINO'S DOCKING AREA AND DO NOT DEVIATE FROM YOUR COURSE.
I MUST SAY, I THOROUGHLY ENJOYED THAT.
I DO SO LIKE A SPOT OF DRAMA.

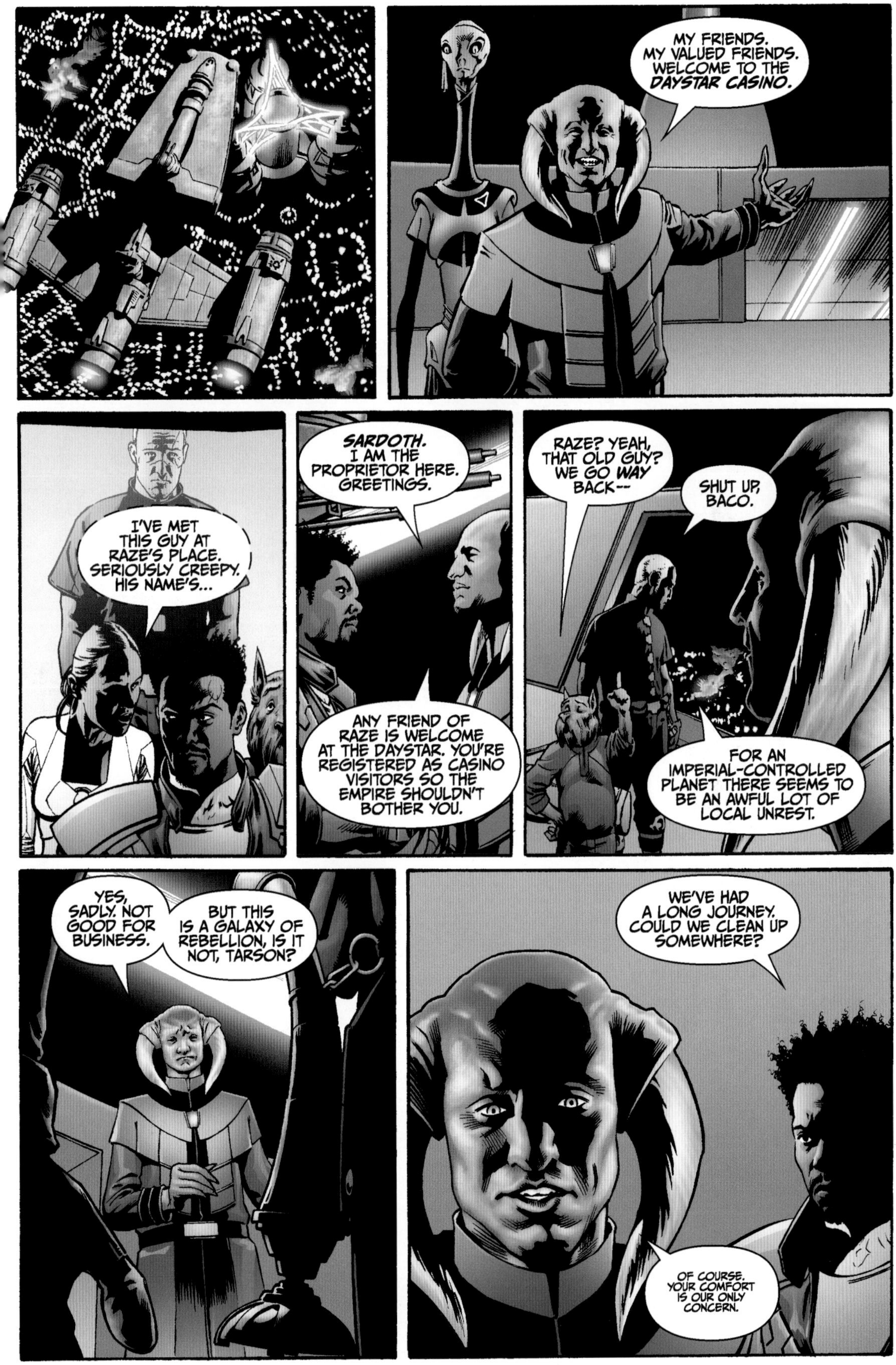
MY FRIENDS. MY VALUED FRIENDS. WELCOME TO THE DAYSTAR CASINO.
I'VE MET THIS GUY AT RAZE'S PLACE. SERIOUSLY CREEPY. HIS NAME'S...
SARDOTH. I AM THE PROPRIETOR HERE. GREETINGS.
ANY FRIEND OF RAZE IS WELCOME AT THE DAYSTAR. YOU'RE REGISTERED AS CASINO VISITORS SO THE EMPIRE SHOULDN'T BOTHER YOU.
RAZE? YEAH, THAT OLD GUY? WE GO WAY BACK--
SHUT UP, BACO.
FOR AN IMPERIAL-CONTROLLED PLANET THERE SEEMS TO BE AN AWFUL LOT OF LOCAL UNREST.
YES, SADLY. NOT GOOD FOR BUSINESS.
BUT THIS IS A GALAXY OF REBELLION, IS IT NOT, TARSON?
WE'VE HAD A LONG JOURNEY. COULD WE CLEAN UP SOMEWHERE?
OF COURSE. YOUR COMFORT IS OUR ONLY CONCERN.

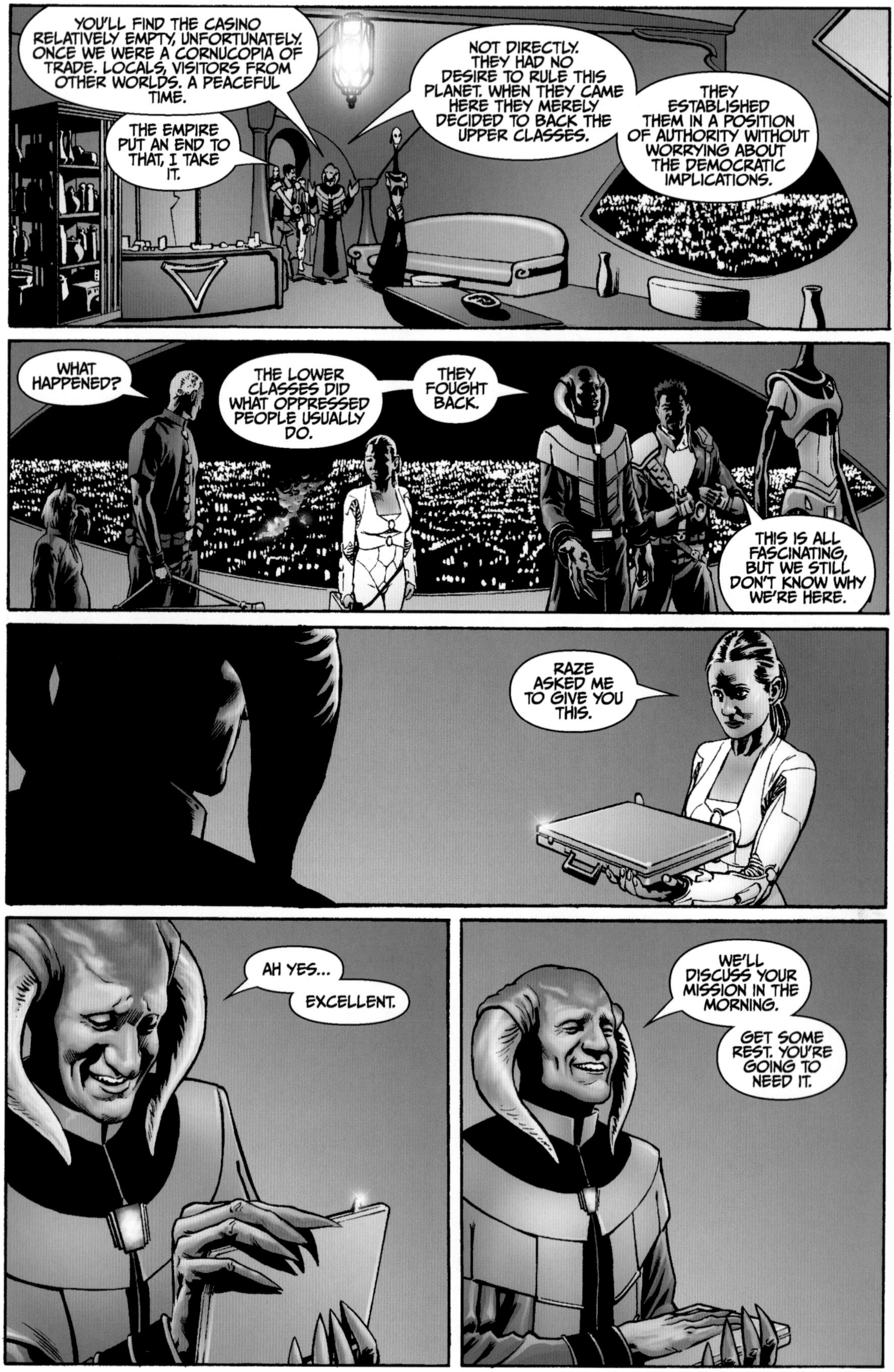
YOU'LL FIND THE CASINO RELATIVELY EMPTY, UNFORTUNATELY. ONCE WE WERE A CORNUCOPIA OF TRADE. LOCALS, VISITORS FROM OTHER WORLDS. A PEACEFUL TIME.
THE EMPIRE PUT AN END TO THAT, I TAKE IT.
NOT DIRECTLY. THEY HAD NO DESIRE TO RULE THIS PLANET. WHEN THEY CAME HERE THEY MERELY DECIDED TO BACK THE UPPER CLASSES.
THEY ESTABLISHED THEM IN A POSITION OF AUTHORITY WITHOUT WORRYING ABOUT THE DEMOCRATIC IMPLICATIONS.
WHAT HAPPENED?
THE LOWER CLASSES DID WHAT OPPRESSED PEOPLE USUALLY DO.
THEY FOUGHT BACK.
THIS IS ALL FASCINATING, BUT WE STILL DON'T KNOW WHY WE'RE HERE.
RAZE ASKED ME TO GIVE YOU THIS.
AH YES...
EXCELLENT.
WE'LL DISCUSS YOUR MISSION IN THE MORNING.
GET SOME REST. YOU'RE GOING TO NEED IT.

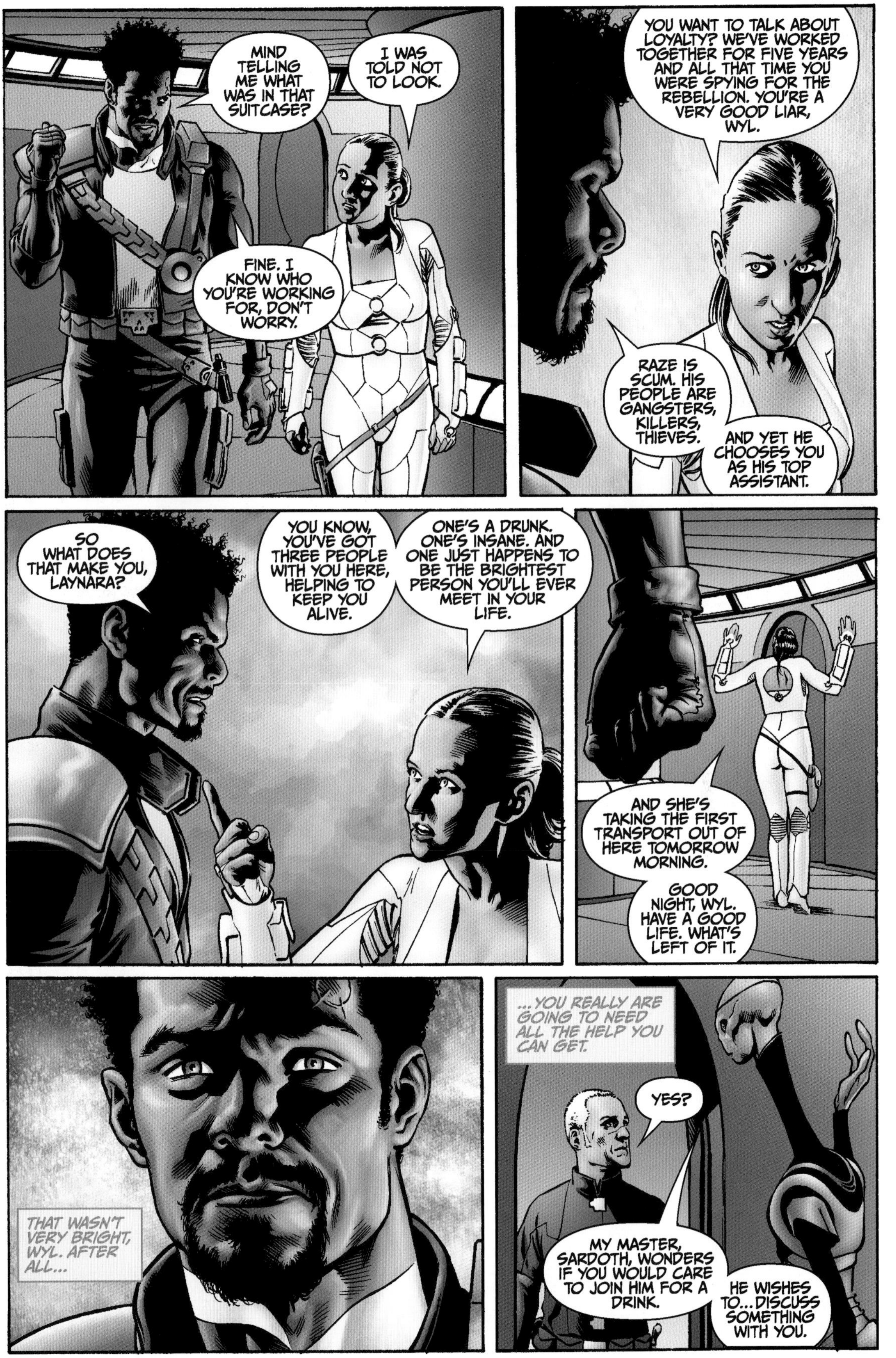
MIND TELLING ME WHAT WAS IN THAT SUITCASE?
I WAS TOLD NOT TO LOOK.
FINE. I KNOW WHO YOU'RE WORKING FOR, DON'T WORRY.
YOU WANT TO TALK ABOUT LOYALTY? WE'VE WORKED TOGETHER FOR FIVE YEARS AND ALL THAT TIME YOU WERE SPYING FOR THE REBELLION. YOU'RE A VERY GOOD LIAR, WYL.
RAZE IS SCUM. HIS PEOPLE ARE GANGSTERS, KILLERS, THIEVES.
AND YET HE CHOOSES YOU AS HIS TOP ASSISTANT.
SO WHAT DOES THAT MAKE YOU, LAYNARA?
YOU KNOW, YOU'VE GOT THREE PEOPLE WITH YOU HERE, HELPING TO KEEP YOU ALIVE.
ONE'S A DRUNK. ONE'S INSANE. AND ONE JUST HAPPENS TO BE THE BRIGHTEST PERSON YOU'LL EVER MEET IN YOUR LIFE.
AND SHE'S TAKING THE FIRST TRANSPORT OUT OF HERE TOMORROW MORNING.
GOOD NIGHT, WYL. HAVE A GOOD LIFE. WHAT'S LEFT OF IT.
THAT WASN'T VERY BRIGHT, WYL. AFTER ALL...
...YOU REALLY ARE GOING TO NEED ALL THE HELP YOU CAN GET.
YES?
MY MASTER, SARDOTH, WONDERS IF YOU WOULD CARE TO JOIN HIM FOR A DRINK.
HE WISHES TO... DISCUSS SOMETHING WITH YOU.

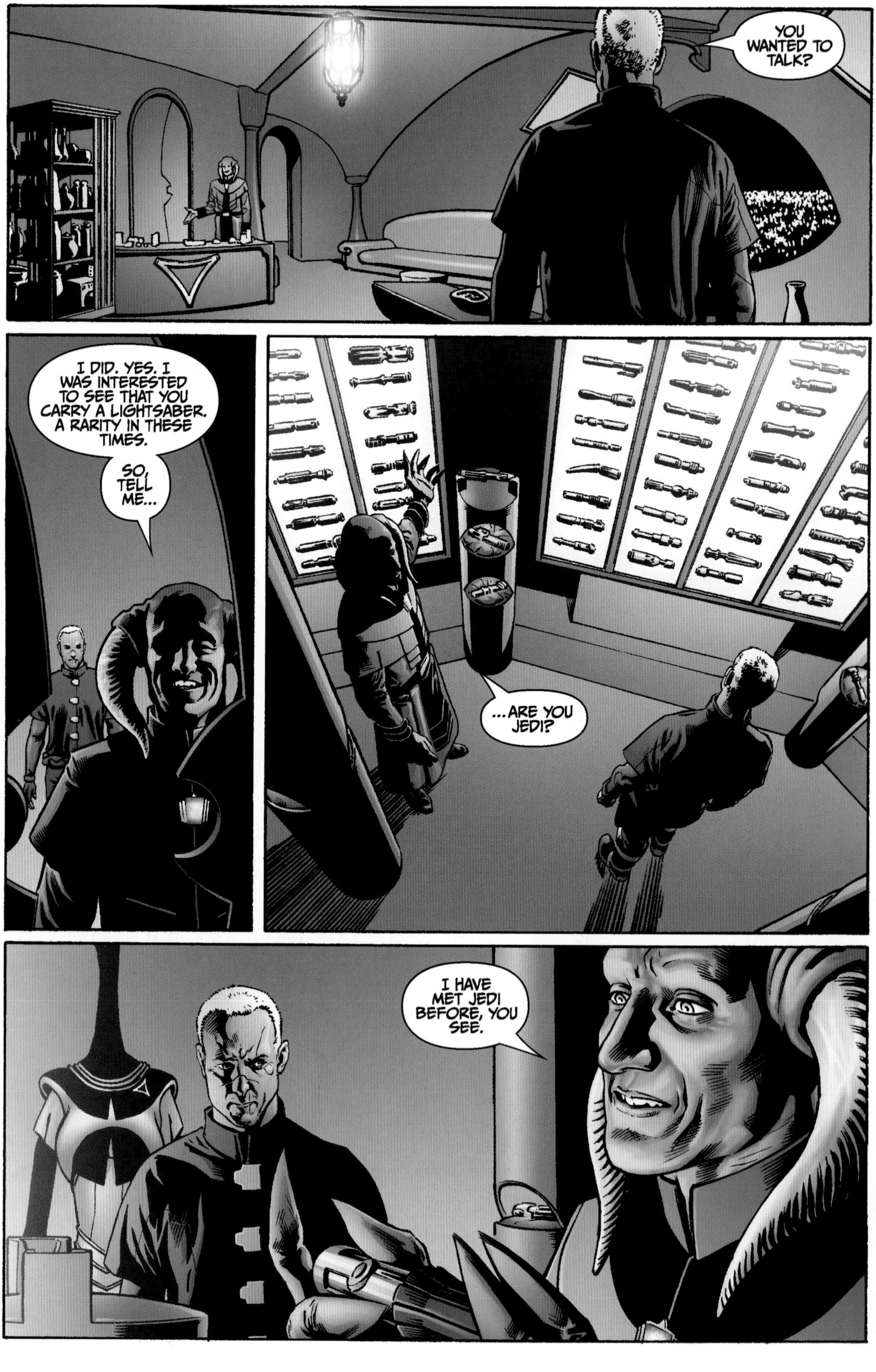
YOU WANTED TO TALK?
I DID. YES. I WAS INTERESTED TO SEE THAT YOU CARRY A LIGHTSABER. A RARITY IN THESE TIMES.
SO, TELL ME...
...ARE YOU JEDI?
I HAVE MET JEDI BEFORE, YOU SEE.

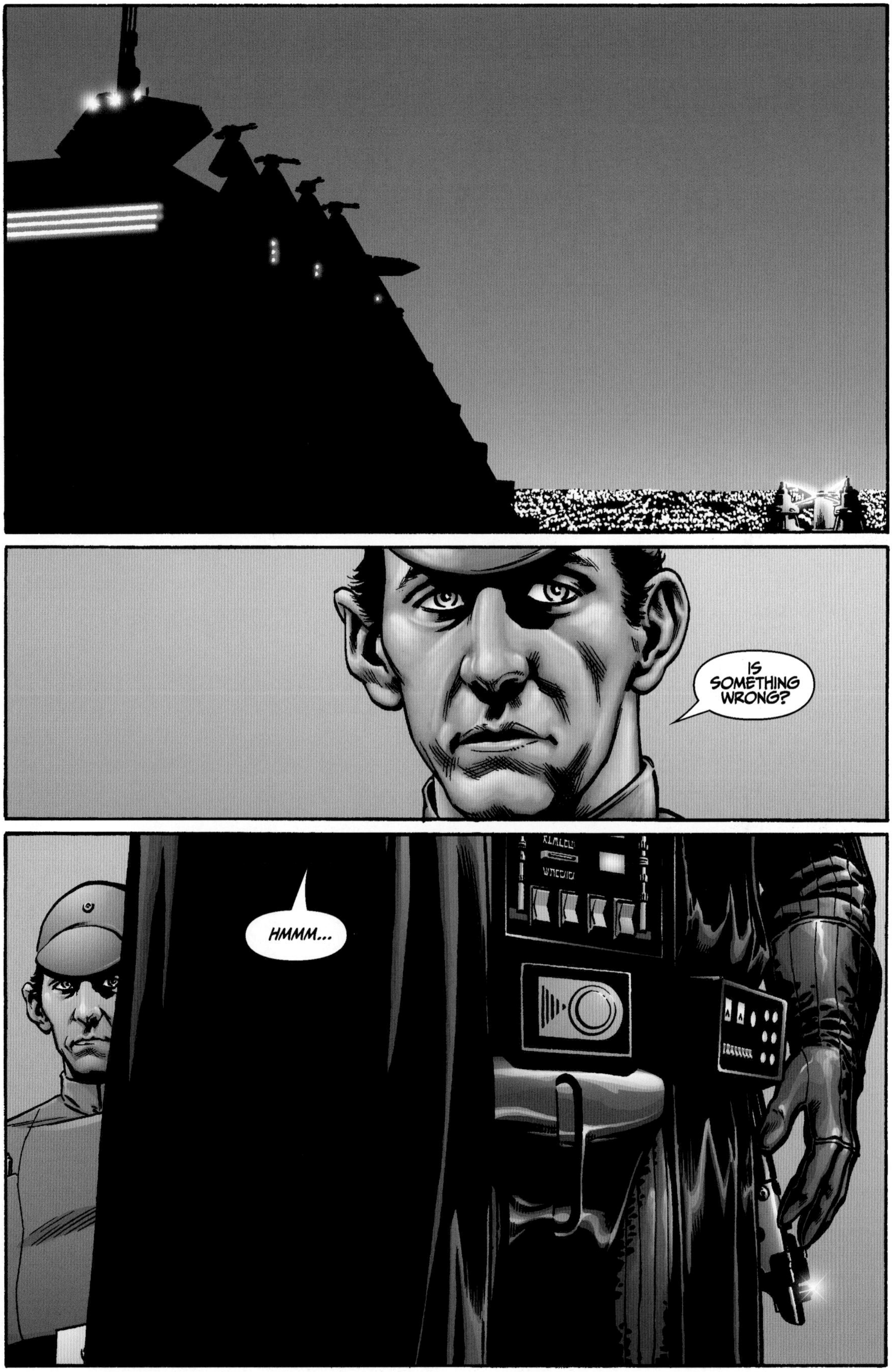
IS SOMETHING WRONG?
HMMM...

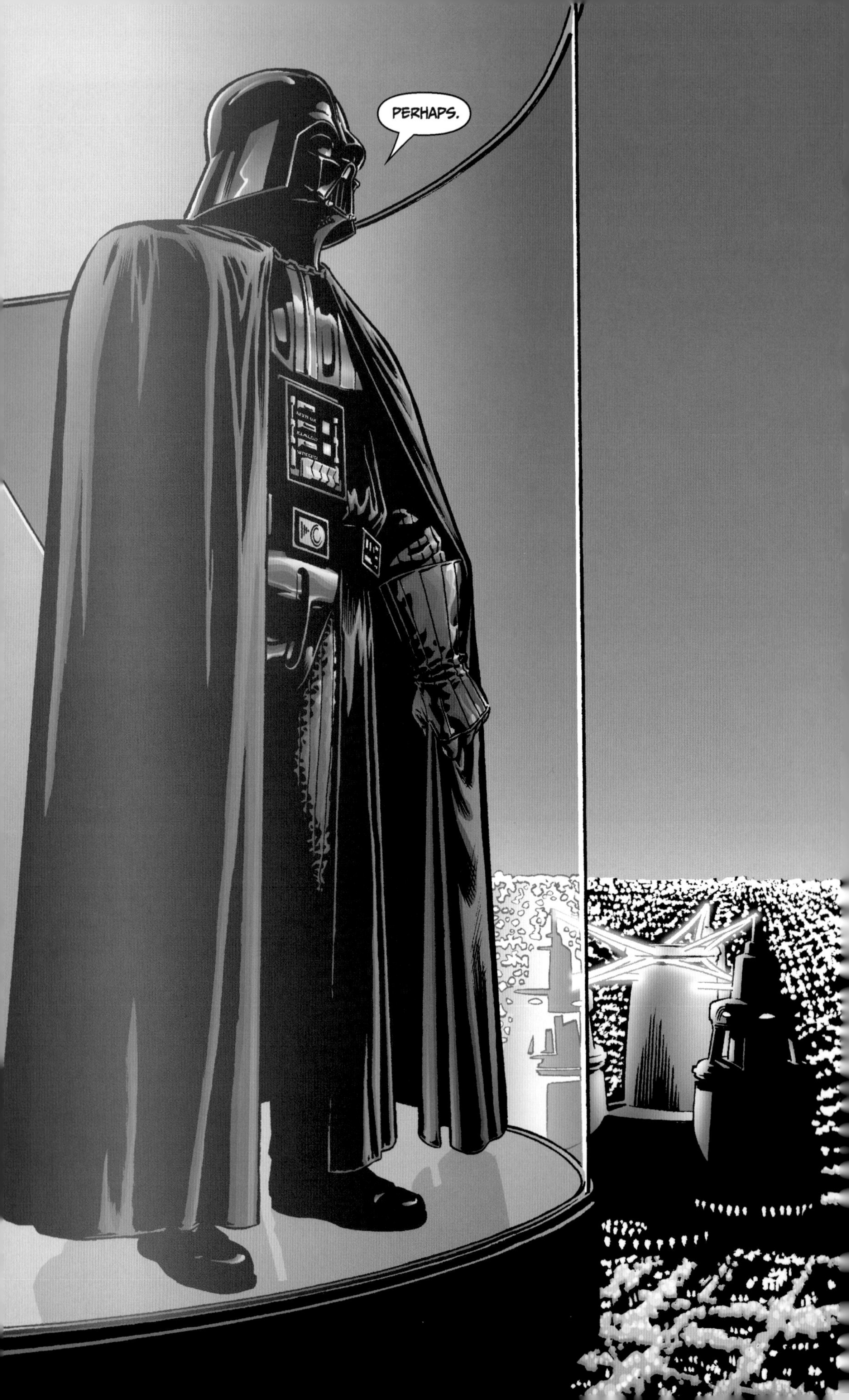
PERHAPS.

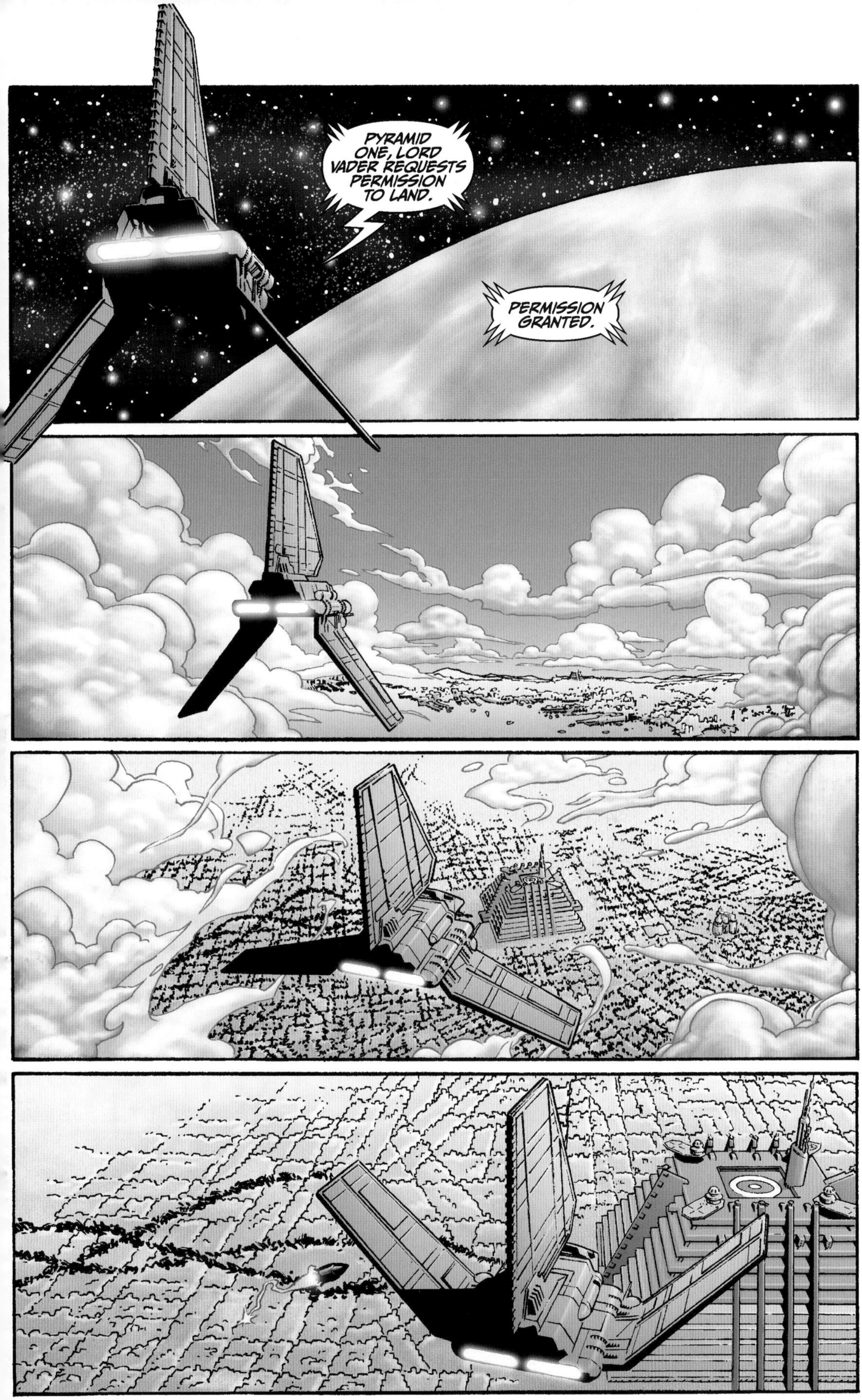
PYRAMID ONE, LORD VADER REQUESTS PERMISSION TO LAND.
PERMISSION GRANTED.

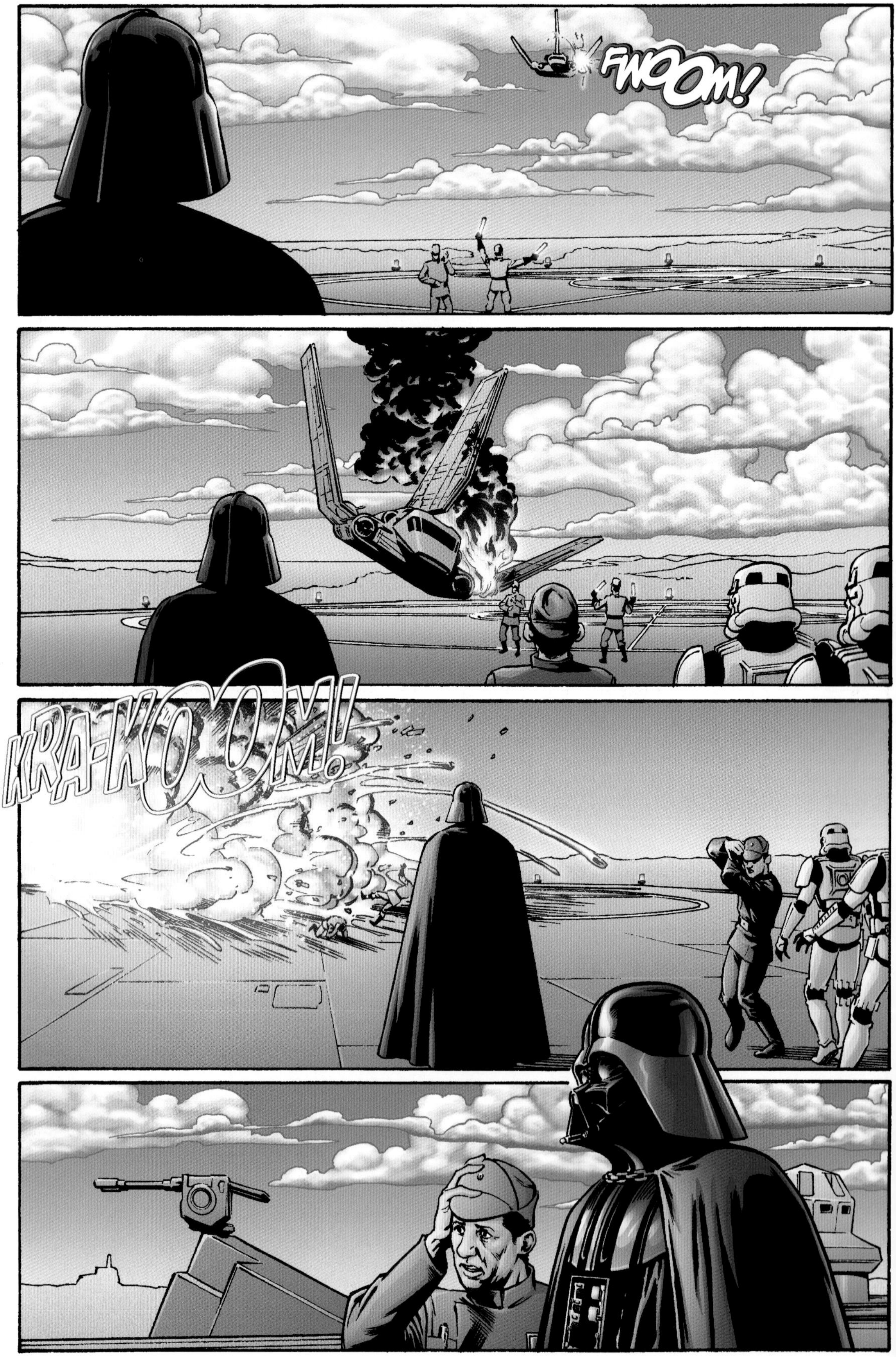
FWOOM!
KRA-KOOM!

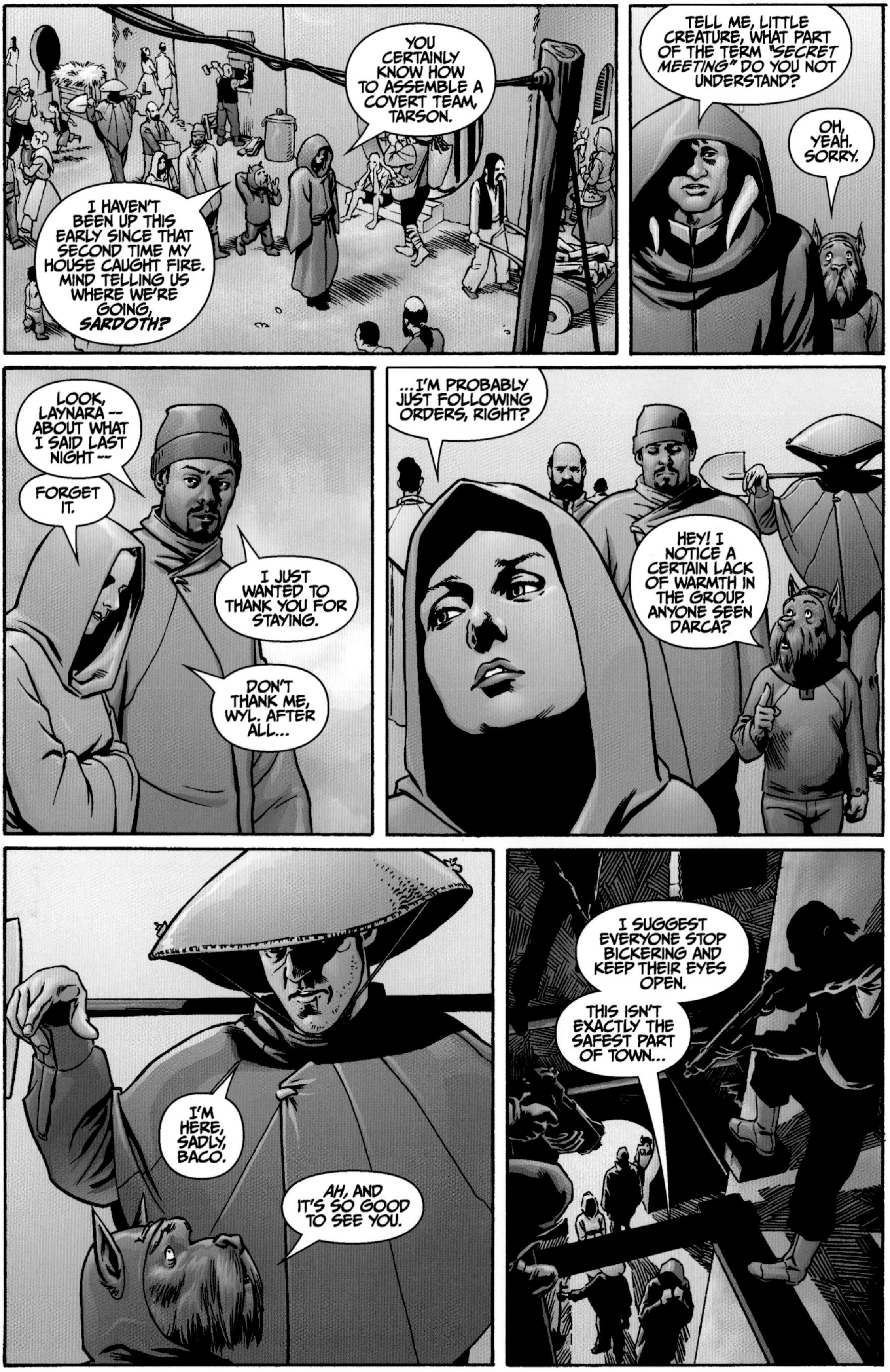
YOU CERTAINLY KNOW HOW TO ASSEMBLE A COVERT TEAM, TARSON.
I HAVEN'T BEEN UP THIS EARLY SINCE THAT SECOND TIME MY HOUSE CAUGHT FIRE. MIND TELLING US WHERE WE'RE GOING, SARDOTH?
TELL ME, LITTLE CREATURE, WHAT PART OF THE TERM "SECRET MEETING" DO YOU NOT UNDERSTAND?
OH, YEAH. SORRY.
LOOK, LAYNARA -- ABOUT WHAT I SAID LAST NIGHT --
FORGET IT.
I JUST WANTED TO THANK YOU FOR STAYING.
DON'T THANK ME, WYL. AFTER ALL...
...I'M PROBABLY JUST FOLLOWING ORDERS, RIGHT?
HEY! I NOTICE A CERTAIN LACK OF WARMTH IN THE GROUP. ANYONE SEEN DARCA?
I'M HERE, SADLY, BACO.
AH, AND IT'S SO GOOD TO SEE YOU.
I SUGGEST EVERYONE STOP BICKERING AND KEEP THEIR EYES OPEN.
THIS ISN'T EXACTLY THE SAFEST PART OF TOWN...

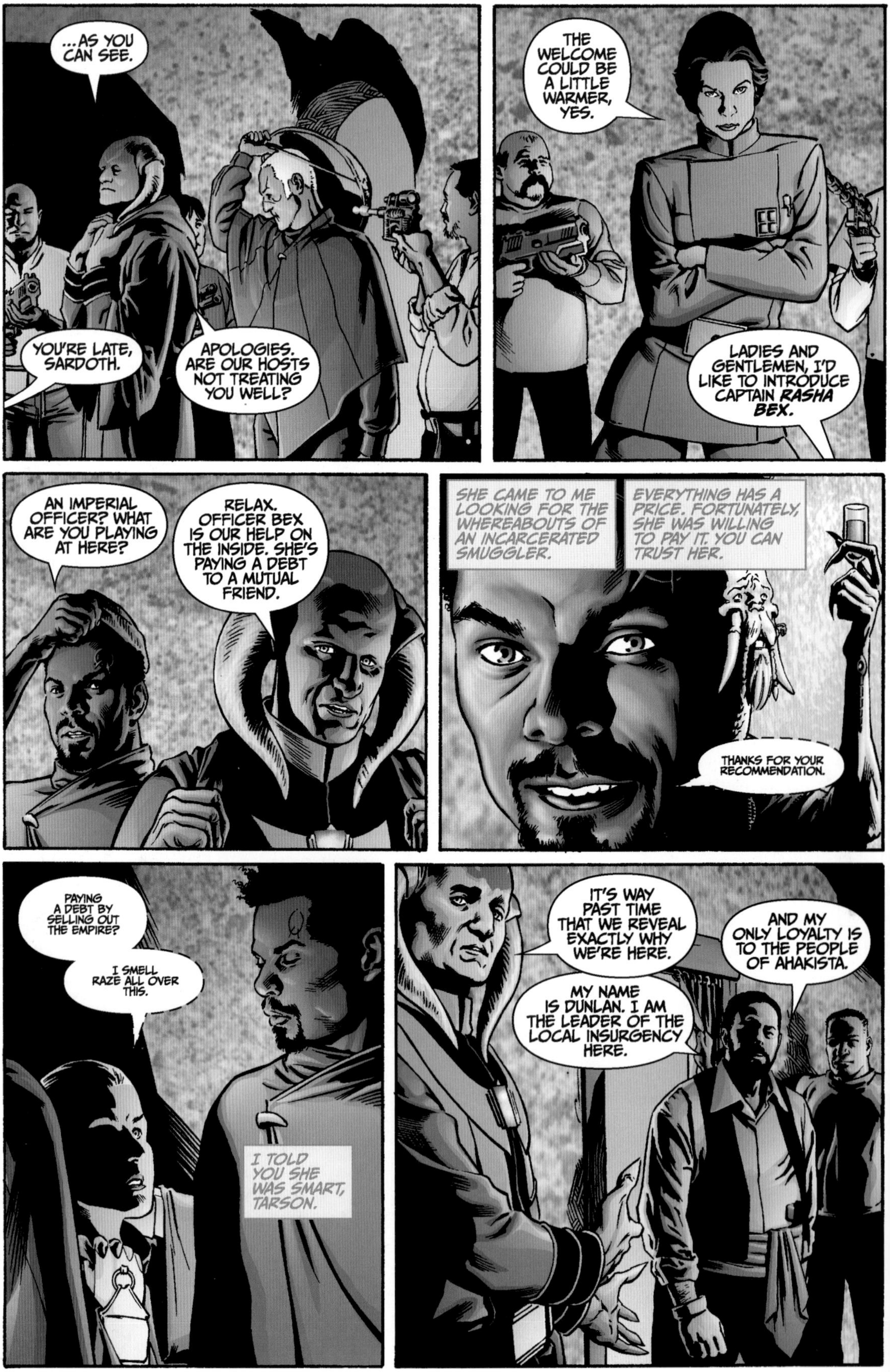

...AS YOU CAN SEE.
YOU'RE LATE, SARDOTH.
APOLOGIES. ARE OUR HOSTS NOT TREATING YOU WELL?
THE WELCOME COULD BE A LITTLE WARMER, YES.
LADIES AND GENTLEMEN, I'D LIKE TO INTRODUCE CAPTAIN RASHA BEX.
AN IMPERIAL OFFICER? WHAT ARE YOU PLAYING AT HERE?
RELAX. OFFICER BEX IS OUR HELP ON THE INSIDE. SHE'S PAYING A DEBT TO A MUTUAL FRIEND.
SHE CAME TO ME LOOKING FOR THE WHEREABOUTS OF AN INCARCERATED SMUGGLER.
EVERYTHING HAS A PRICE. FORTUNATELY, SHE WAS WILLING TO PAY IT. YOU CAN TRUST HER.
THANKS FOR YOUR RECOMMENDATION.
PAYING A DEBT BY SELLING OUT THE EMPIRE?
I SMELL RAZE ALL OVER THIS.
I TOLD YOU SHE WAS SMART, TARSON.
IT'S WAY PAST TIME THAT WE REVEAL EXACTLY WHY WE'RE HERE.
MY NAME IS DUNLAN. I AM THE LEADER OF THE LOCAL INSURGENCY HERE.
AND MY ONLY LOYALTY IS TO THE PEOPLE OF AHAKISTA.

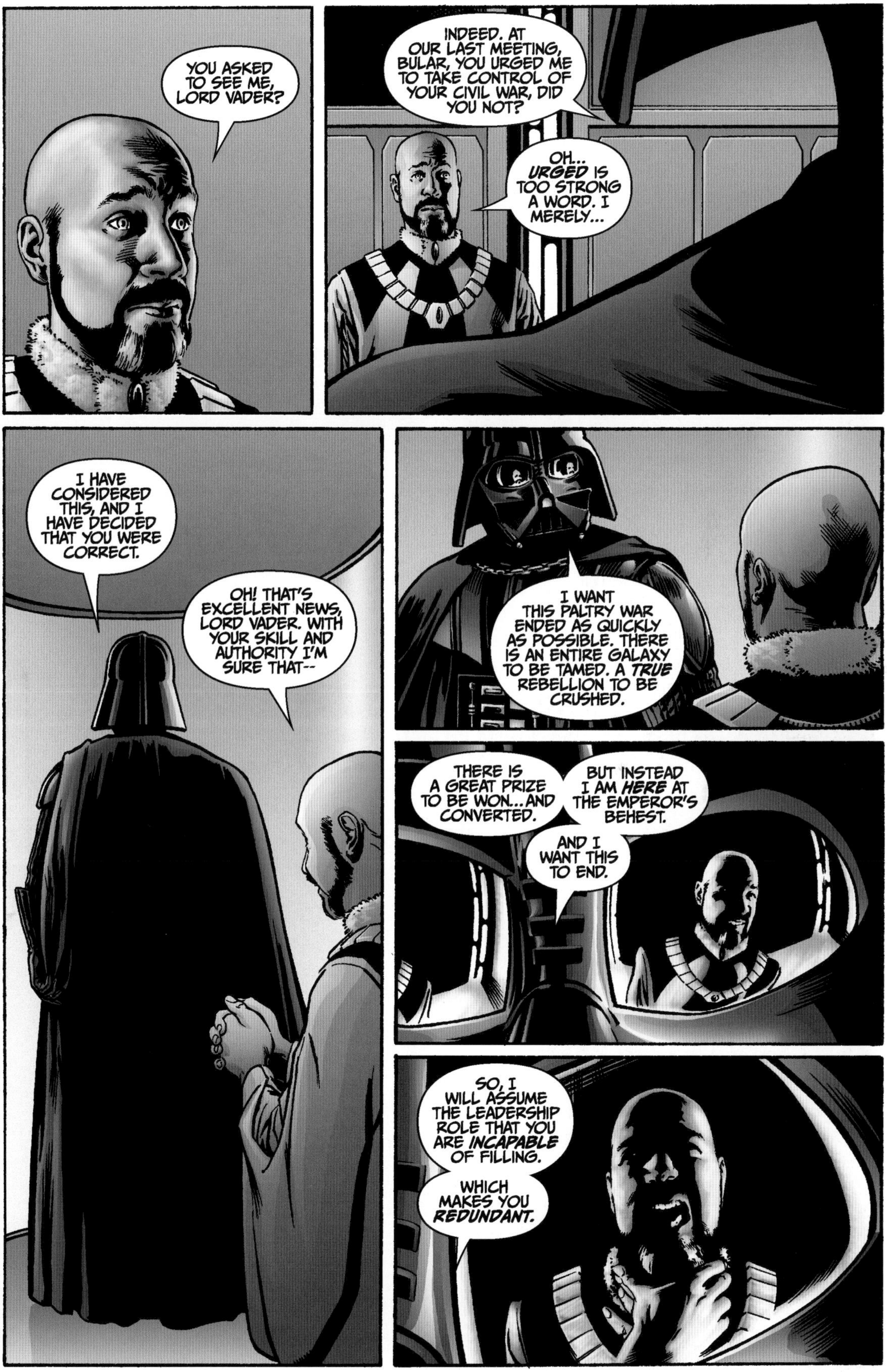
YOU ASKED TO SEE ME, LORD VADER?
INDEED. AT OUR LAST MEETING, BULAR, YOU URGED ME TO TAKE CONTROL OF YOUR CIVIL WAR, DID YOU NOT?
OH... *URGED* IS TOO STRONG A WORD. I MERELY...
I HAVE CONSIDERED THIS, AND I HAVE DECIDED THAT YOU WERE CORRECT.
OH! THAT'S EXCELLENT NEWS, LORD VADER. WITH YOUR SKILL AND AUTHORITY I'M SURE THAT--
I WANT THIS PALTRY WAR ENDED AS QUICKLY AS POSSIBLE. THERE IS AN ENTIRE GALAXY TO BE TAMED. A *TRUE* REBELLION TO BE CRUSHED.
THERE IS A GREAT PRIZE TO BE WON...AND CONVERTED.
BUT INSTEAD I AM *HERE* AT THE EMPEROR'S BEHEST.
AND I WANT THIS TO END.
SO, I WILL ASSUME THE LEADERSHIP ROLE THAT YOU ARE *INCAPABLE* OF FILLING.
WHICH MAKES YOU *REDUNDANT*.

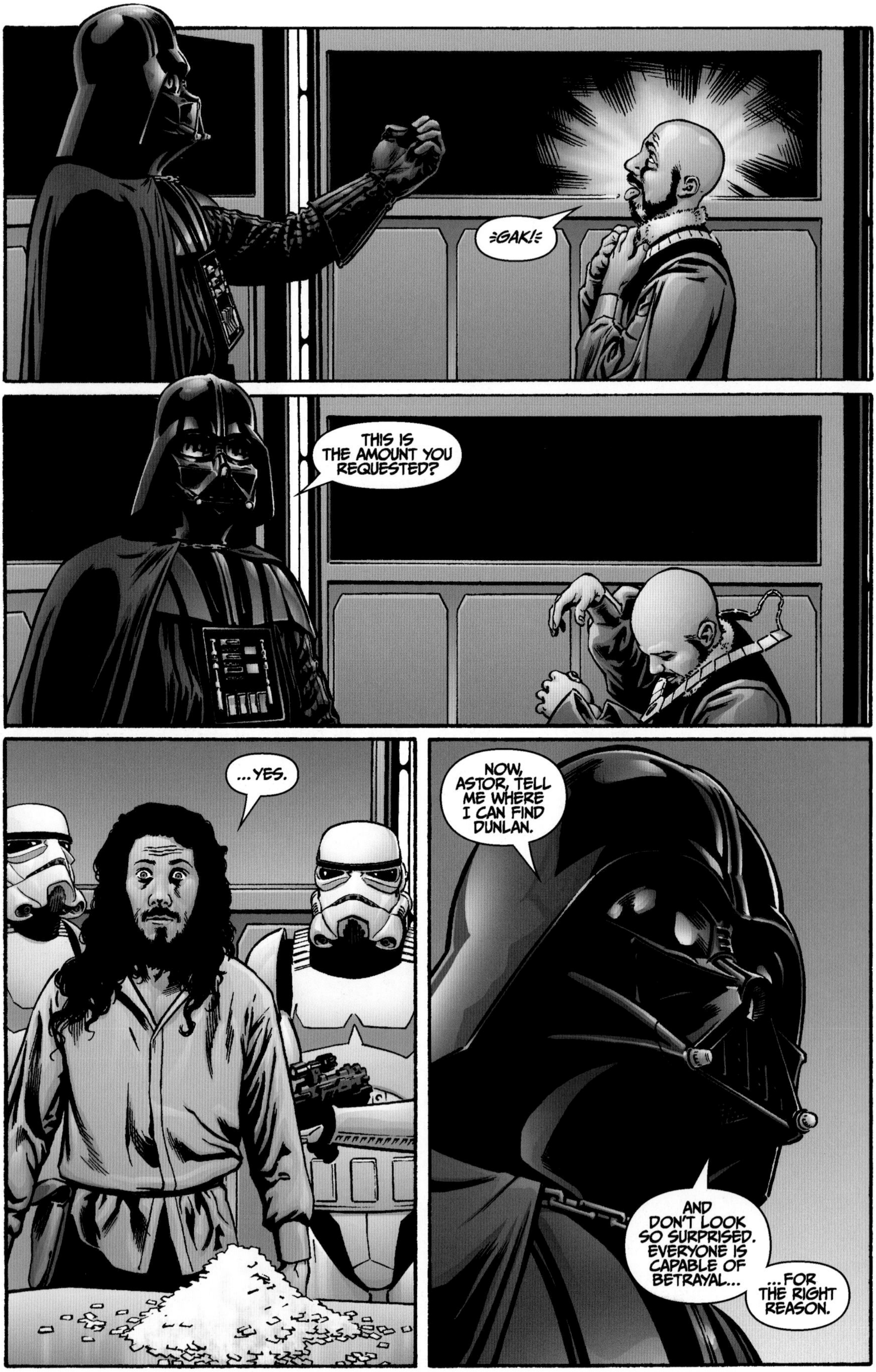
GAK!
THIS IS THE AMOUNT YOU REQUESTED?
...YES.
NOW, ASTOR, TELL ME WHERE I CAN FIND DUNLAN.
AND DON'T LOOK SO SURPRISED. EVERYONE IS CAPABLE OF BETRAYAL...
...FOR THE RIGHT REASON.

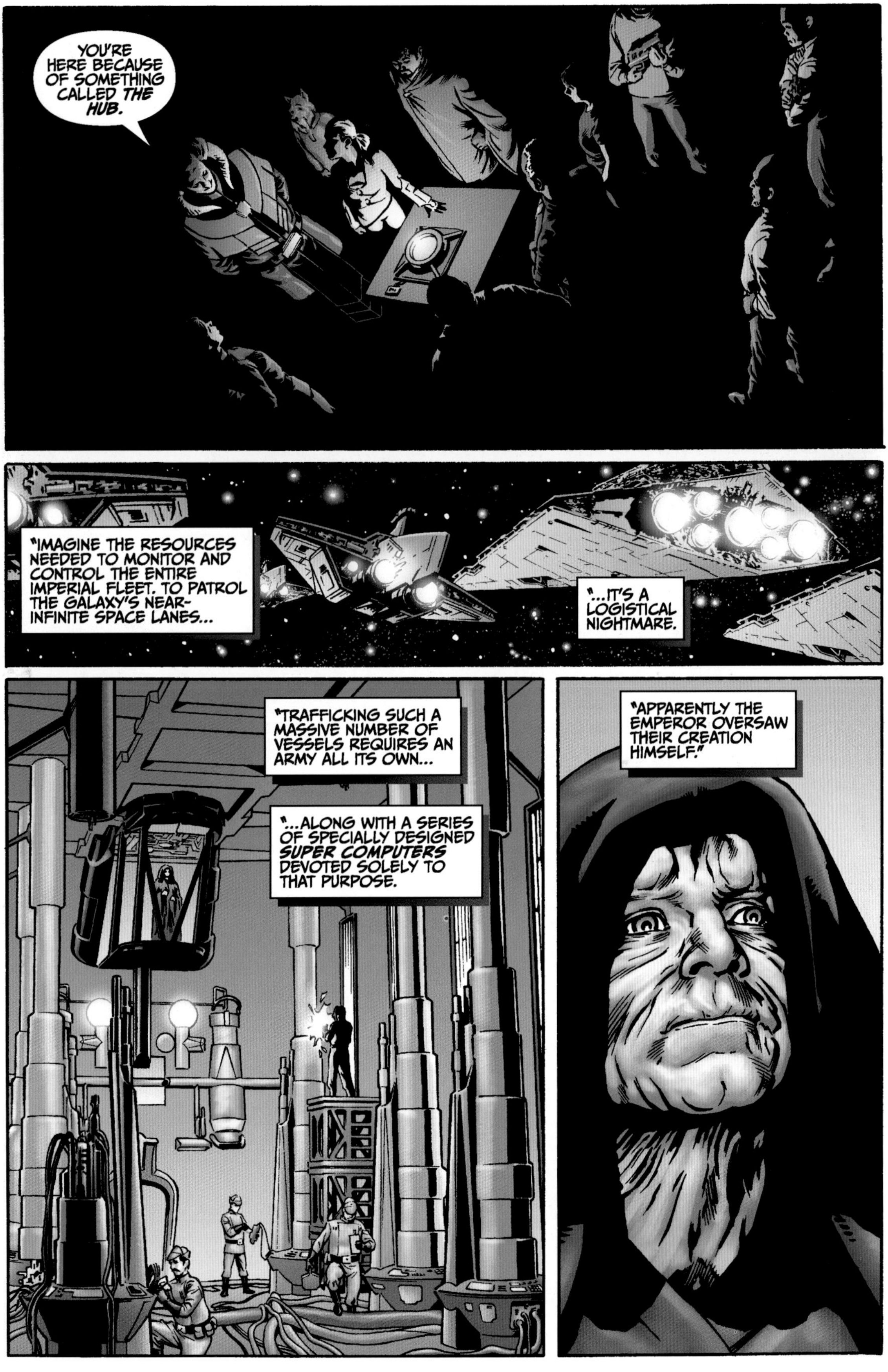
YOU'RE HERE BECAUSE OF SOMETHING CALLED THE HUB.
"IMAGINE THE RESOURCES NEEDED TO MONITOR AND CONTROL THE ENTIRE IMPERIAL FLEET. TO PATROL THE GALAXY'S NEAR-INFINITE SPACE LANES...
"...IT'S A LOGISTICAL NIGHTMARE.
"TRAFFICKING SUCH A MASSIVE NUMBER OF VESSELS REQUIRES AN ARMY ALL ITS OWN...
"...ALONG WITH A SERIES OF SPECIALLY DESIGNED SUPER COMPUTERS DEVOTED SOLELY TO THAT PURPOSE.
"APPARENTLY THE EMPEROR OVERSAW THEIR CREATION HIMSELF."

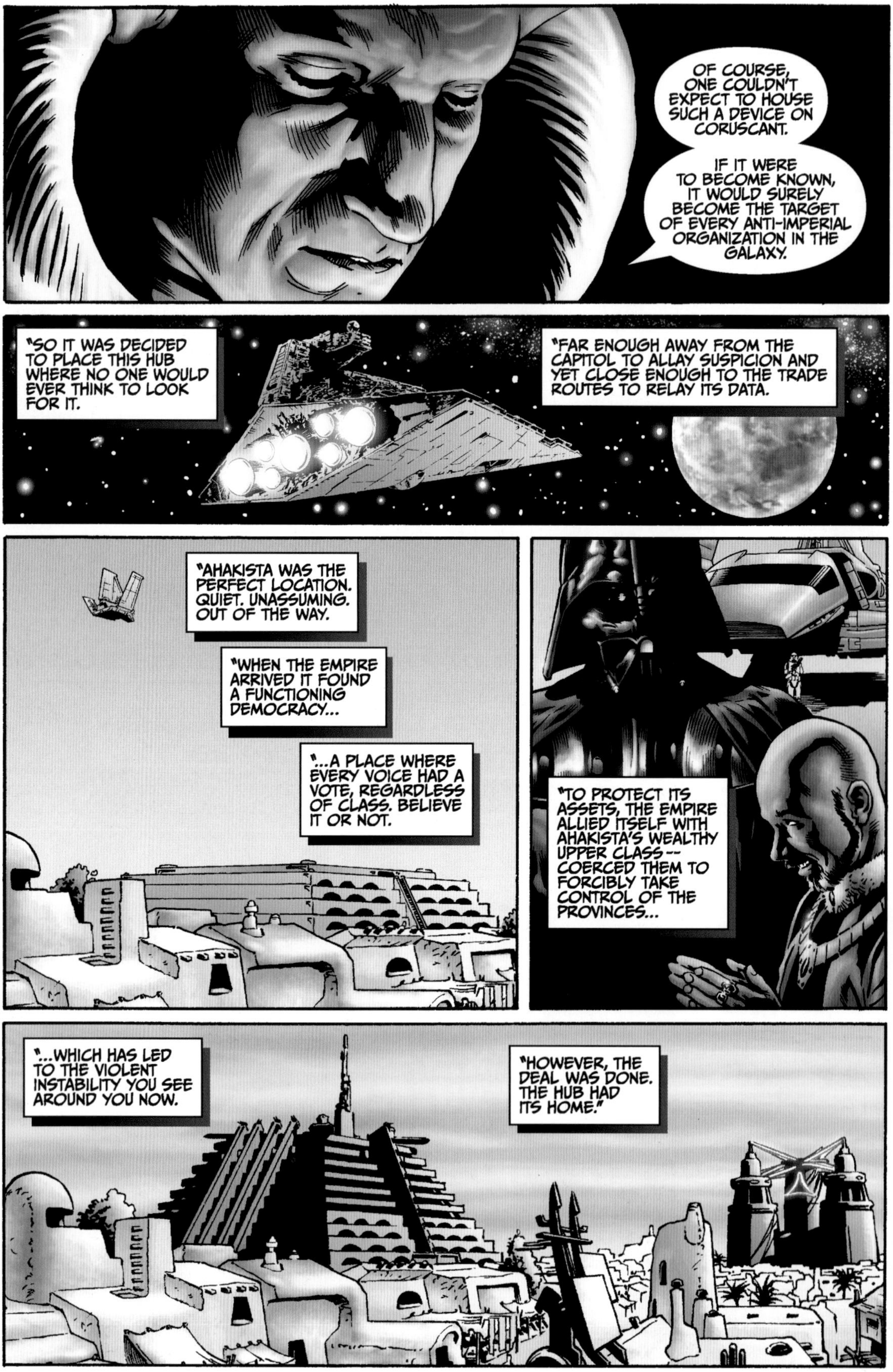

OF COURSE, ONE COULDN'T EXPECT TO HOUSE SUCH A DEVICE ON CORUSCANT.
IF IT WERE TO BECOME KNOWN, IT WOULD SURELY BECOME THE TARGET OF EVERY ANTI-IMPERIAL ORGANIZATION IN THE GALAXY.
"SO IT WAS DECIDED TO PLACE THIS HUB WHERE NO ONE WOULD EVER THINK TO LOOK FOR IT.
"FAR ENOUGH AWAY FROM THE CAPITOL TO ALLAY SUSPICION AND YET CLOSE ENOUGH TO THE TRADE ROUTES TO RELAY ITS DATA.
"AHAKISTA WAS THE PERFECT LOCATION. QUIET. UNASSUMING. OUT OF THE WAY.
"WHEN THE EMPIRE ARRIVED IT FOUND A FUNCTIONING DEMOCRACY...
"...A PLACE WHERE EVERY VOICE HAD A VOTE, REGARDLESS OF CLASS. BELIEVE IT OR NOT.
"TO PROTECT ITS ASSETS, THE EMPIRE ALLIED ITSELF WITH AHAKISTA'S WEALTHY UPPER CLASS-- COERCED THEM TO FORCIBLY TAKE CONTROL OF THE PROVINCES...
"...WHICH HAS LED TO THE VIOLENT INSTABILITY YOU SEE AROUND YOU NOW.
"HOWEVER, THE DEAL WAS DONE. THE HUB HAD ITS HOME."

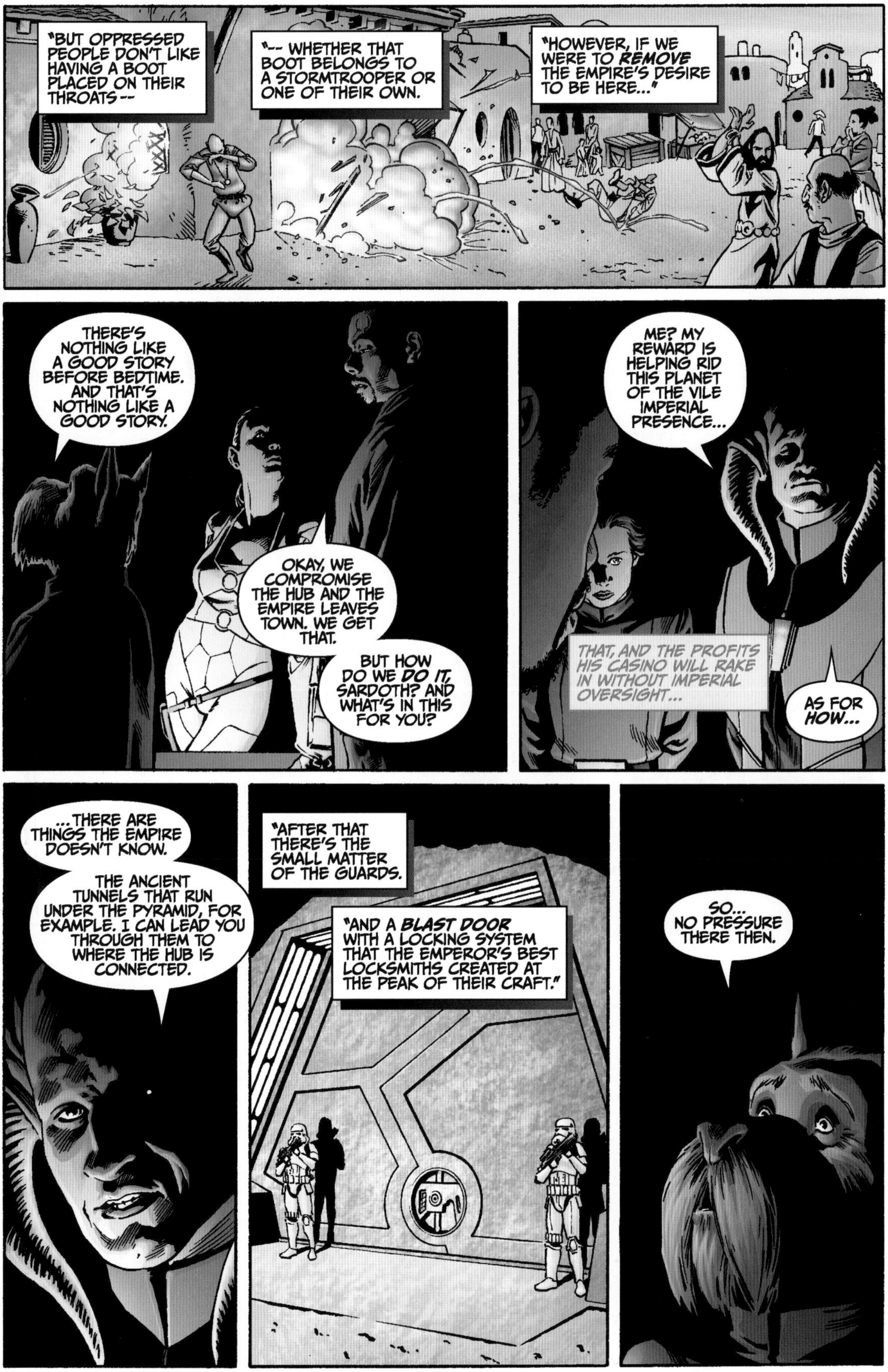
"BUT OPPRESSED PEOPLE DON'T LIKE HAVING A BOOT PLACED ON THEIR THROATS--
"-- WHETHER THAT BOOT BELONGS TO A STORMTROOPER OR ONE OF THEIR OWN.
"HOWEVER, IF WE WERE TO REMOVE THE EMPIRE'S DESIRE TO BE HERE..."
THERE'S NOTHING LIKE A GOOD STORY BEFORE BEDTIME. AND THAT'S NOTHING LIKE A GOOD STORY.
OKAY, WE COMPROMISE THE HUB AND THE EMPIRE LEAVES TOWN. WE GET THAT.
BUT HOW DO WE DO IT, SARDOTH? AND WHAT'S IN THIS FOR YOU?
ME? MY REWARD IS HELPING RID THIS PLANET OF THE VILE IMPERIAL PRESENCE...
THAT, AND THE PROFITS HIS CASINO WILL RAKE IN WITHOUT IMPERIAL OVERSIGHT...
AS FOR HOW...
...THERE ARE THINGS THE EMPIRE DOESN'T KNOW.
THE ANCIENT TUNNELS THAT RUN UNDER THE PYRAMID, FOR EXAMPLE. I CAN LEAD YOU THROUGH THEM TO WHERE THE HUB IS CONNECTED.
"AFTER THAT THERE'S THE SMALL MATTER OF THE GUARDS.
"AND A BLAST DOOR WITH A LOCKING SYSTEM THAT THE EMPEROR'S BEST LOCKSMITHS CREATED AT THE PEAK OF THEIR CRAFT."
SO... NO PRESSURE THERE THEN.

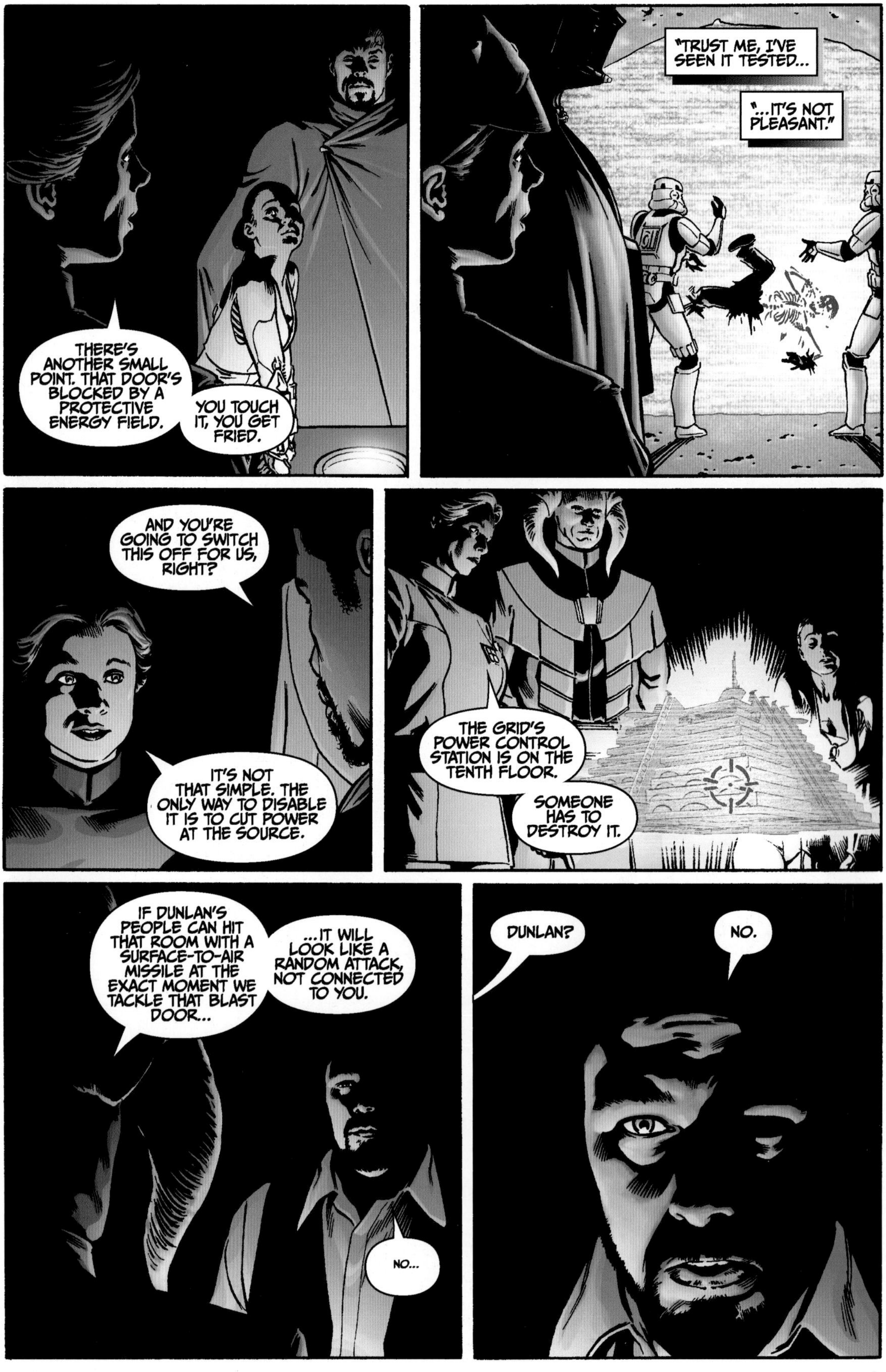
THERE'S ANOTHER SMALL POINT. THAT DOOR'S BLOCKED BY A PROTECTIVE ENERGY FIELD.
YOU TOUCH IT, YOU GET FRIED.
"TRUST ME, I'VE SEEN IT TESTED...
"...IT'S NOT PLEASANT."
AND YOU'RE GOING TO SWITCH THIS OFF FOR US, RIGHT?
IT'S NOT THAT SIMPLE. THE ONLY WAY TO DISABLE IT IS TO CUT POWER AT THE SOURCE.
THE GRID'S POWER CONTROL STATION IS ON THE TENTH FLOOR.
SOMEONE HAS TO DESTROY IT.
IF DUNLAN'S PEOPLE CAN HIT THAT ROOM WITH A SURFACE-TO-AIR MISSILE AT THE EXACT MOMENT WE TACKLE THAT BLAST DOOR...
...IT WILL LOOK LIKE A RANDOM ATTACK, NOT CONNECTED TO YOU.
NO...
DUNLAN?
NO.

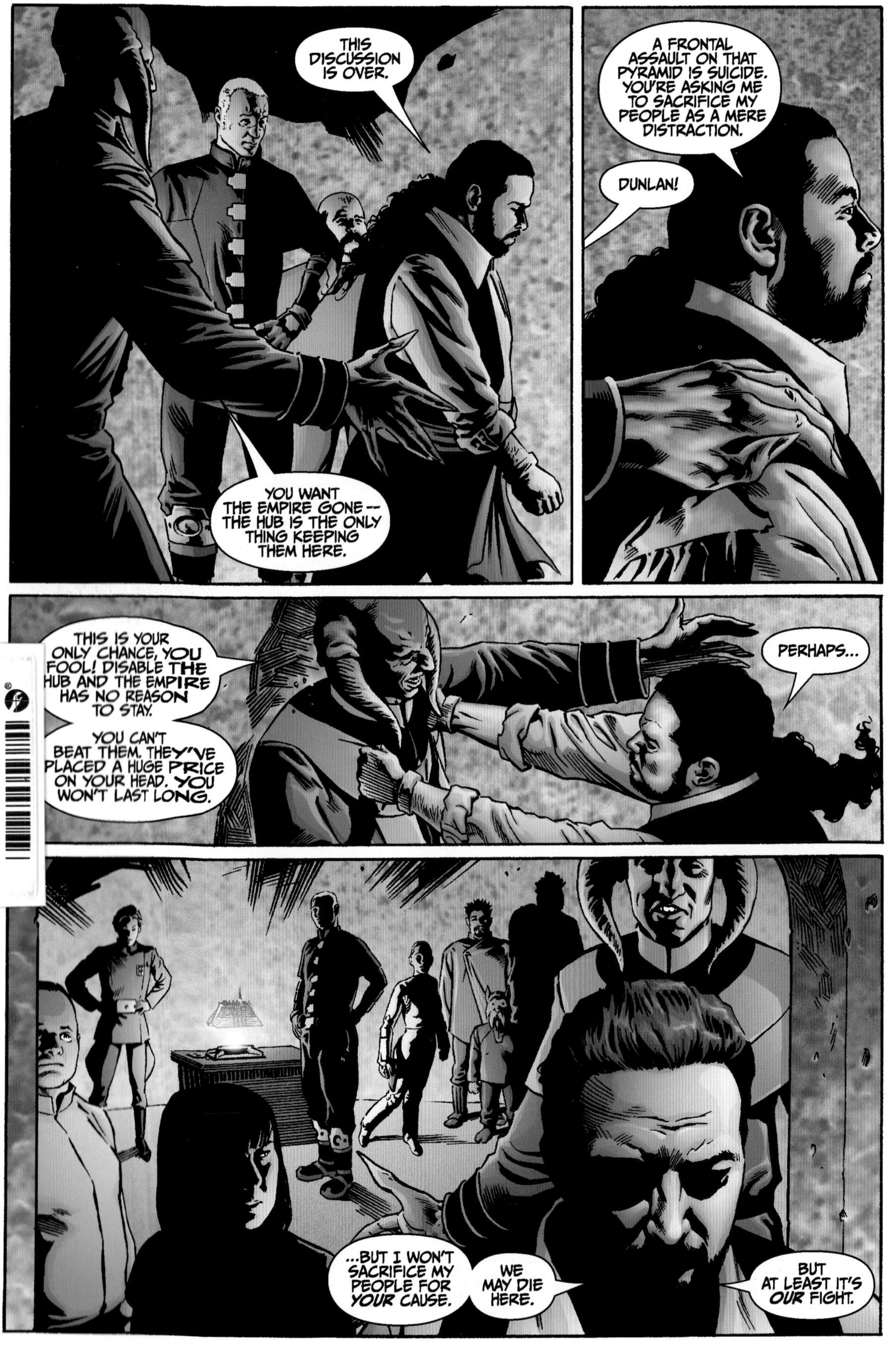
THIS DISCUSSION IS OVER.
YOU WANT THE EMPIRE GONE -- THE HUB IS THE ONLY THING KEEPING THEM HERE.
A FRONTAL ASSAULT ON THAT PYRAMID IS SUICIDE. YOU'RE ASKING ME TO SACRIFICE MY PEOPLE AS A MERE DISTRACTION.
DUNLAN!
THIS IS YOUR ONLY CHANCE, YOU FOOL! DISABLE THE HUB AND THE EMPIRE HAS NO REASON TO STAY.
YOU CAN'T BEAT THEM. THEY'VE PLACED A HUGE PRICE ON YOUR HEAD. YOU WON'T LAST LONG.
PERHAPS...
...BUT I WON'T SACRIFICE MY PEOPLE FOR YOUR CAUSE.
WE MAY DIE HERE.
BUT AT LEAST IT'S OUR FIGHT.

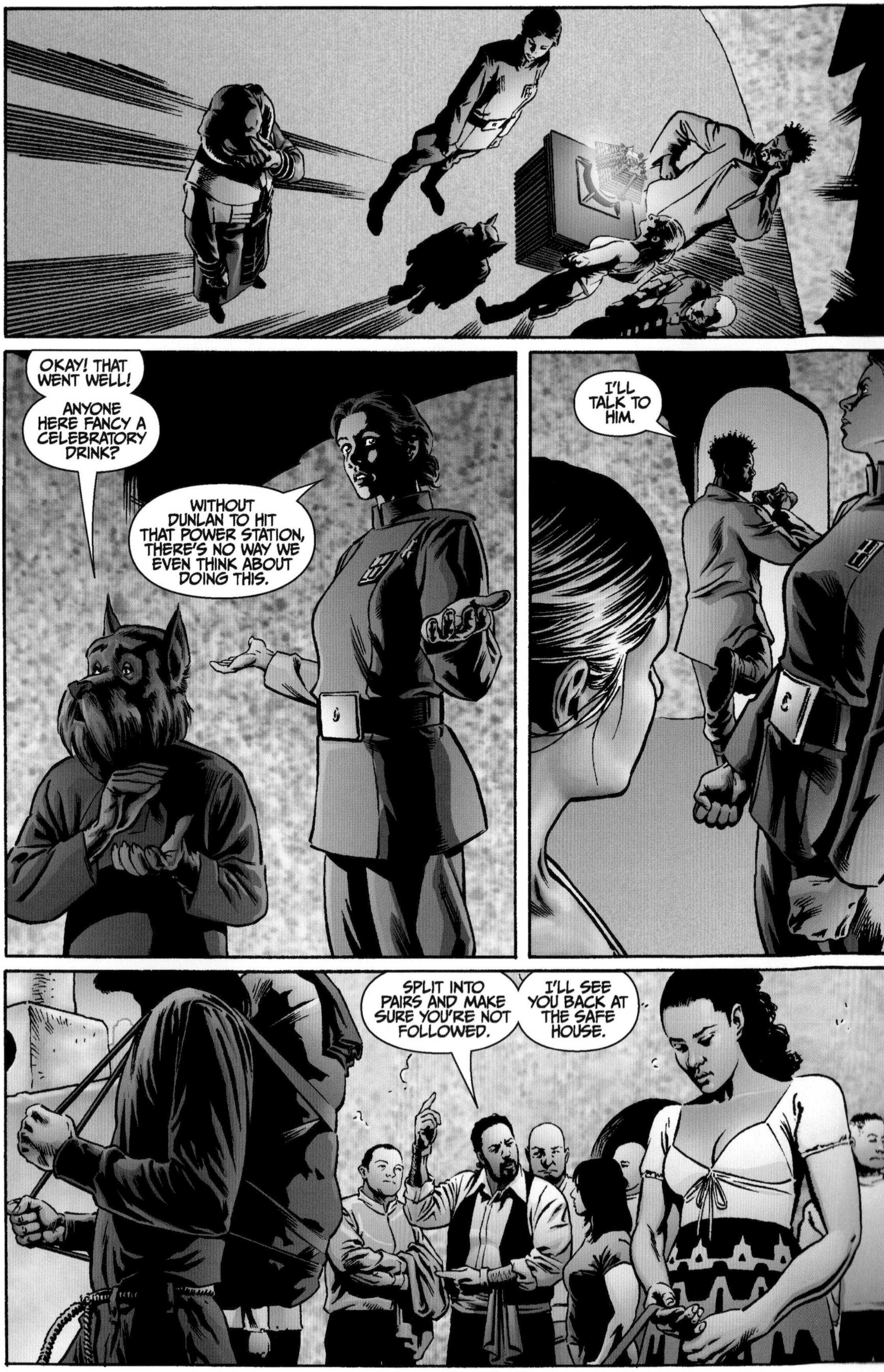
OKAY! THAT WENT WELL!
ANYONE HERE FANCY A CELEBRATORY DRINK?
WITHOUT DUNLAN TO HIT THAT POWER STATION, THERE'S NO WAY WE EVEN THINK ABOUT DOING THIS.
I'LL TALK TO HIM.
SPLIT INTO PAIRS AND MAKE SURE YOU'RE NOT FOLLOWED.
I'LL SEE YOU BACK AT THE SAFE HOUSE.

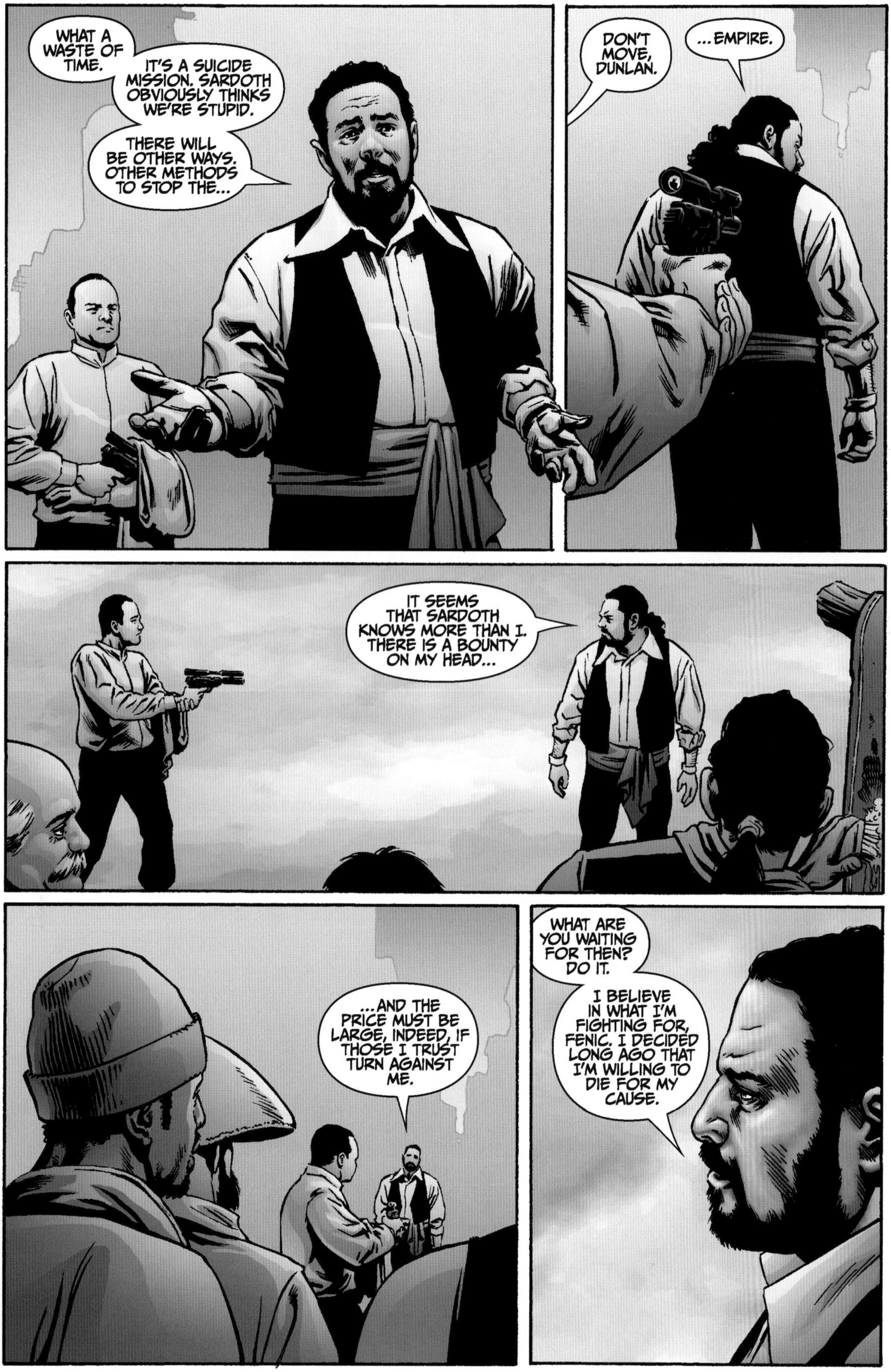
WHAT A WASTE OF TIME.
IT'S A SUICIDE MISSION. SARDOTH OBVIOUSLY THINKS WE'RE STUPID.
THERE WILL BE OTHER WAYS. OTHER METHODS TO STOP THE...
DON'T MOVE, DUNLAN.
...EMPIRE.
IT SEEMS THAT SARDOTH KNOWS MORE THAN I. THERE IS A BOUNTY ON MY HEAD...
...AND THE PRICE MUST BE LARGE, INDEED, IF THOSE I TRUST TURN AGAINST ME.
WHAT ARE YOU WAITING FOR THEN? DO IT.
I BELIEVE IN WHAT I'M FIGHTING FOR, FENIC. I DECIDED LONG AGO THAT I'M WILLING TO DIE FOR MY CAUSE.

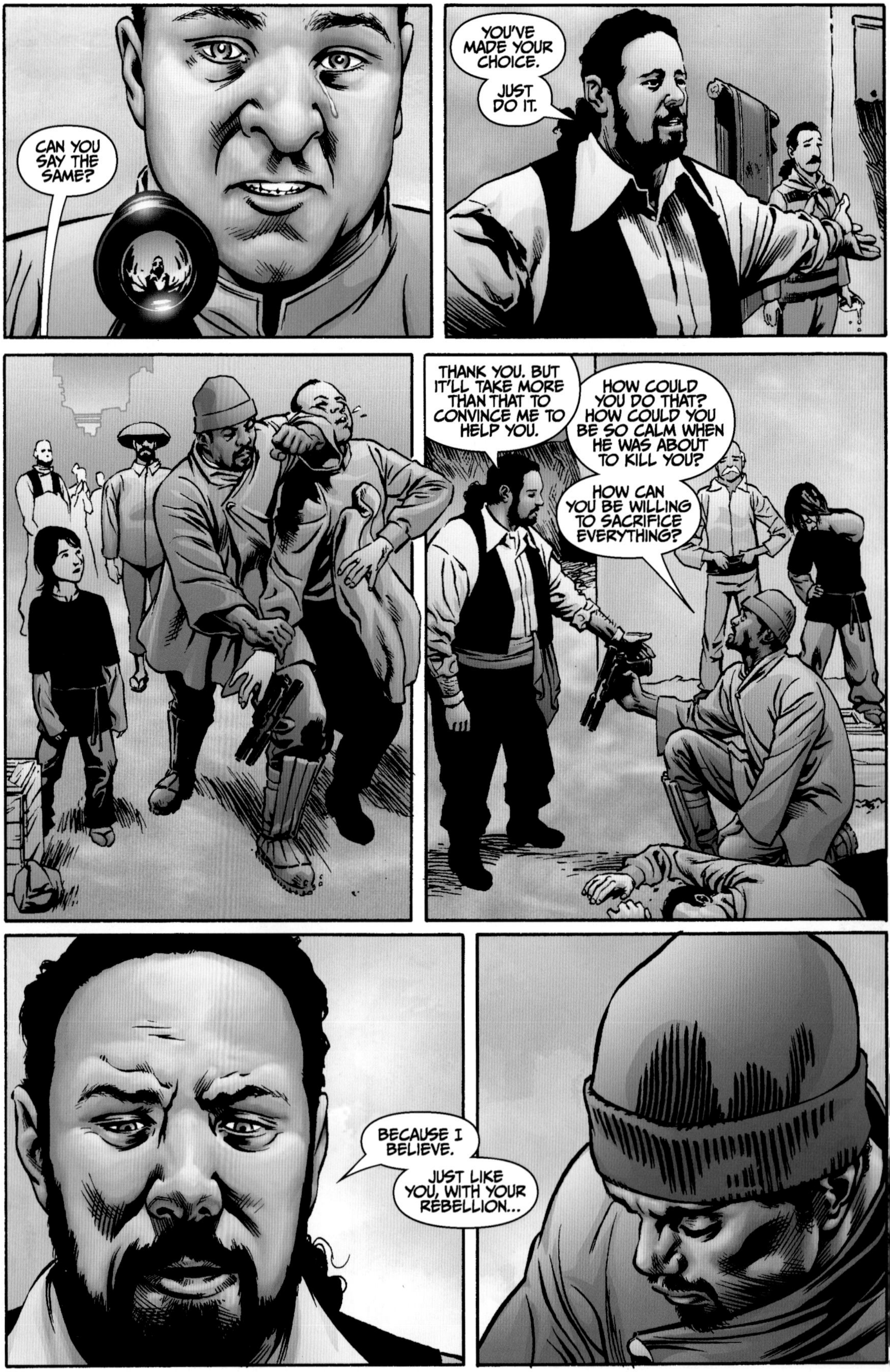
YOU'VE MADE YOUR CHOICE.
JUST DO IT.
CAN YOU SAY THE SAME?
THANK YOU. BUT IT'LL TAKE MORE THAN THAT TO CONVINCE ME TO HELP YOU.
HOW COULD YOU DO THAT? HOW COULD YOU BE SO CALM WHEN HE WAS ABOUT TO KILL YOU?
HOW CAN YOU BE WILLING TO SACRIFICE EVERYTHING?
BECAUSE I BELIEVE.
JUST LIKE YOU, WITH YOUR REBELLION...

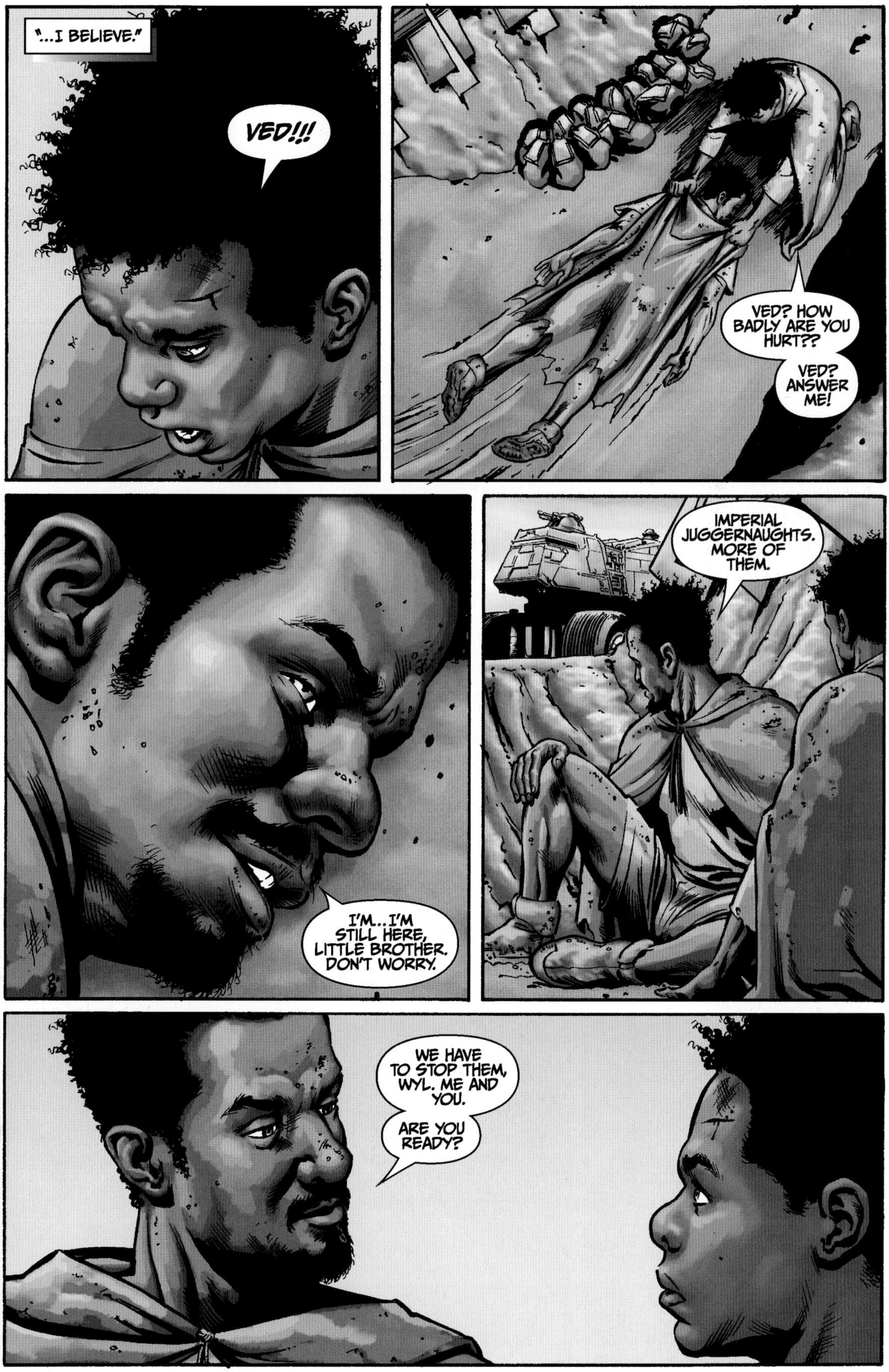
"...I BELIEVE."
VED!!!
VED? HOW BADLY ARE YOU HURT??
VED? ANSWER ME!
I'M...I'M STILL HERE, LITTLE BROTHER. DON'T WORRY.
IMPERIAL JUGGERNAUGHTS. MORE OF THEM.
WE HAVE TO STOP THEM, WYL. ME AND YOU.
ARE YOU READY?

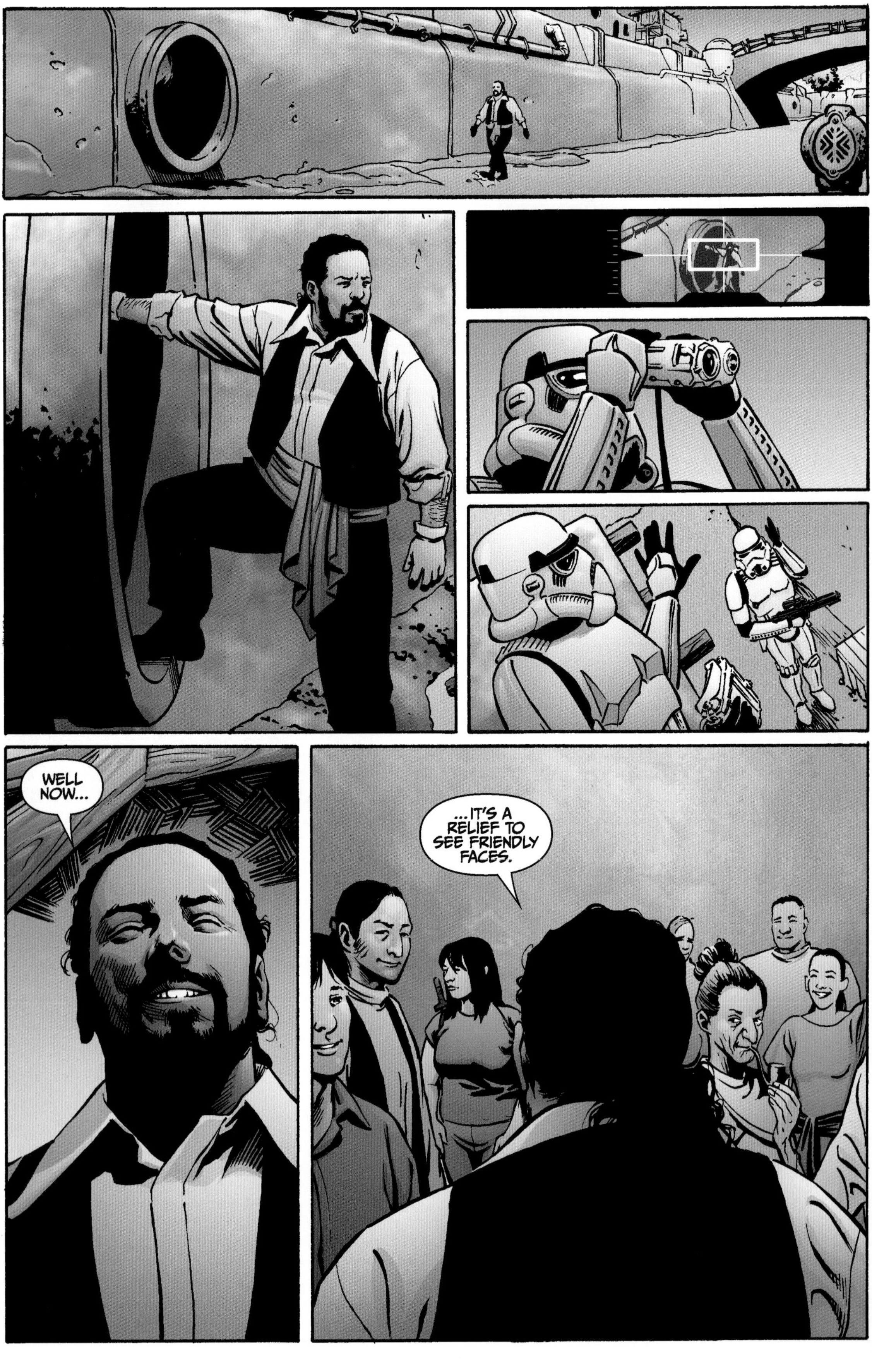
WELL NOW...
...IT'S A RELIEF TO SEE FRIENDLY FACES.

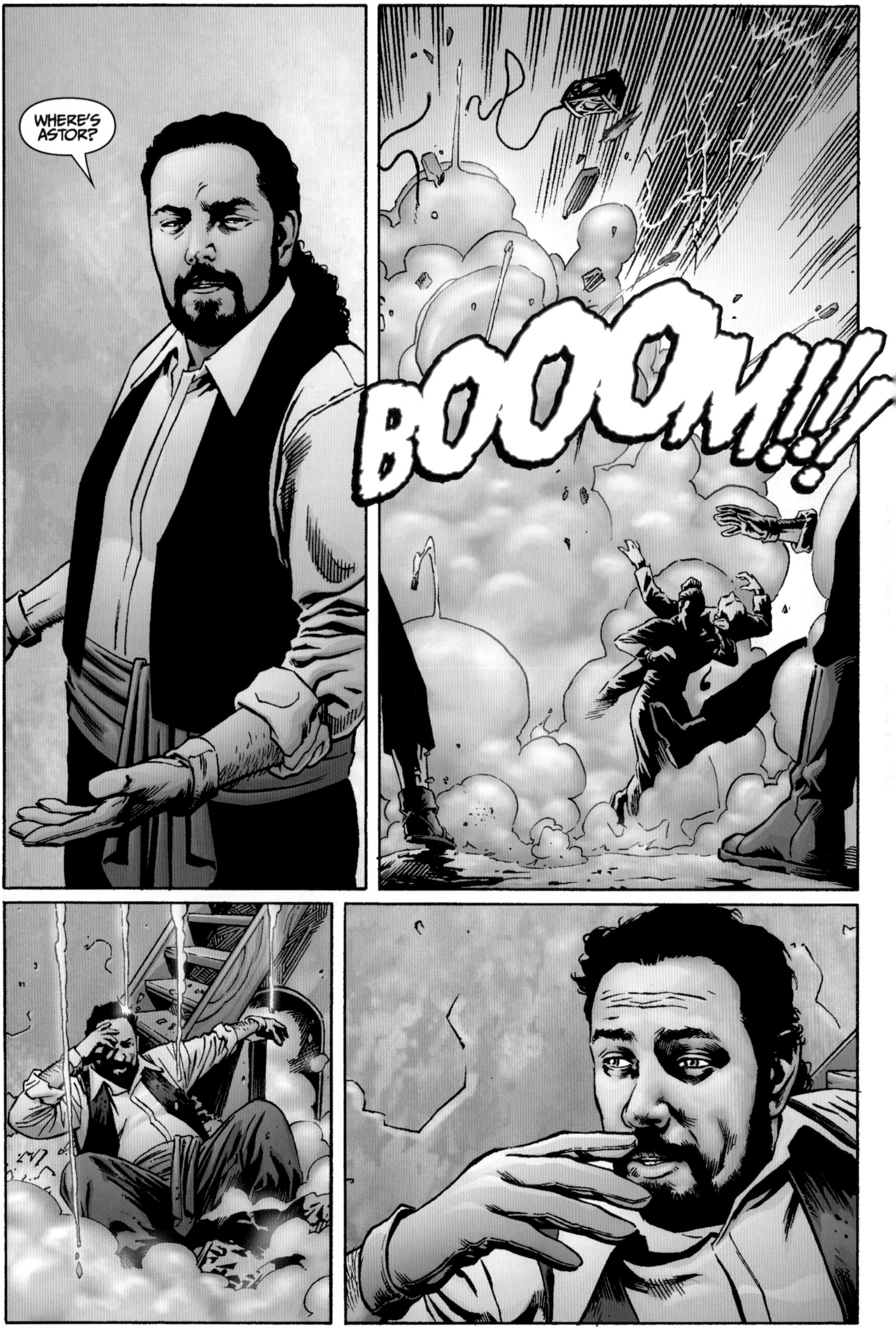
WHERE'S ASTOR?
BOOOM!!!

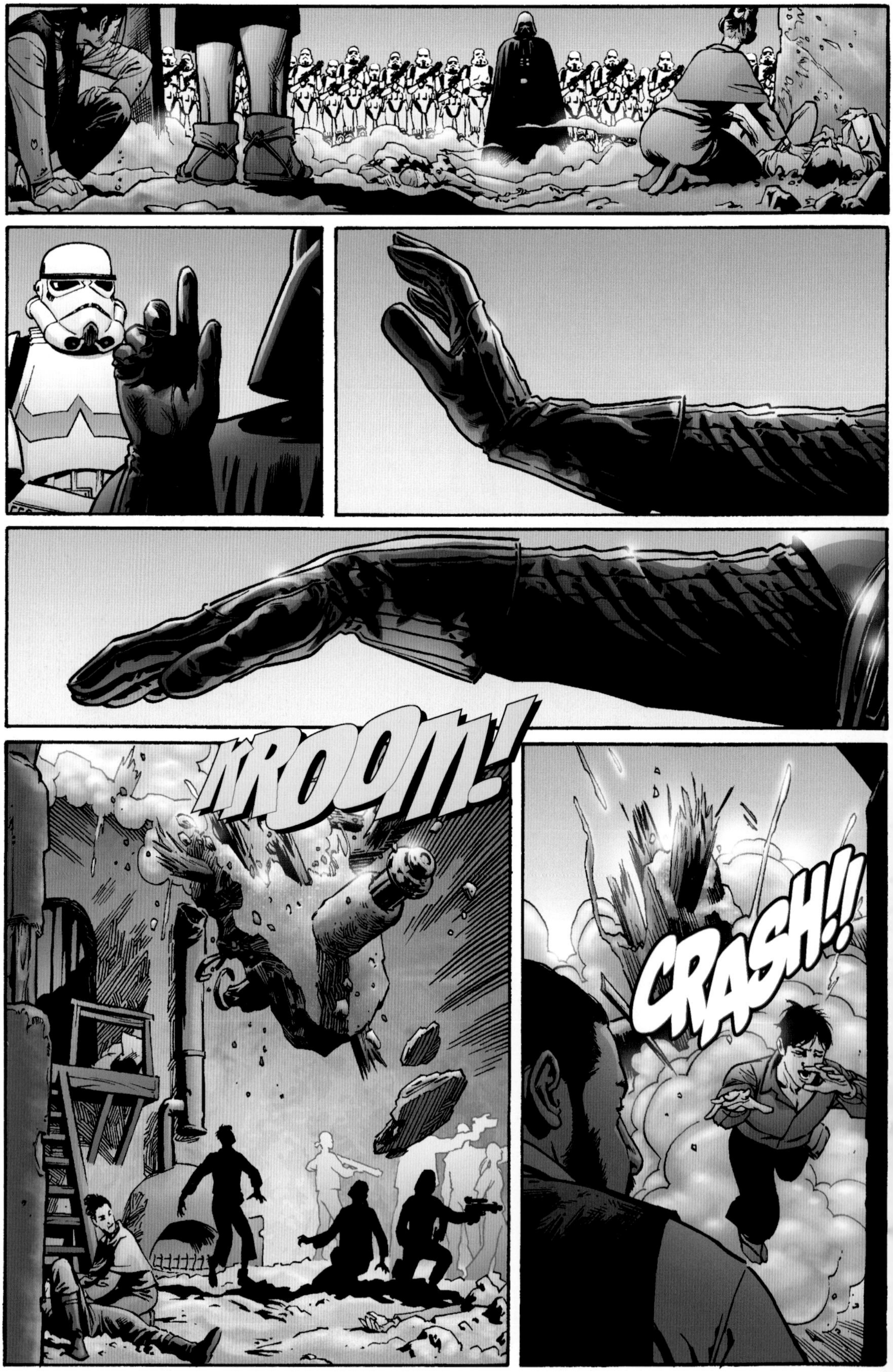
KROOM!
CRASH!!

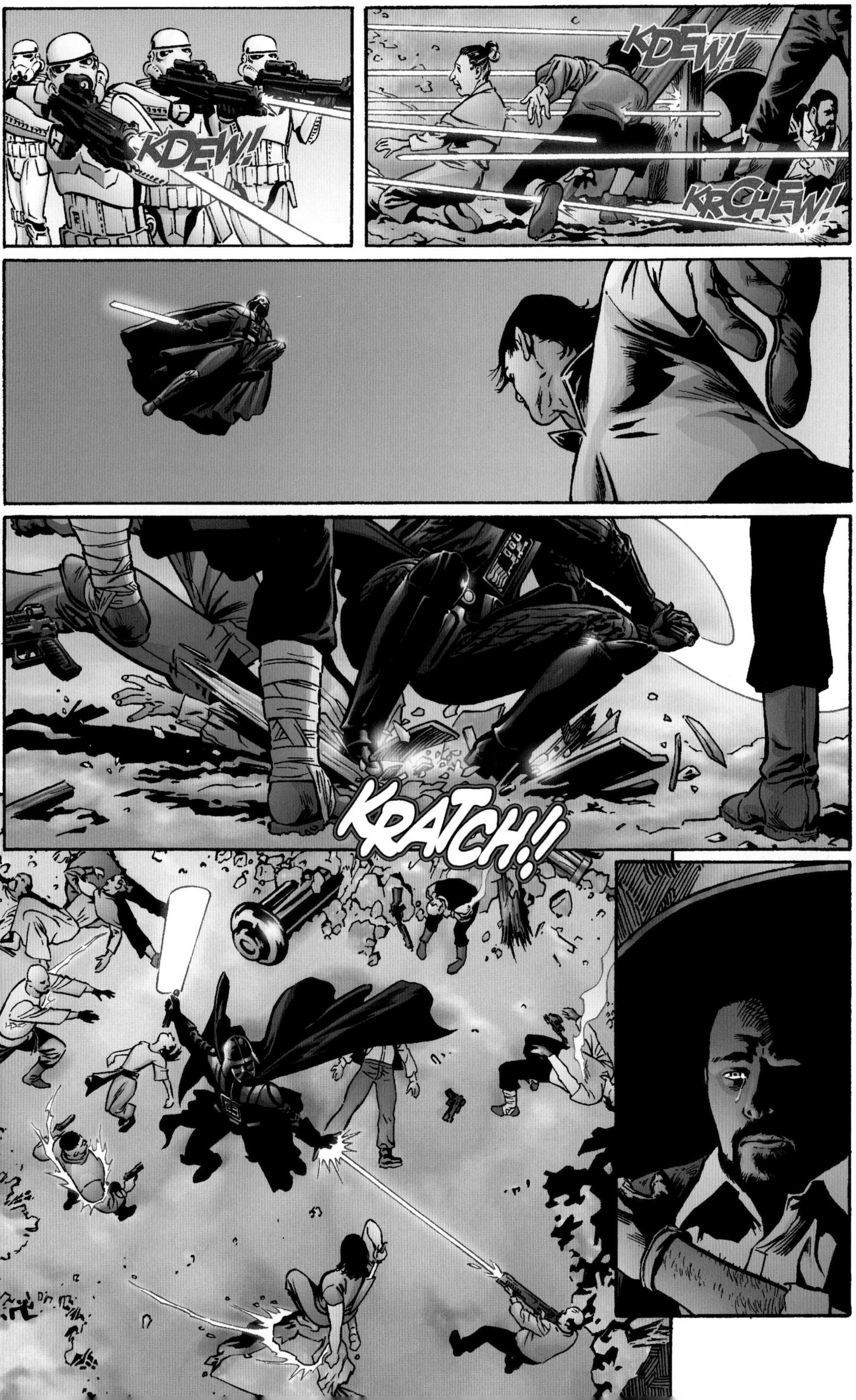
KDEW!
KDEW!
KRCHEW!
KRATCH!!

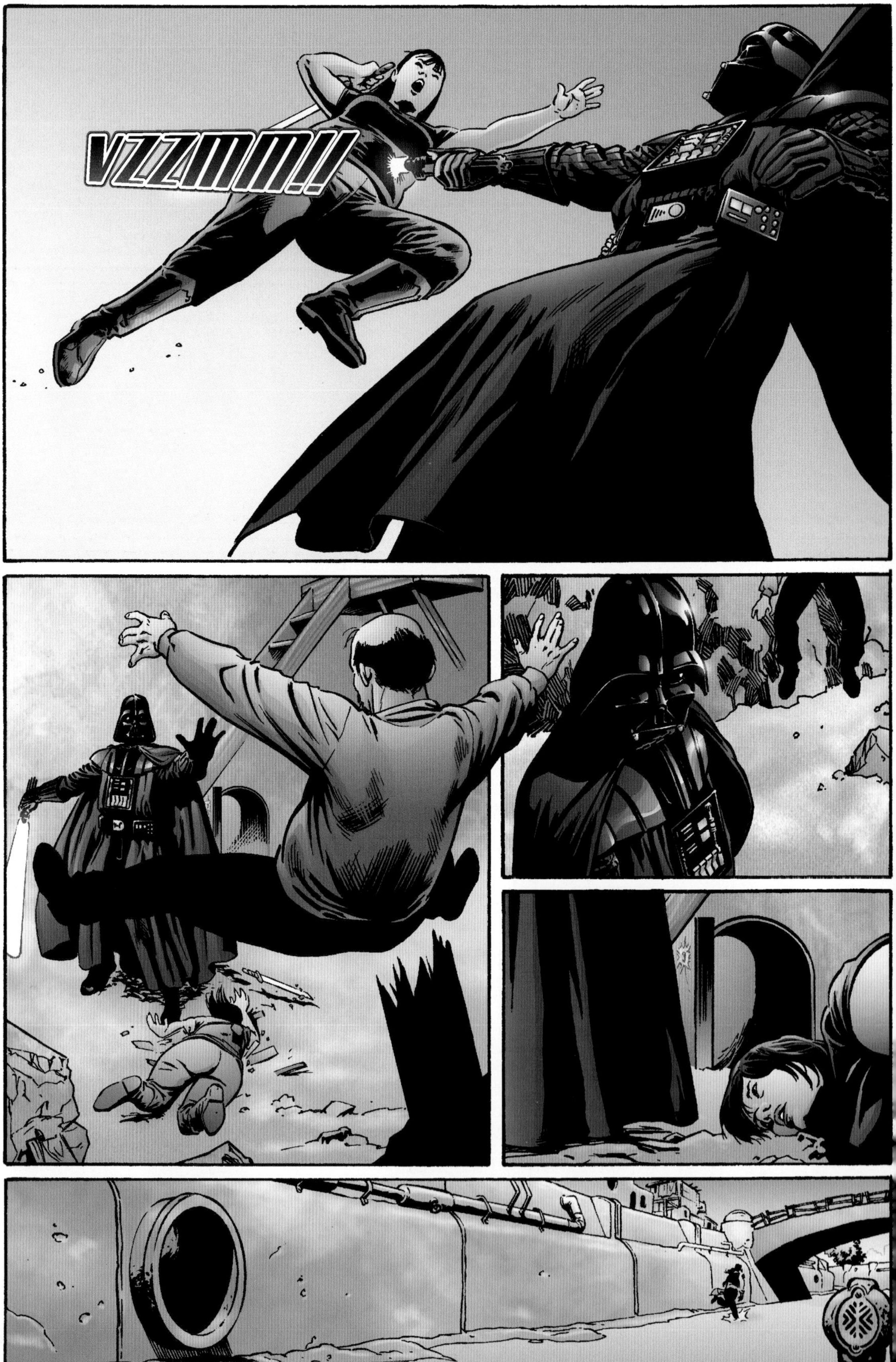
VZZMMM!!

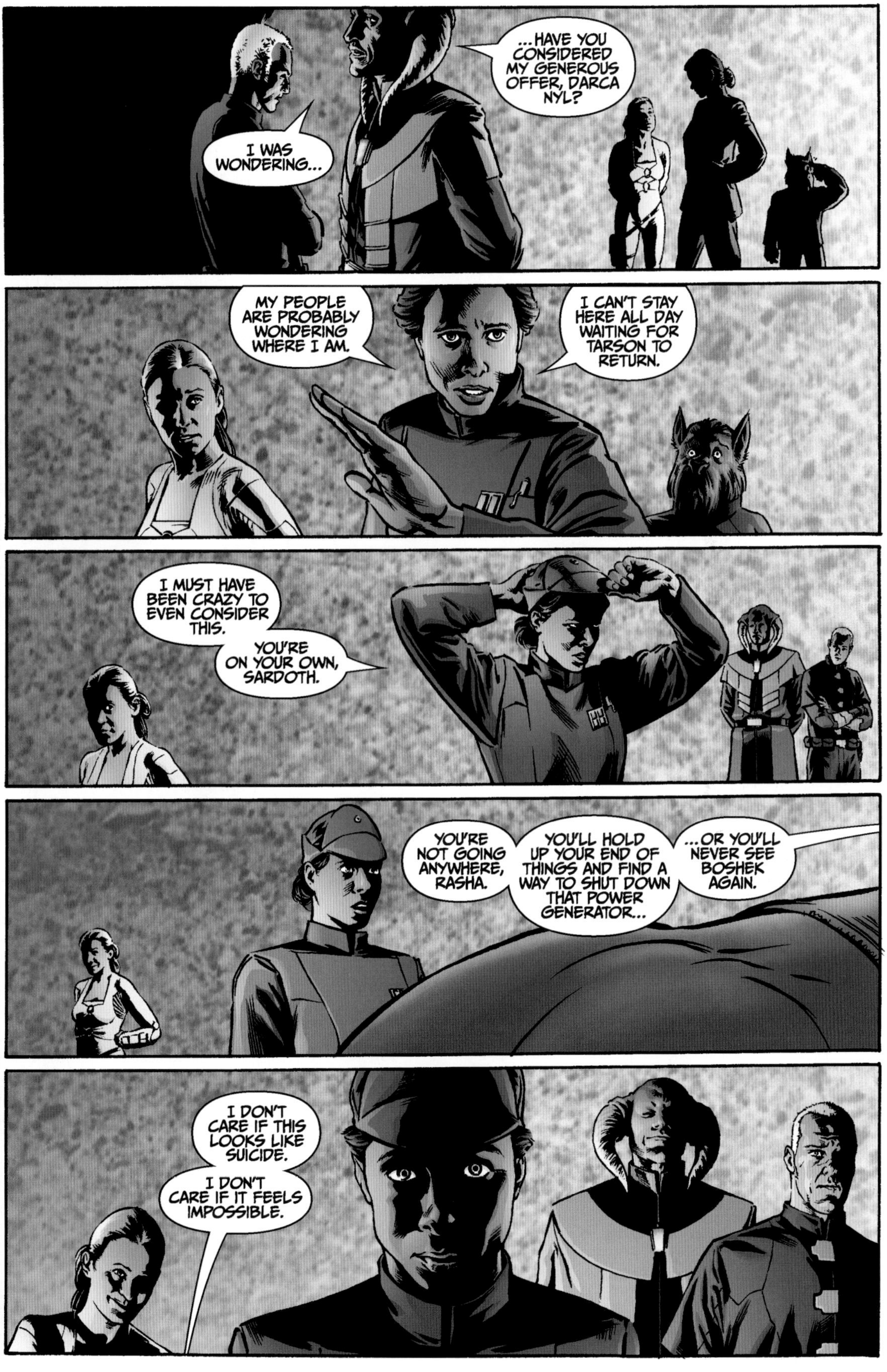
...HAVE YOU CONSIDERED MY GENEROUS OFFER, DARCA NYL?
I WAS WONDERING...
MY PEOPLE ARE PROBABLY WONDERING WHERE I AM.
I CAN'T STAY HERE ALL DAY WAITING FOR TARSON TO RETURN.
I MUST HAVE BEEN CRAZY TO EVEN CONSIDER THIS.
YOU'RE ON YOUR OWN, SARDOTH.
YOU'RE NOT GOING ANYWHERE, RASHA.
YOU'LL HOLD UP YOUR END OF THINGS AND FIND A WAY TO SHUT DOWN THAT POWER GENERATOR...
...OR YOU'LL NEVER SEE BOSHEK AGAIN.
I DON'T CARE IF THIS LOOKS LIKE SUICIDE.
I DON'T CARE IF IT FEELS IMPOSSIBLE.

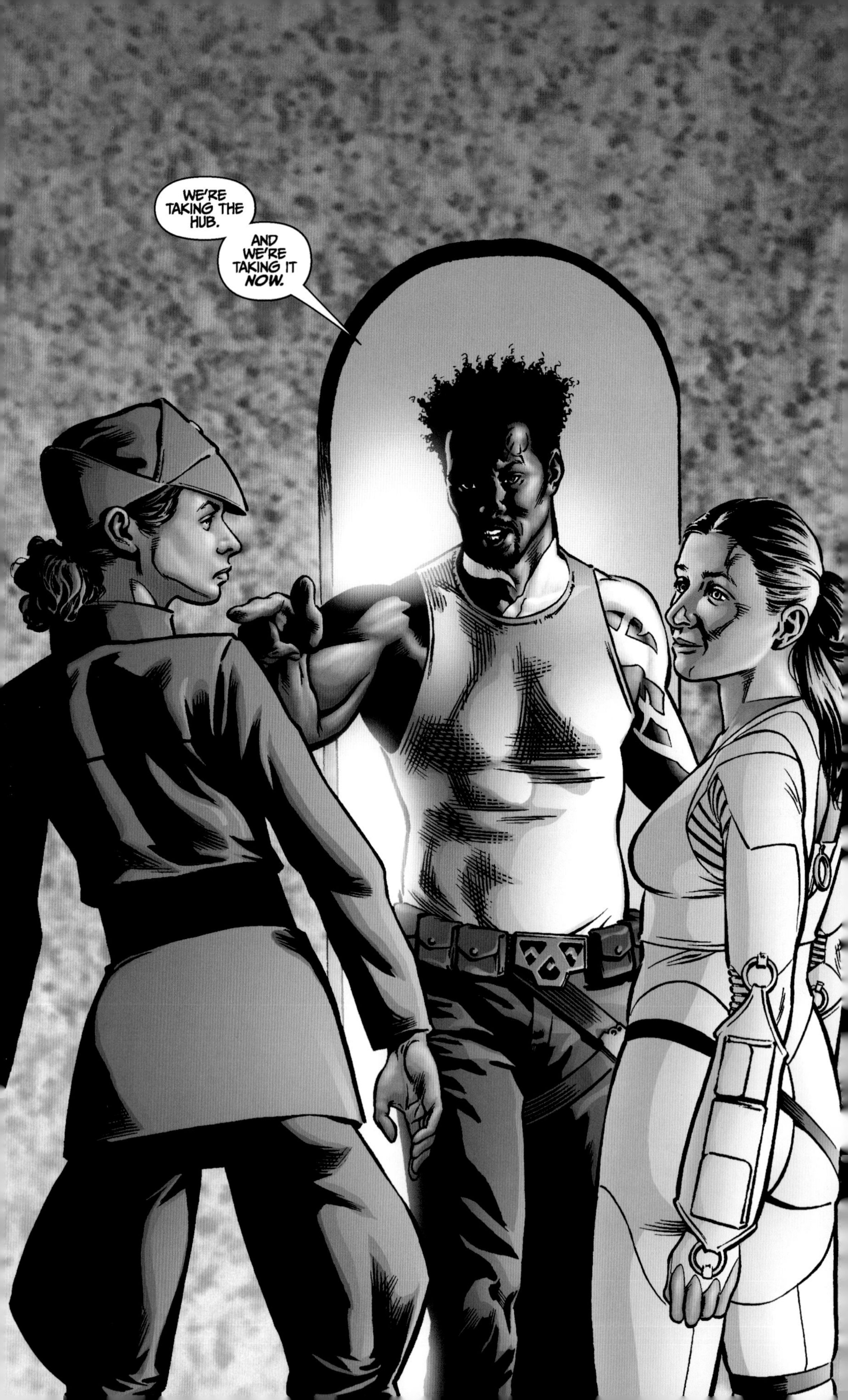
WE'RE TAKING THE HUB.
AND WE'RE TAKING IT NOW.

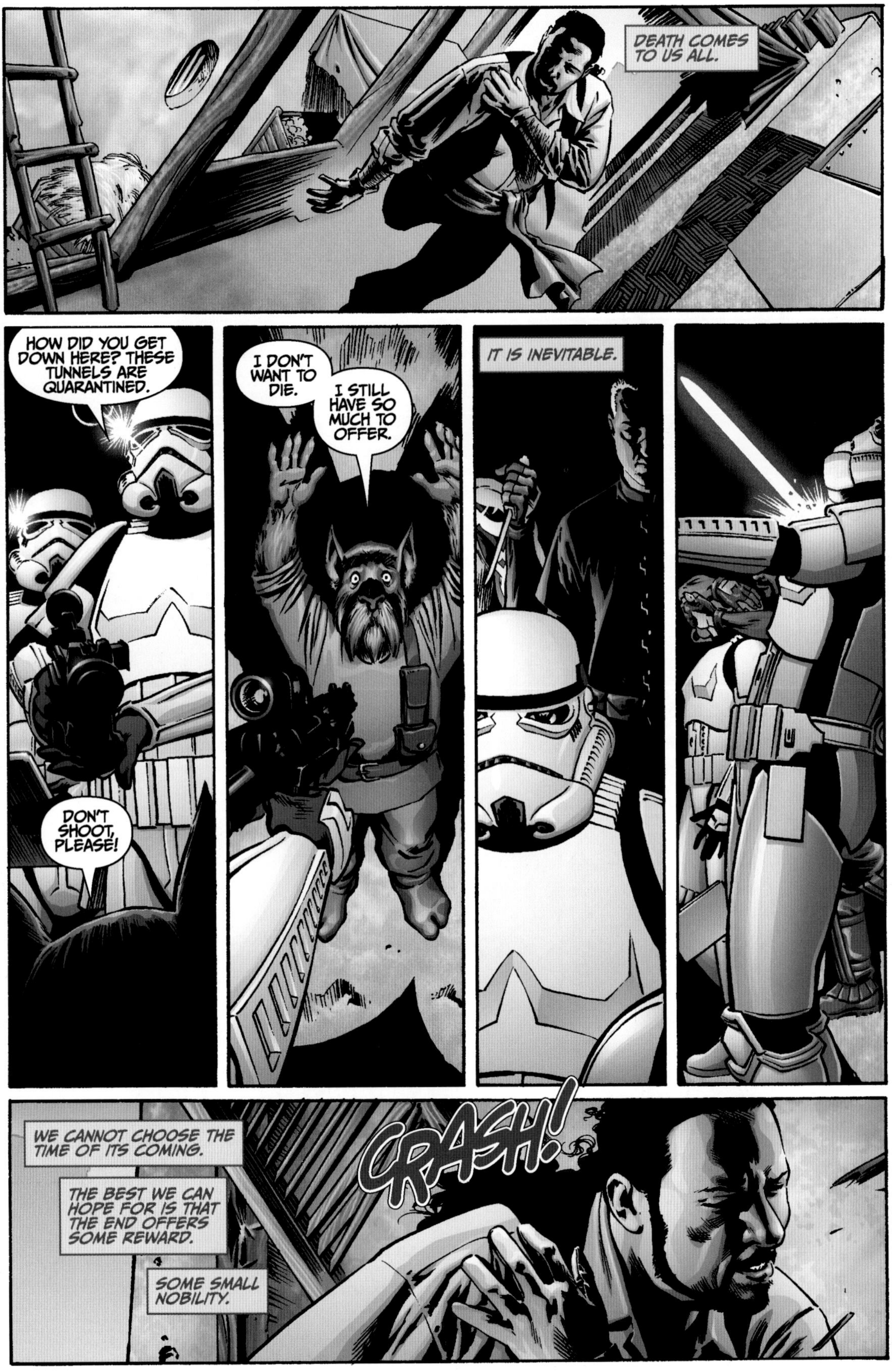
DEATH COMES TO US ALL.
HOW DID YOU GET DOWN HERE? THESE TUNNELS ARE QUARANTINED.
DON'T SHOOT, PLEASE!
I DON'T WANT TO DIE.
I STILL HAVE SO MUCH TO OFFER.
IT IS INEVITABLE.
WE CANNOT CHOOSE THE TIME OF ITS COMING.
CRASH!
THE BEST WE CAN HOPE FOR IS THAT THE END OFFERS SOME REWARD.
SOME SMALL NOBILITY.

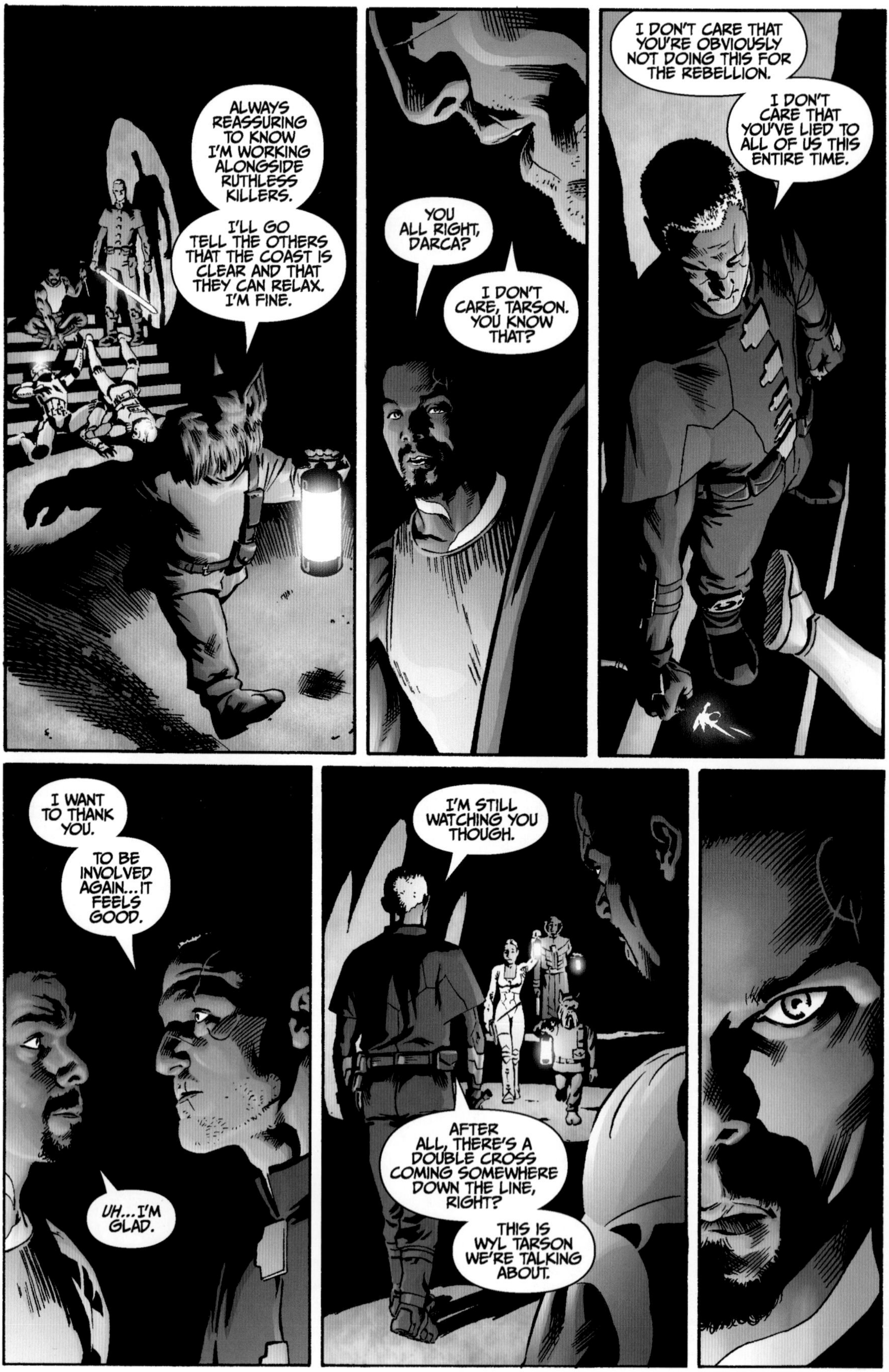

ALWAYS REASSURING TO KNOW I'M WORKING ALONGSIDE RUTHLESS KILLERS.
I'LL GO TELL THE OTHERS THAT THE COAST IS CLEAR AND THAT THEY CAN RELAX. I'M FINE.
YOU ALL RIGHT, DARCA?
I DON'T CARE, TARSON. YOU KNOW THAT?
I DON'T CARE THAT YOU'RE OBVIOUSLY NOT DOING THIS FOR THE REBELLION.
I DON'T CARE THAT YOU'VE LIED TO ALL OF US THIS ENTIRE TIME.
I WANT TO THANK YOU.
TO BE INVOLVED AGAIN...IT FEELS GOOD.
UH...I'M GLAD.
I'M STILL WATCHING YOU THOUGH.
AFTER ALL, THERE'S A DOUBLE CROSS COMING SOMEWHERE DOWN THE LINE, RIGHT?
THIS IS WYL TARSON WE'RE TALKING ABOUT.

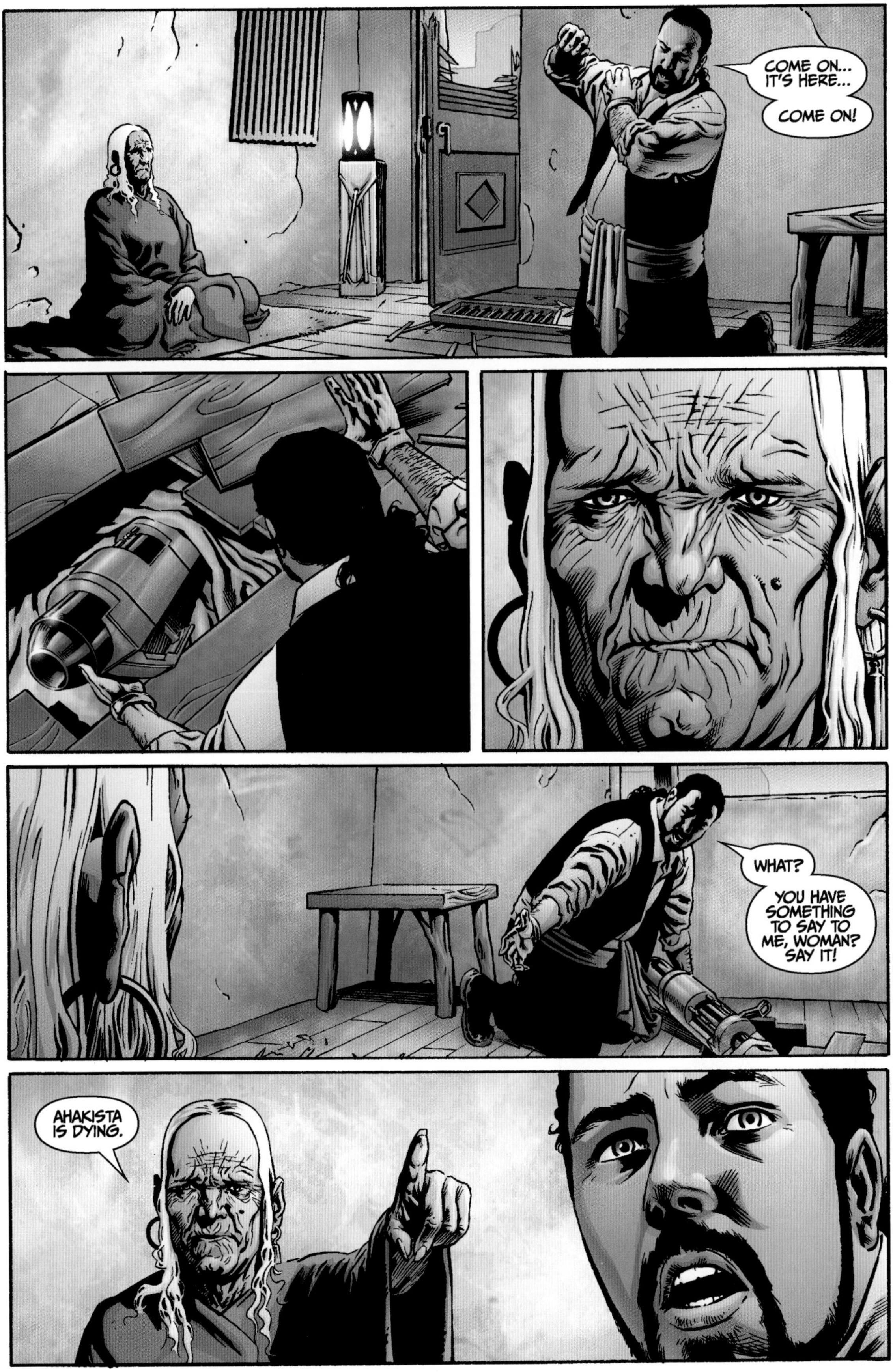
COME ON... IT'S HERE...
COME ON!
WHAT?
YOU HAVE SOMETHING TO SAY TO ME, WOMAN? SAY IT!
AHAKISTA IS DYING.

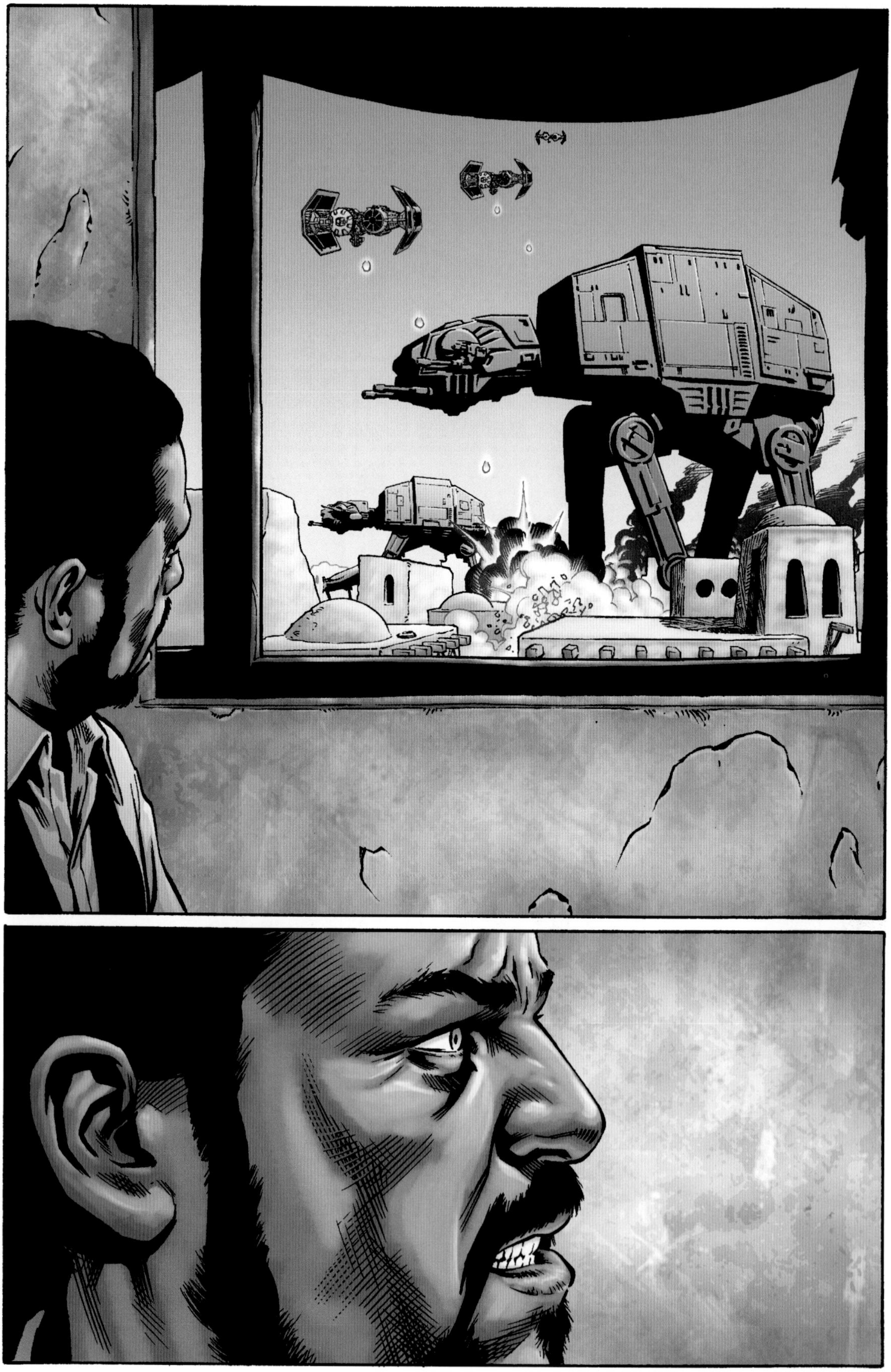

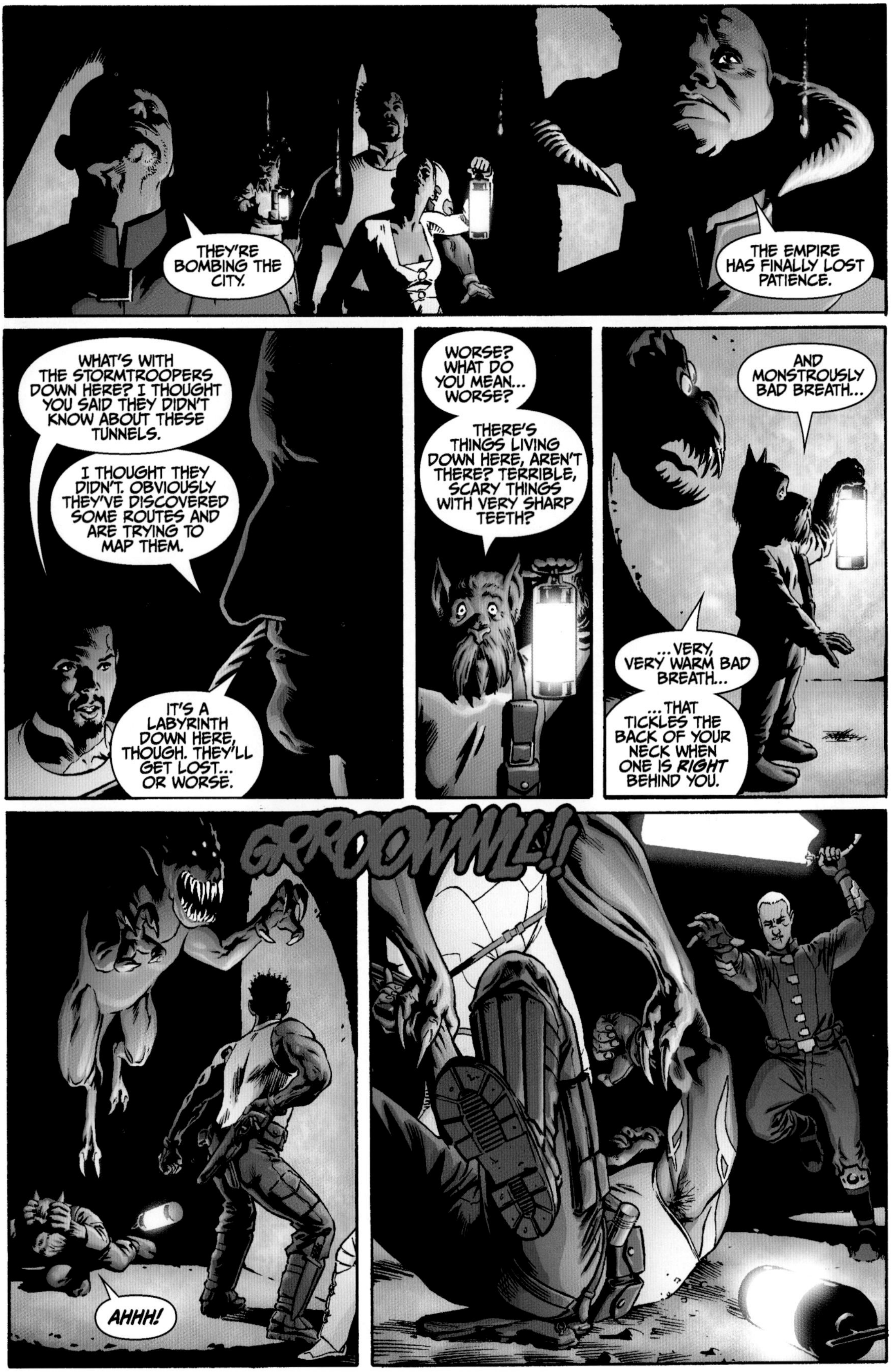
THEY'RE BOMBING THE CITY.
THE EMPIRE HAS FINALLY LOST PATIENCE.
WHAT'S WITH THE STORMTROOPERS DOWN HERE? I THOUGHT YOU SAID THEY DIDN'T KNOW ABOUT THESE TUNNELS.
I THOUGHT THEY DIDN'T. OBVIOUSLY THEY'VE DISCOVERED SOME ROUTES AND ARE TRYING TO MAP THEM.
IT'S A LABYRINTH DOWN HERE, THOUGH. THEY'LL GET LOST... OR WORSE.
WORSE? WHAT DO YOU MEAN... WORSE?
THERE'S THINGS LIVING DOWN HERE, AREN'T THERE? TERRIBLE, SCARY THINGS WITH VERY SHARP TEETH?
AND MONSTROUSLY BAD BREATH...
...VERY, VERY WARM BAD BREATH...
...THAT TICKLES THE BACK OF YOUR NECK WHEN ONE IS RIGHT BEHIND YOU.
GRROOWWL!!
AHHH!

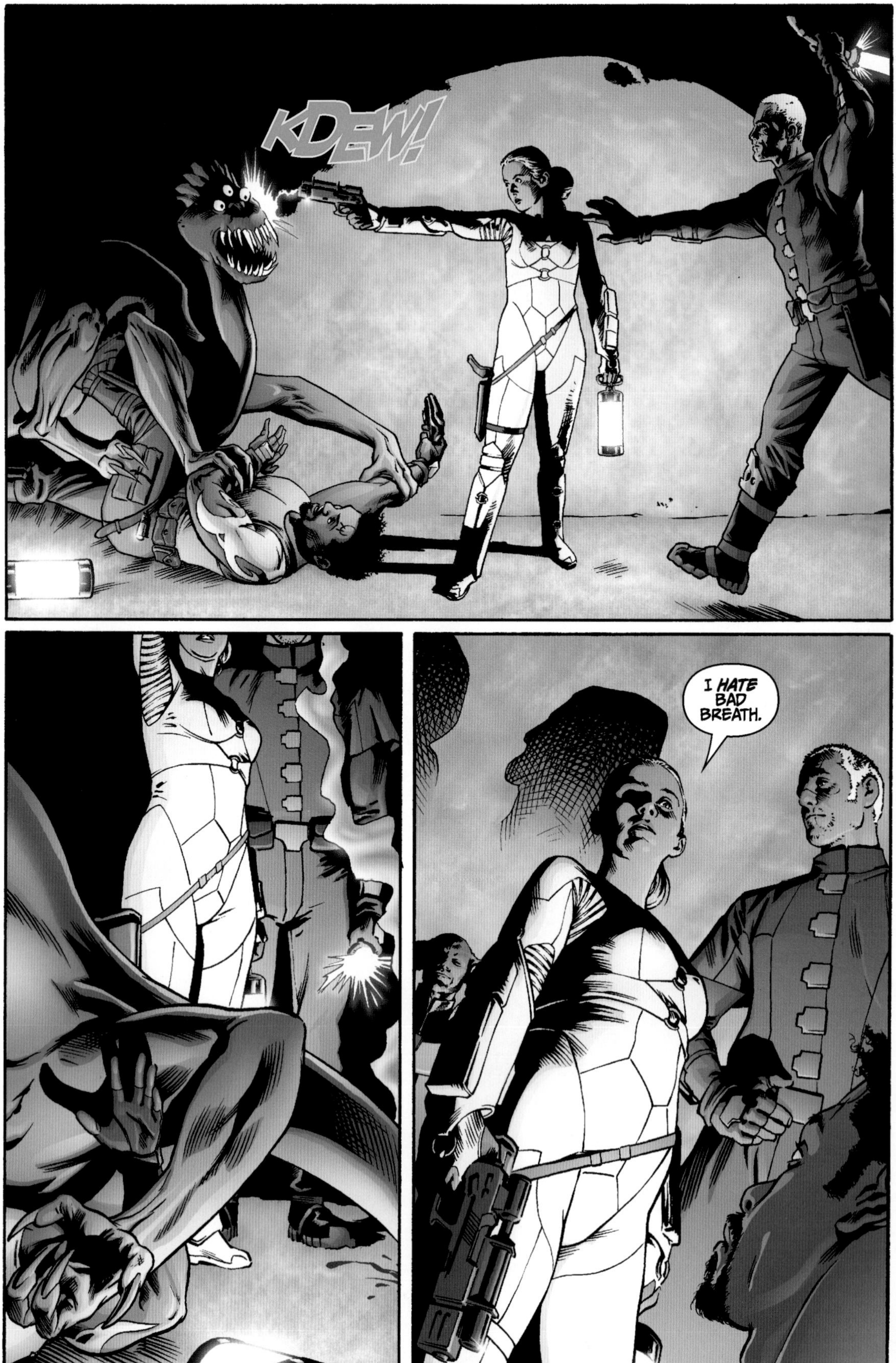
KDEW!
I HATE BAD BREATH.

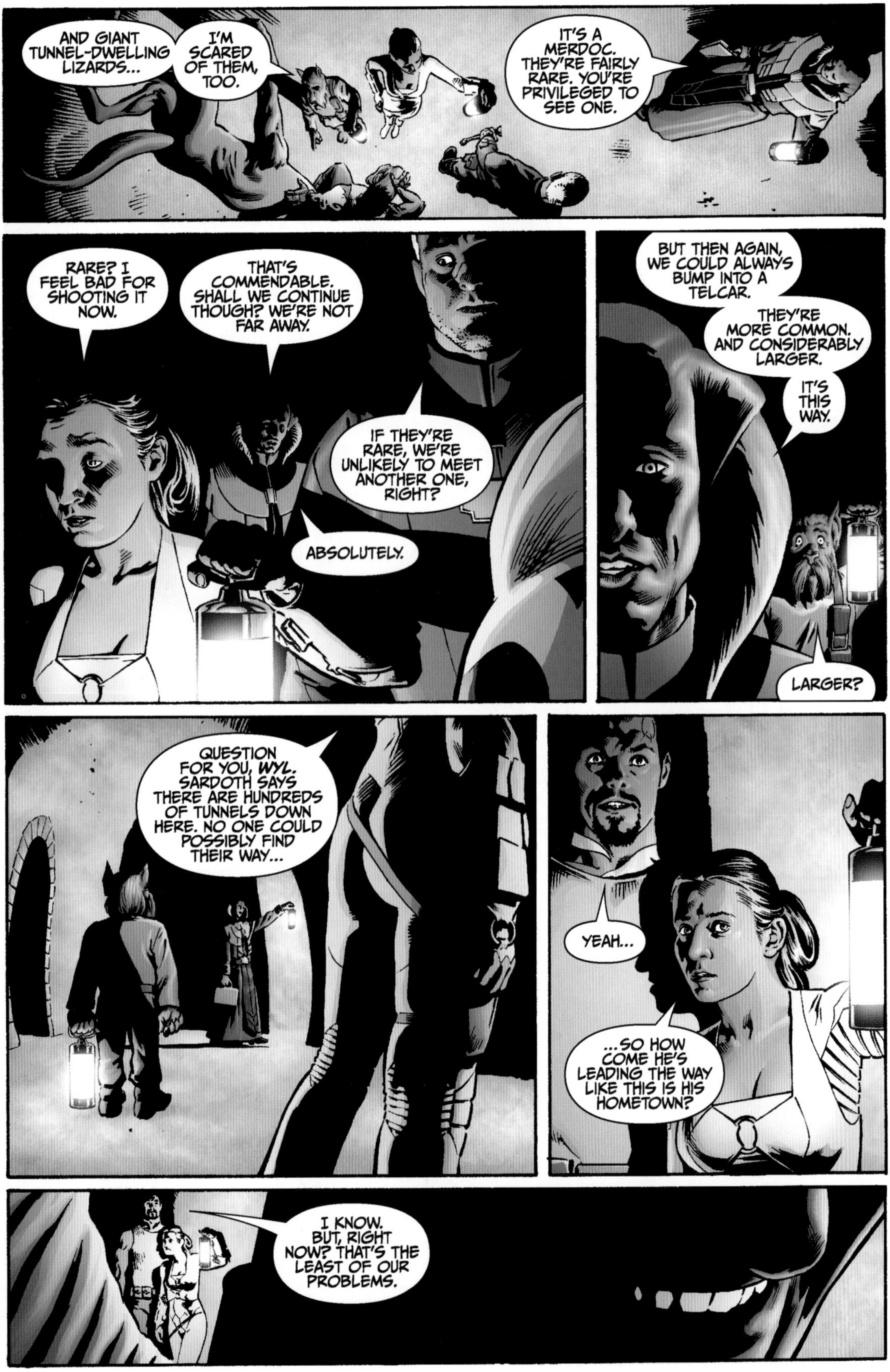
AND GIANT TUNNEL-DWELLING LIZARDS...
I'M SCARED OF THEM, TOO.
IT'S A MERDOC. THEY'RE FAIRLY RARE. YOU'RE PRIVILEGED TO SEE ONE.
RARE? I FEEL BAD FOR SHOOTING IT NOW.
THAT'S COMMENDABLE. SHALL WE CONTINUE THOUGH? WE'RE NOT FAR AWAY.
IF THEY'RE RARE, WE'RE UNLIKELY TO MEET ANOTHER ONE, RIGHT?
ABSOLUTELY.
BUT THEN AGAIN, WE COULD ALWAYS BUMP INTO A TELCAR.
THEY'RE MORE COMMON. AND CONSIDERABLY LARGER.
IT'S THIS WAY.
LARGER?
QUESTION FOR YOU, WYL. SARDOTH SAYS THERE ARE HUNDREDS OF TUNNELS DOWN HERE. NO ONE COULD POSSIBLY FIND THEIR WAY...
YEAH...
...SO HOW COME HE'S LEADING THE WAY LIKE THIS IS HIS HOMETOWN?
I KNOW. BUT, RIGHT NOW? THAT'S THE LEAST OF OUR PROBLEMS.

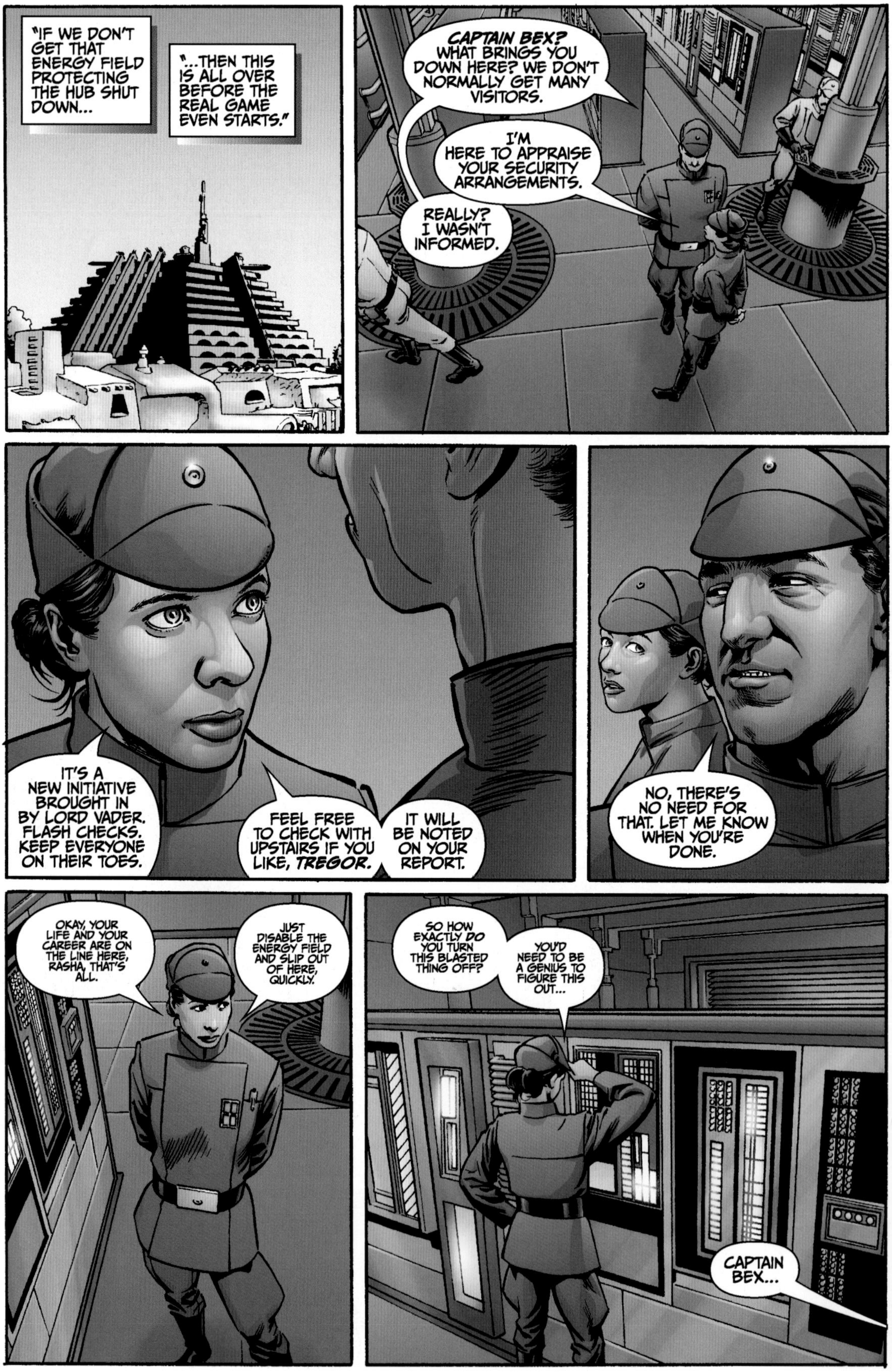
"IF WE DON'T GET THAT ENERGY FIELD PROTECTING THE HUB SHUT DOWN...
"...THEN THIS IS ALL OVER BEFORE THE REAL GAME EVEN STARTS."
CAPTAIN BEX? WHAT BRINGS YOU DOWN HERE? WE DON'T NORMALLY GET MANY VISITORS.
I'M HERE TO APPRAISE YOUR SECURITY ARRANGEMENTS.
REALLY? I WASN'T INFORMED.
IT'S A NEW INITIATIVE BROUGHT IN BY LORD VADER. FLASH CHECKS. KEEP EVERYONE ON THEIR TOES.
FEEL FREE TO CHECK WITH UPSTAIRS IF YOU LIKE, TREGOR.
IT WILL BE NOTED ON YOUR REPORT.
NO, THERE'S NO NEED FOR THAT. LET ME KNOW WHEN YOU'RE DONE.
OKAY, YOUR LIFE AND YOUR CAREER ARE ON THE LINE HERE, RASHA, THAT'S ALL.
JUST DISABLE THE ENERGY FIELD AND SLIP OUT OF HERE, QUICKLY.
SO HOW EXACTLY DO YOU TURN THIS BLASTED THING OFF?
YOU'D NEED TO BE A GENIUS TO FIGURE THIS OUT...
CAPTAIN BEX...

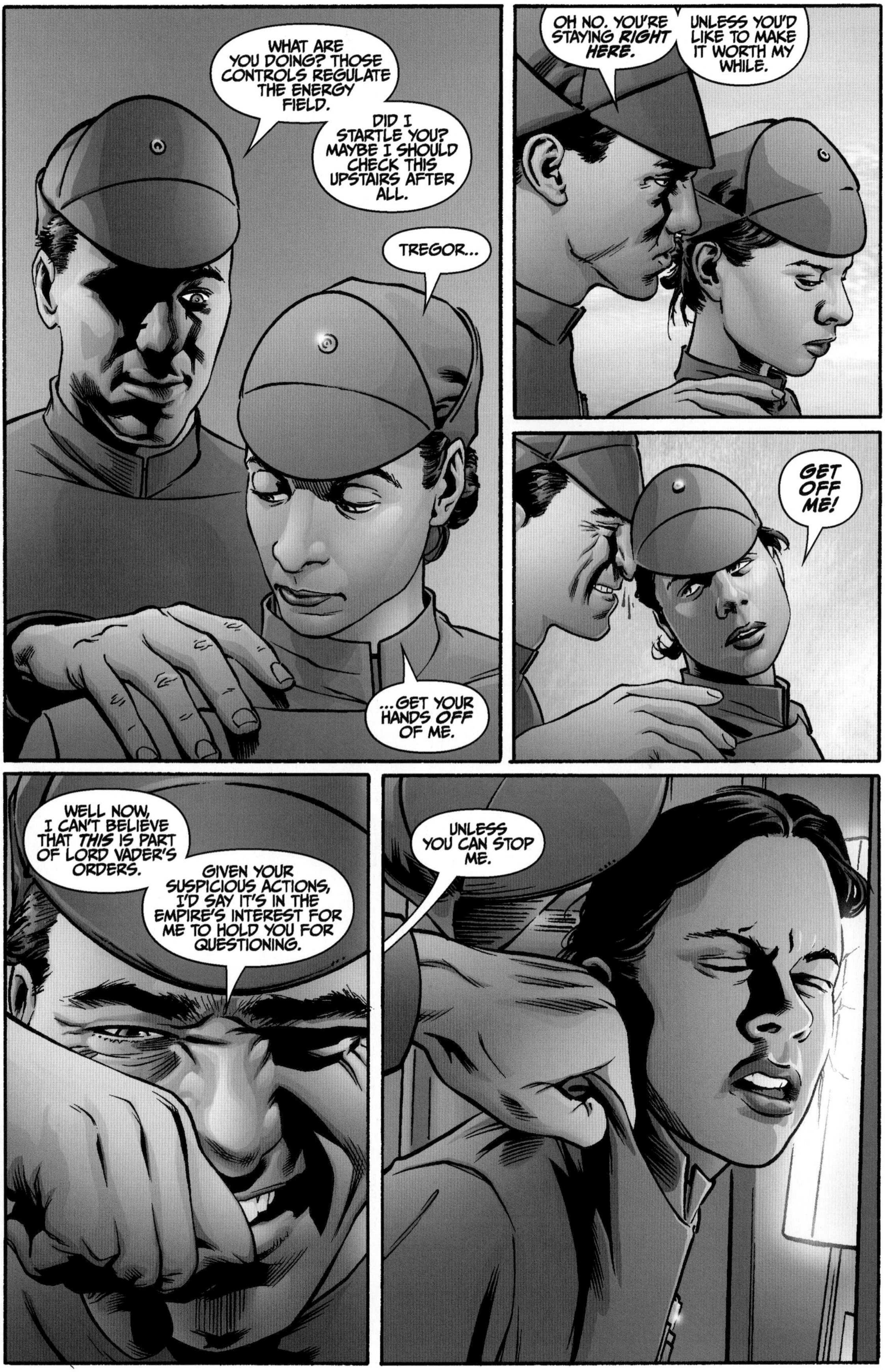
WHAT ARE YOU DOING? THOSE CONTROLS REGULATE THE ENERGY FIELD.
DID I STARTLE YOU? MAYBE I SHOULD CHECK THIS UPSTAIRS AFTER ALL.
TREGOR...
...GET YOUR HANDS OFF OF ME.
OH NO. YOU'RE STAYING RIGHT HERE.
UNLESS YOU'D LIKE TO MAKE IT WORTH MY WHILE.
GET OFF ME!
WELL NOW, I CAN'T BELIEVE THAT THIS IS PART OF LORD VADER'S ORDERS.
GIVEN YOUR SUSPICIOUS ACTIONS, I'D SAY IT'S IN THE EMPIRE'S INTEREST FOR ME TO HOLD YOU FOR QUESTIONING.
UNLESS YOU CAN STOP ME.

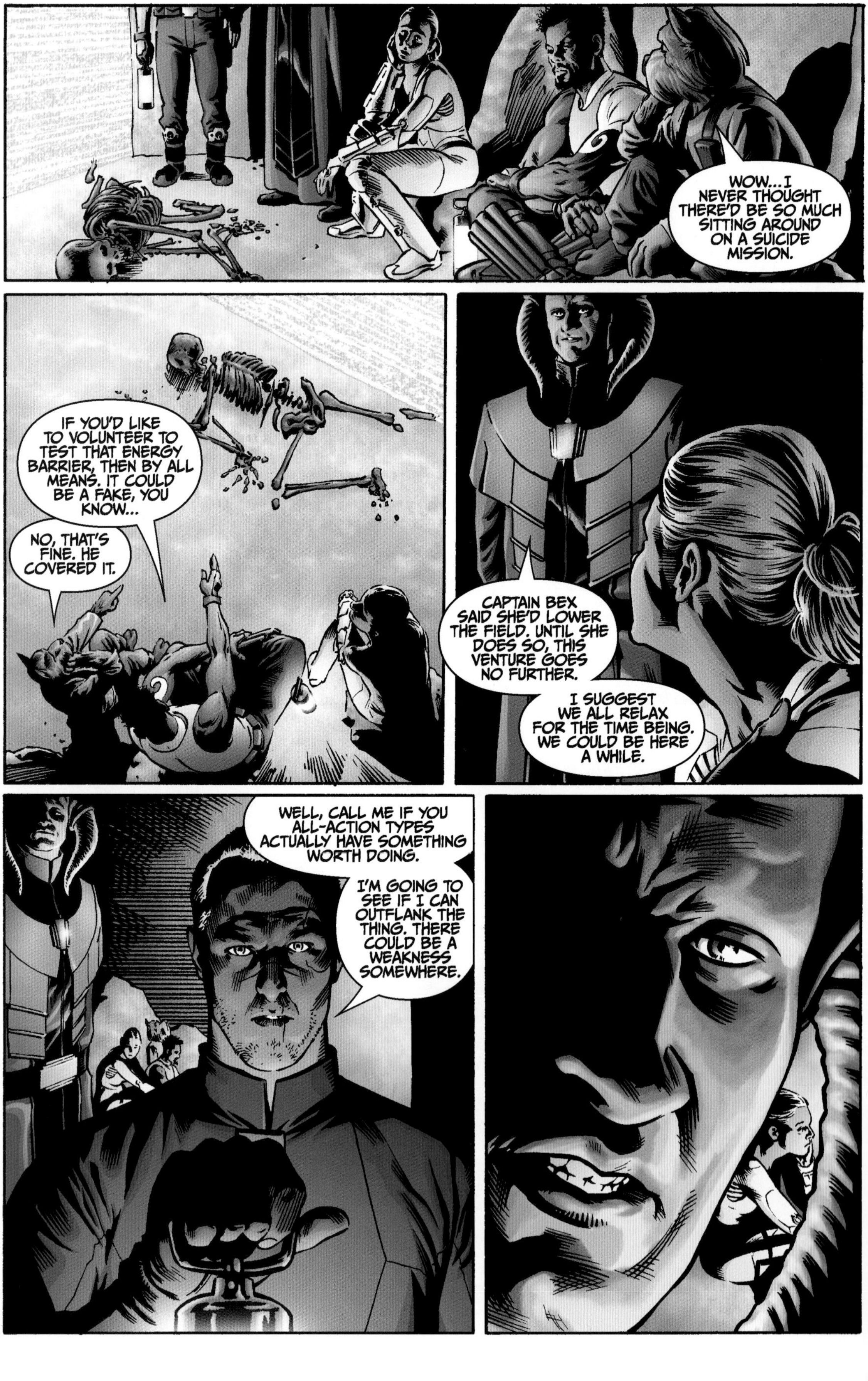
WOW... I NEVER THOUGHT THERE'D BE SO MUCH SITTING AROUND ON A SUICIDE MISSION.
IF YOU'D LIKE TO VOLUNTEER TO TEST THAT ENERGY BARRIER, THEN BY ALL MEANS. IT COULD BE A FAKE, YOU KNOW...
NO, THAT'S FINE. HE COVERED IT.
CAPTAIN BEX SAID SHE'D LOWER THE FIELD. UNTIL SHE DOES SO, THIS VENTURE GOES NO FURTHER.
I SUGGEST WE ALL RELAX FOR THE TIME BEING. WE COULD BE HERE A WHILE.
WELL, CALL ME IF YOU ALL-ACTION TYPES ACTUALLY HAVE SOMETHING WORTH DOING.
I'M GOING TO SEE IF I CAN OUTFLANK THE THING. THERE COULD BE A WEAKNESS SOMEWHERE.

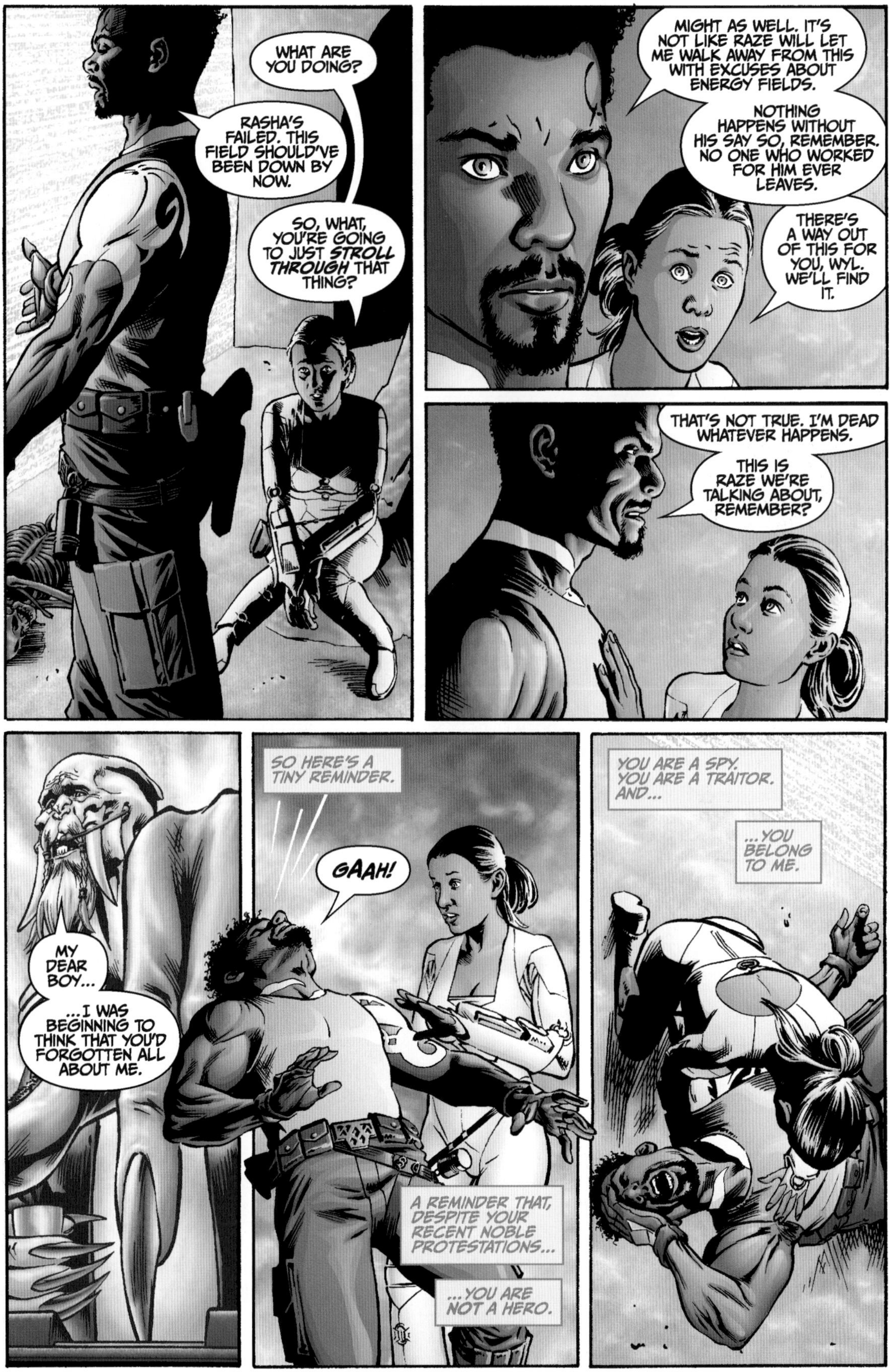
WHAT ARE YOU DOING?
RASHA'S FAILED. THIS FIELD SHOULD'VE BEEN DOWN BY NOW.
SO, WHAT, YOU'RE GOING TO JUST STROLL THROUGH THAT THING?
MIGHT AS WELL. IT'S NOT LIKE RAZE WILL LET ME WALK AWAY FROM THIS WITH EXCUSES ABOUT ENERGY FIELDS.
NOTHING HAPPENS WITHOUT HIS SAY SO, REMEMBER. NO ONE WHO WORKED FOR HIM EVER LEAVES.
THERE'S A WAY OUT OF THIS FOR YOU, WYL. WE'LL FIND IT.
THAT'S NOT TRUE. I'M DEAD WHATEVER HAPPENS.
THIS IS RAZE WE'RE TALKING ABOUT, REMEMBER?
MY DEAR BOY...
...I WAS BEGINNING TO THINK THAT YOU'D FORGOTTEN ALL ABOUT ME.
SO HERE'S A TINY REMINDER.
GAAH!
A REMINDER THAT, DESPITE YOUR RECENT NOBLE PROTESTATIONS...
...YOU ARE NOT A HERO.
YOU ARE A SPY. YOU ARE A TRAITOR. AND...
...YOU BELONG TO ME.

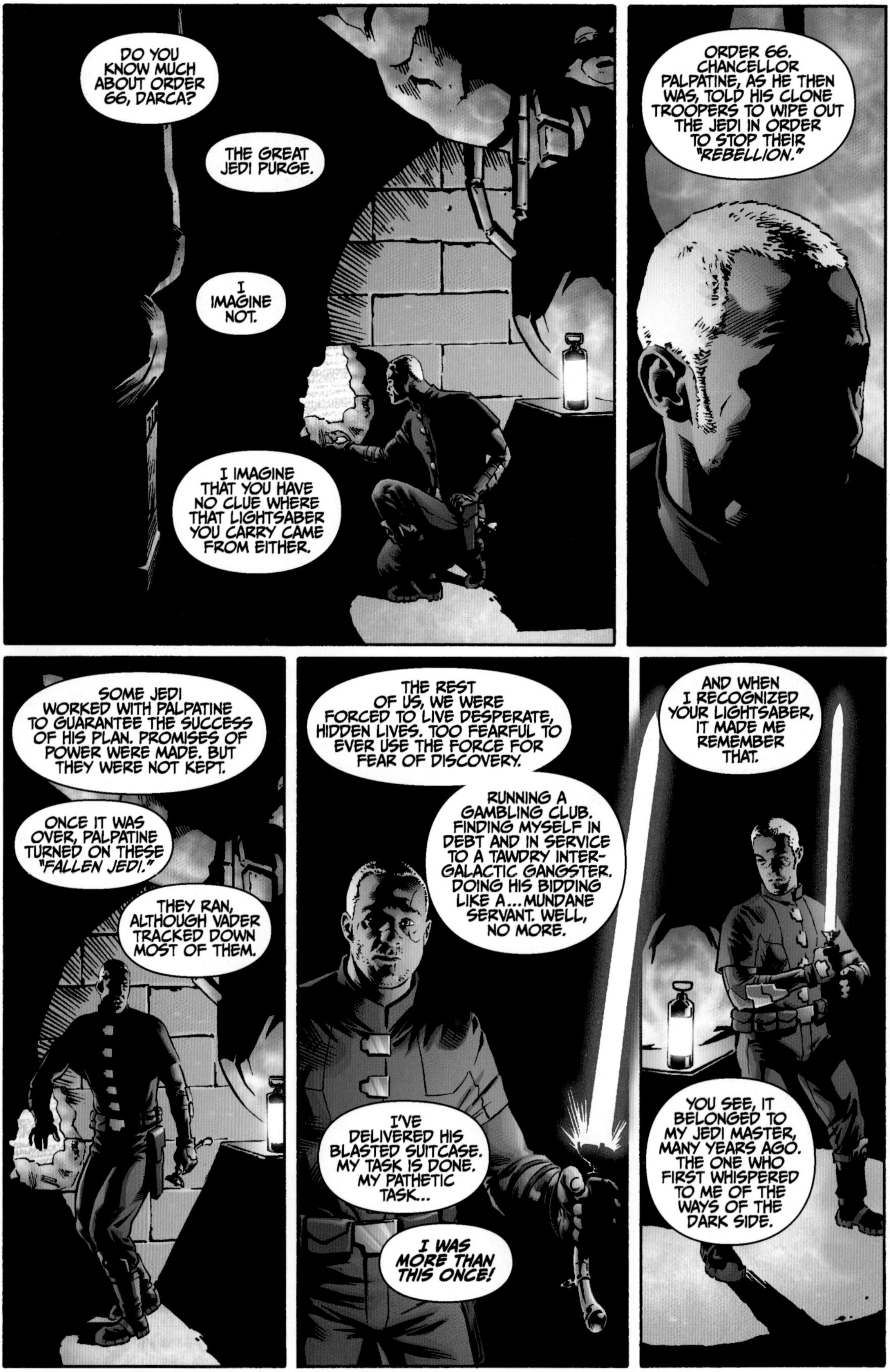
DO YOU KNOW MUCH ABOUT ORDER 66, DARCA?
THE GREAT JEDI PURGE.
I IMAGINE NOT.
I IMAGINE THAT YOU HAVE NO CLUE WHERE THAT LIGHTSABER YOU CARRY CAME FROM EITHER.
ORDER 66. CHANCELLOR PALPATINE, AS HE THEN WAS, TOLD HIS CLONE TROOPERS TO WIPE OUT THE JEDI IN ORDER TO STOP THEIR "REBELLION."
SOME JEDI WORKED WITH PALPATINE TO GUARANTEE THE SUCCESS OF HIS PLAN. PROMISES OF POWER WERE MADE. BUT THEY WERE NOT KEPT.
ONCE IT WAS OVER, PALPATINE TURNED ON THESE "FALLEN JEDI."
THEY RAN, ALTHOUGH VADER TRACKED DOWN MOST OF THEM.
THE REST OF US, WE WERE FORCED TO LIVE DESPERATE, HIDDEN LIVES. TOO FEARFUL TO EVER USE THE FORCE FOR FEAR OF DISCOVERY.
RUNNING A GAMBLING CLUB. FINDING MYSELF IN DEBT AND IN SERVICE TO A TAWDRY INTER-GALACTIC GANGSTER. DOING HIS BIDDING LIKE A... MUNDANE SERVANT. WELL, NO MORE.
I'VE DELIVERED HIS BLASTED SUITCASE. MY TASK IS DONE. MY PATHETIC TASK...
I WAS MORE THAN THIS ONCE!
AND WHEN I RECOGNIZED YOUR LIGHTSABER, IT MADE ME REMEMBER THAT.
YOU SEE, IT BELONGED TO MY JEDI MASTER, MANY YEARS AGO. THE ONE WHO FIRST WHISPERED TO ME OF THE WAYS OF THE DARK SIDE.

HIS NAME WAS LYCAN.

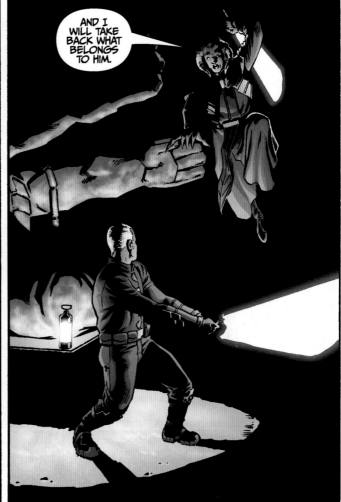

AND I WILL TAKE BACK WHAT BELONGS TO HIM.

WYL!

WYL, LISTEN TO ME!

NNNN!!!

WE CAN DO THIS, WYL. WE CAN PULL THIS OFF...

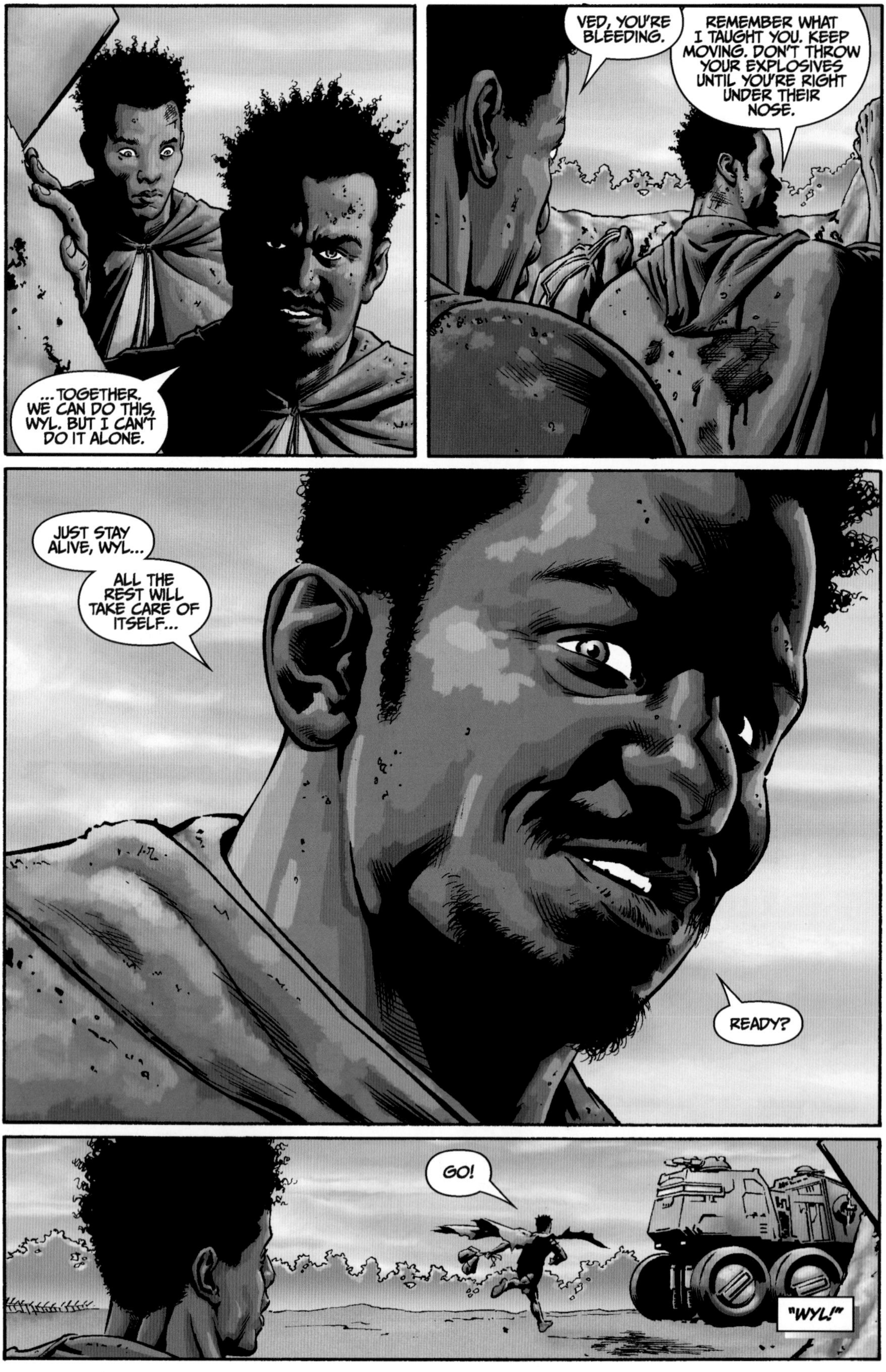
...TOGETHER. WE CAN DO THIS, WYL. BUT I CAN'T DO IT ALONE.
VED, YOU'RE BLEEDING.
REMEMBER WHAT I TAUGHT YOU. KEEP MOVING. DON'T THROW YOUR EXPLOSIVES UNTIL YOU'RE RIGHT UNDER THEIR NOSE.
JUST STAY ALIVE, WYL...
ALL THE REST WILL TAKE CARE OF ITSELF...
READY?
GO!
"WYL!"

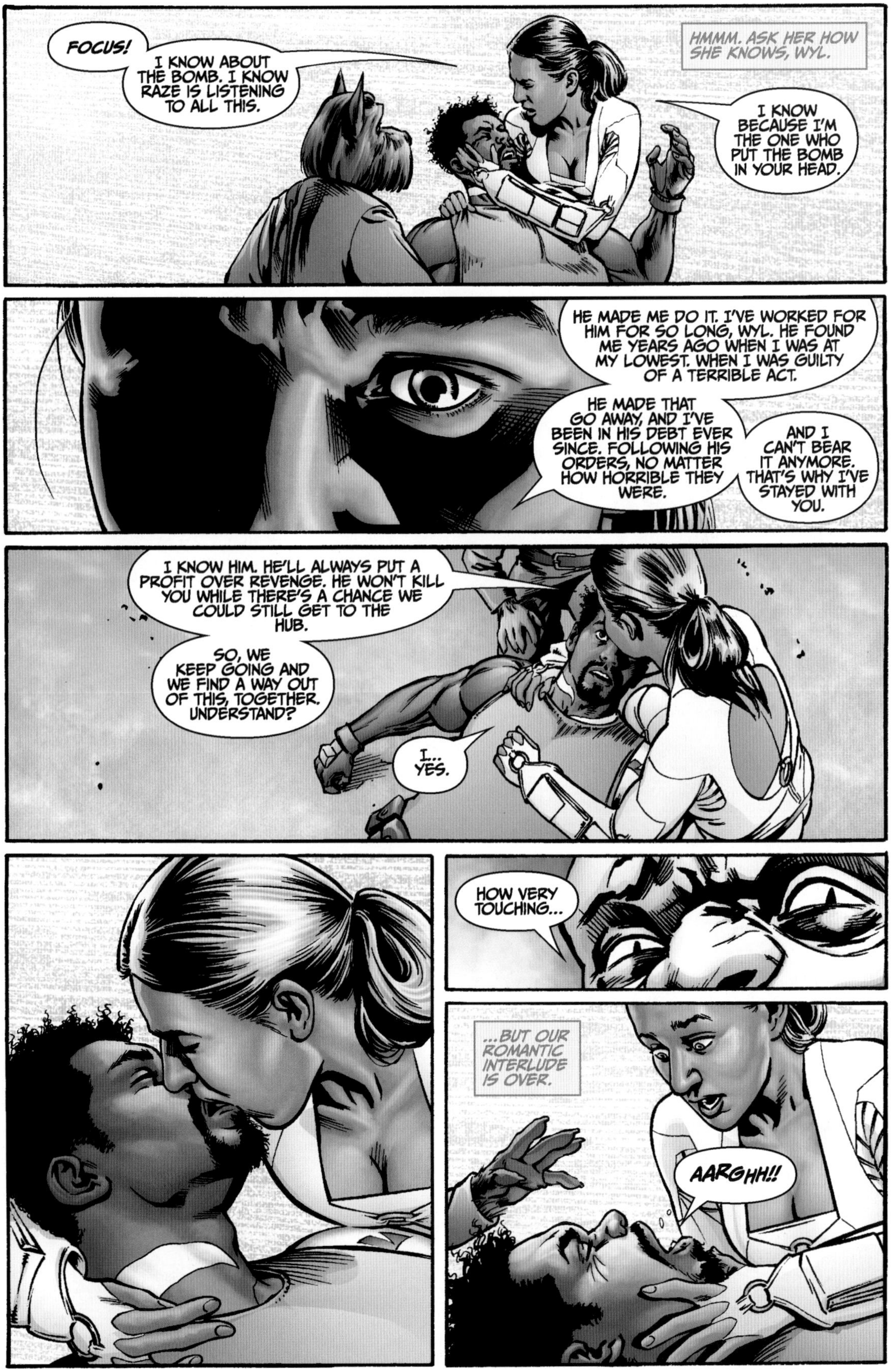
FOCUS!
I KNOW ABOUT THE BOMB. I KNOW RAZE IS LISTENING TO ALL THIS.
HMMM. ASK HER HOW SHE KNOWS, WYL.
I KNOW BECAUSE I'M THE ONE WHO PUT THE BOMB IN YOUR HEAD.
HE MADE ME DO IT. I'VE WORKED FOR HIM FOR SO LONG, WYL. HE FOUND ME YEARS AGO WHEN I WAS AT MY LOWEST. WHEN I WAS GUILTY OF A TERRIBLE ACT.
HE MADE THAT GO AWAY, AND I'VE BEEN IN HIS DEBT EVER SINCE. FOLLOWING HIS ORDERS, NO MATTER HOW HORRIBLE THEY WERE.
AND I CAN'T BEAR IT ANYMORE. THAT'S WHY I'VE STAYED WITH YOU.
I KNOW HIM. HE'LL ALWAYS PUT A PROFIT OVER REVENGE. HE WON'T KILL YOU WHILE THERE'S A CHANCE WE COULD STILL GET TO THE HUB.
SO, WE KEEP GOING AND WE FIND A WAY OUT OF THIS, TOGETHER. UNDERSTAND?
I... YES.
HOW VERY TOUCHING...
...BUT OUR ROMANTIC INTERLUDE IS OVER.
AARGHH!!

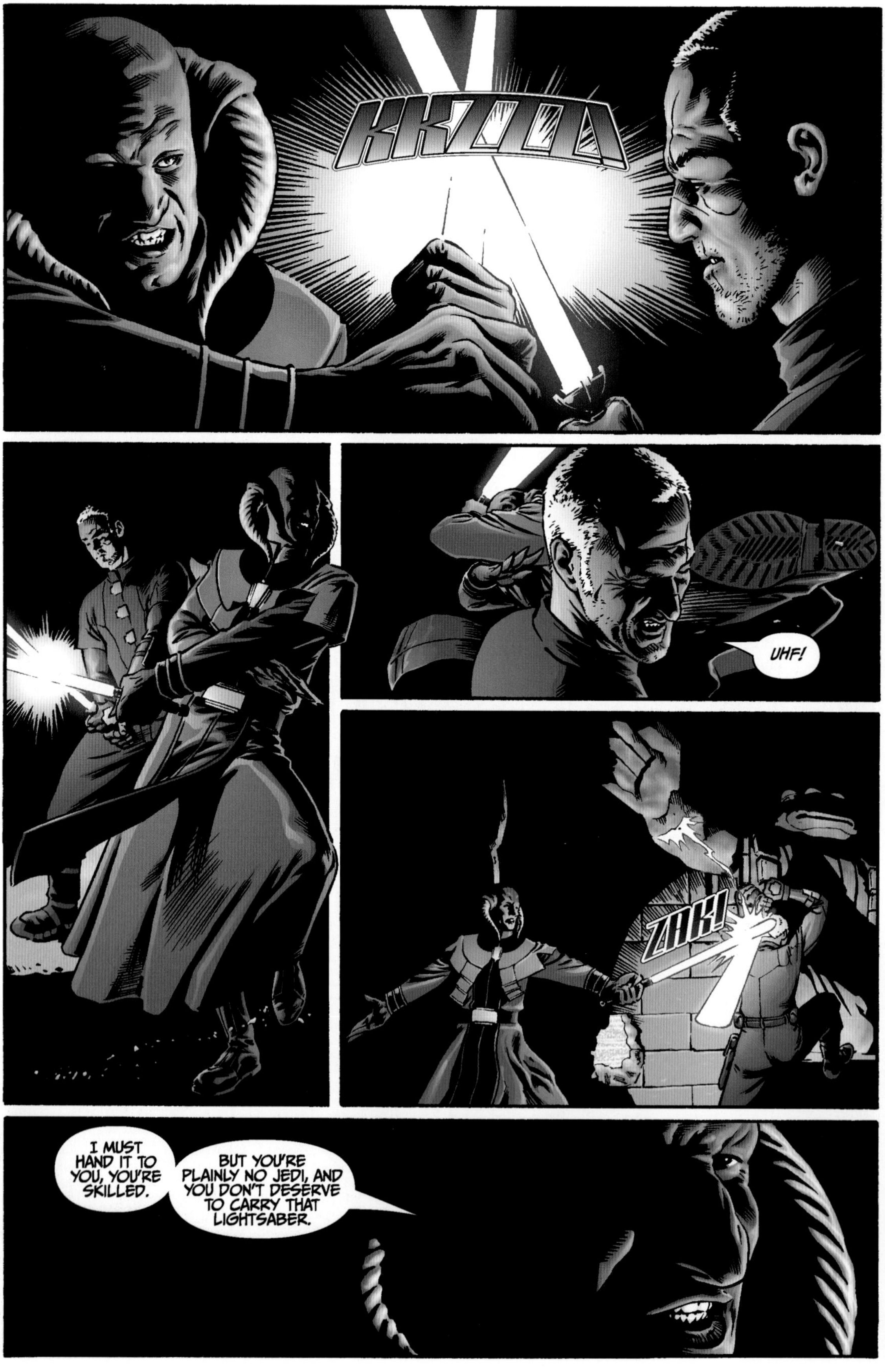
KKZZOW
UHF!
ZAK!
I MUST HAND IT TO YOU, YOU'RE SKILLED.
BUT YOU'RE PLAINLY NO JEDI, AND YOU DON'T DESERVE TO CARRY THAT LIGHTSABER.

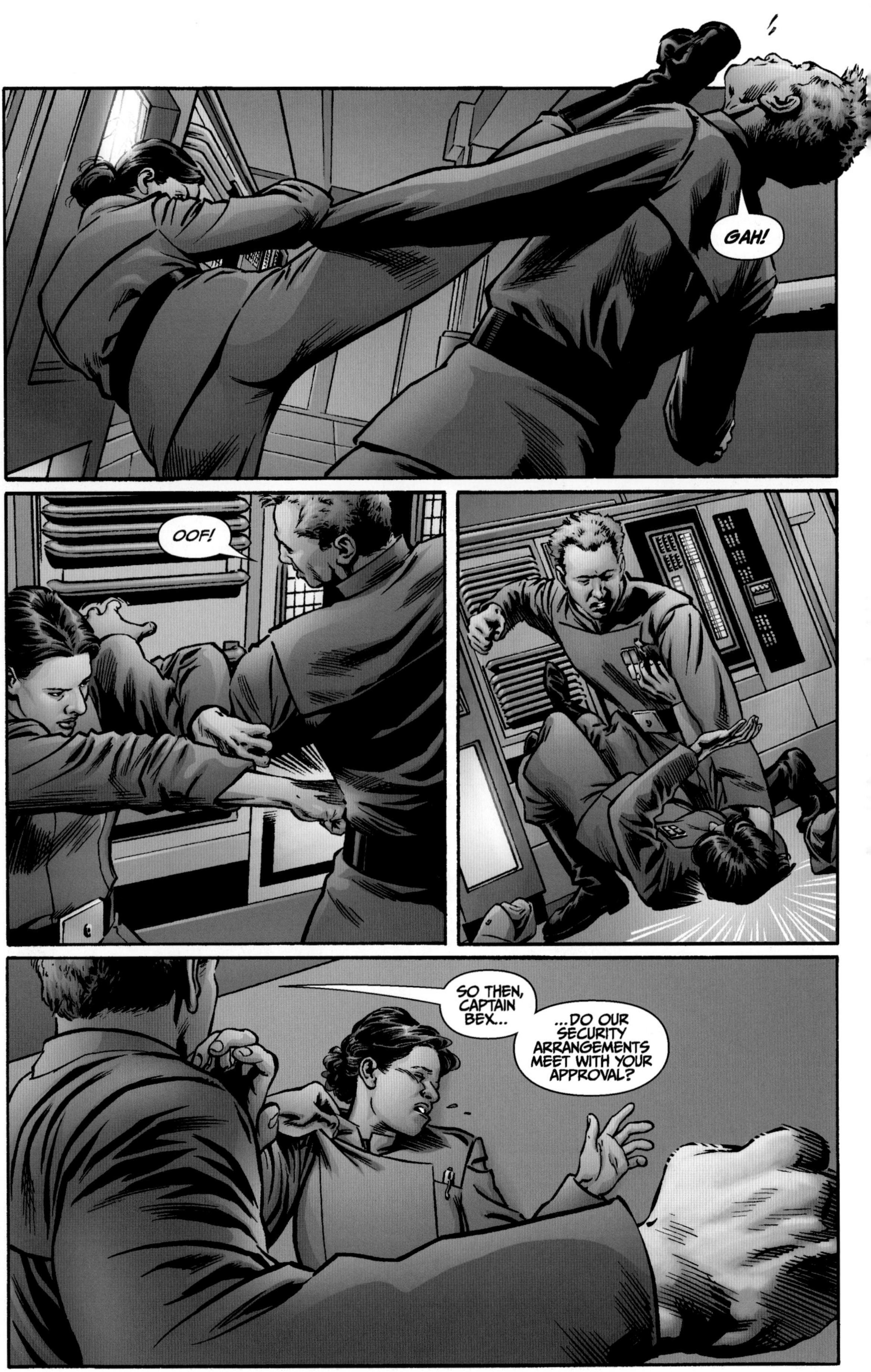
GAH!
OOF!
SO THEN, CAPTAIN BEX...
...DO OUR SECURITY ARRANGEMENTS MEET WITH YOUR APPROVAL?

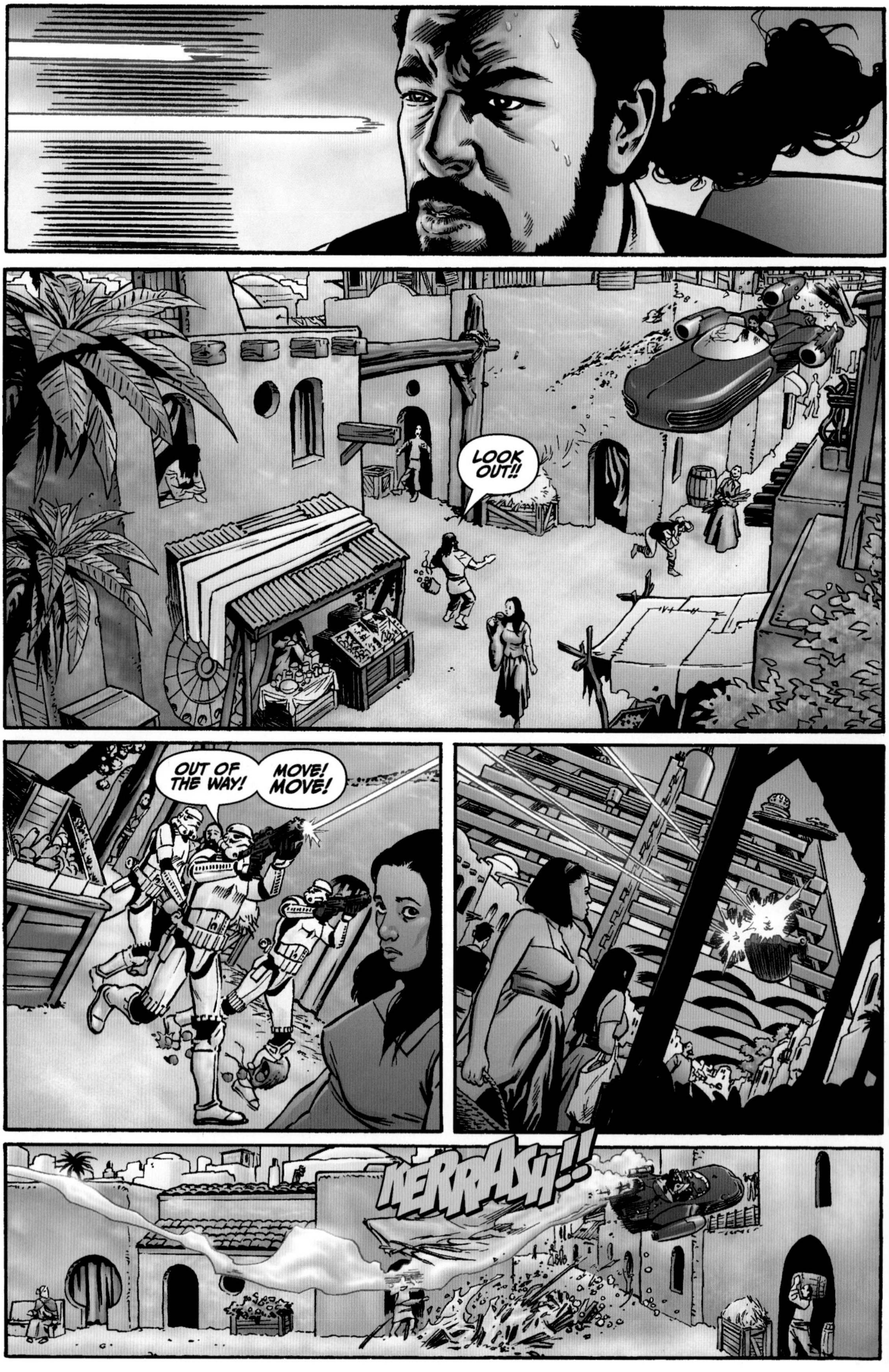
LOOK OUT!!
OUT OF THE WAY!
MOVE! MOVE!
KERRASH!!

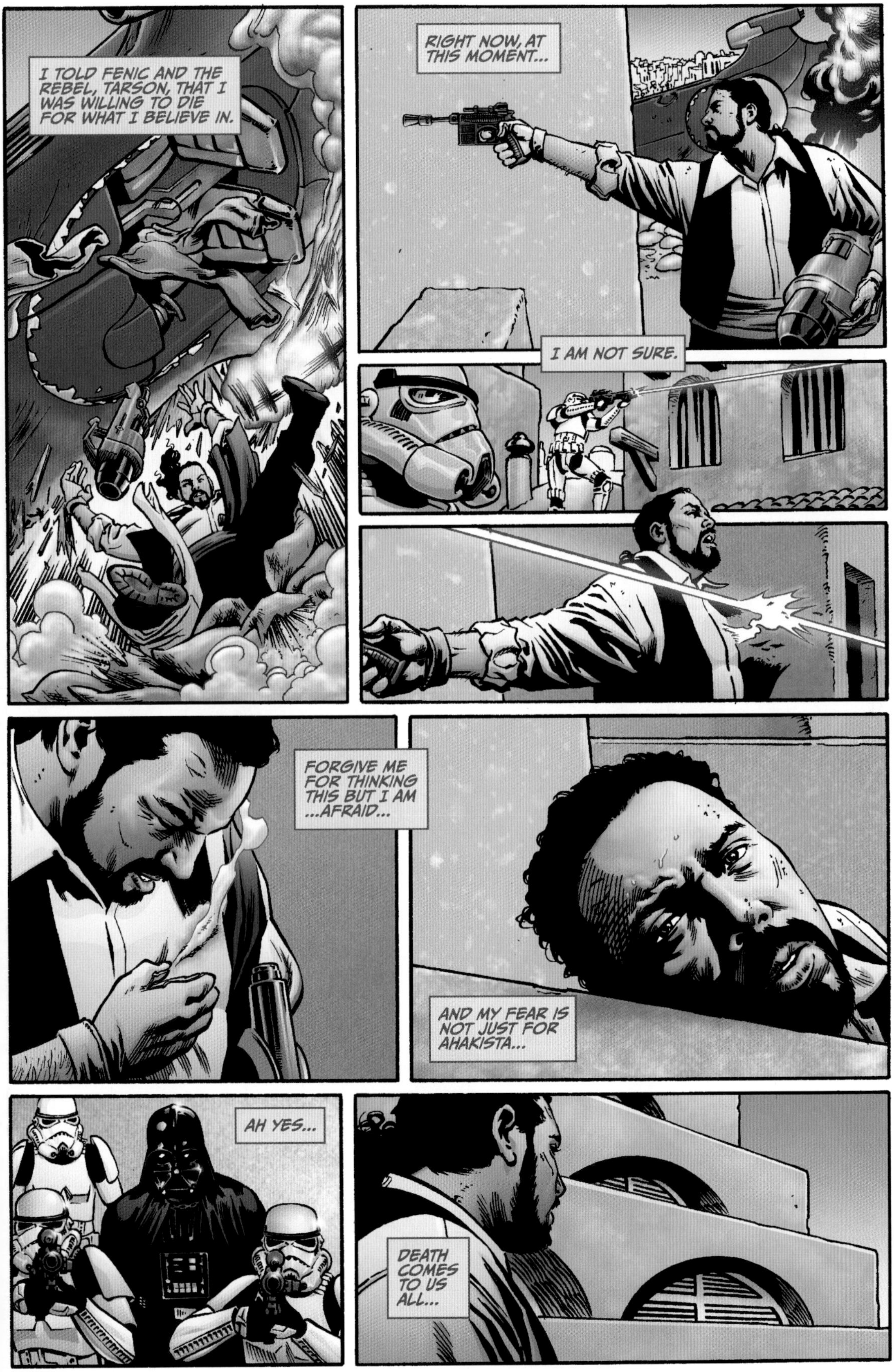
I TOLD FENIC AND THE REBEL, TARSON, THAT I WAS WILLING TO DIE FOR WHAT I BELIEVE IN.
RIGHT NOW, AT THIS MOMENT...
I AM NOT SURE.
FORGIVE ME FOR THINKING THIS BUT I AM ...AFRAID...
AND MY FEAR IS NOT JUST FOR AHAKISTA...
AH YES...
DEATH COMES TO US ALL...

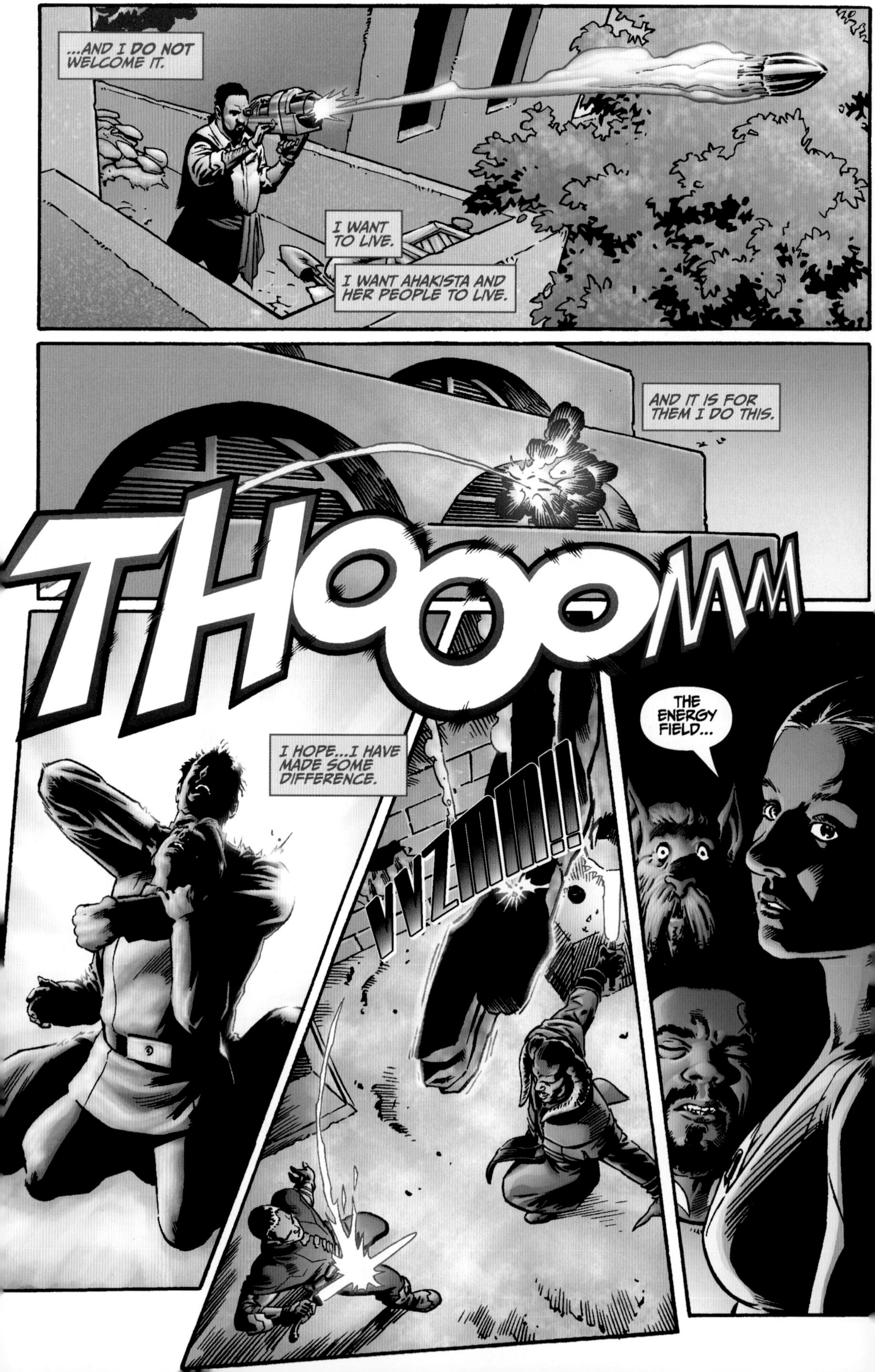
...AND I DO NOT WELCOME IT.
I WANT TO LIVE.
I WANT AHAKISTA AND HER PEOPLE TO LIVE.
AND IT IS FOR THEM I DO THIS.
THOOOMM
I HOPE...I HAVE MADE SOME DIFFERENCE.
VVZMMM!!
THE ENERGY FIELD...

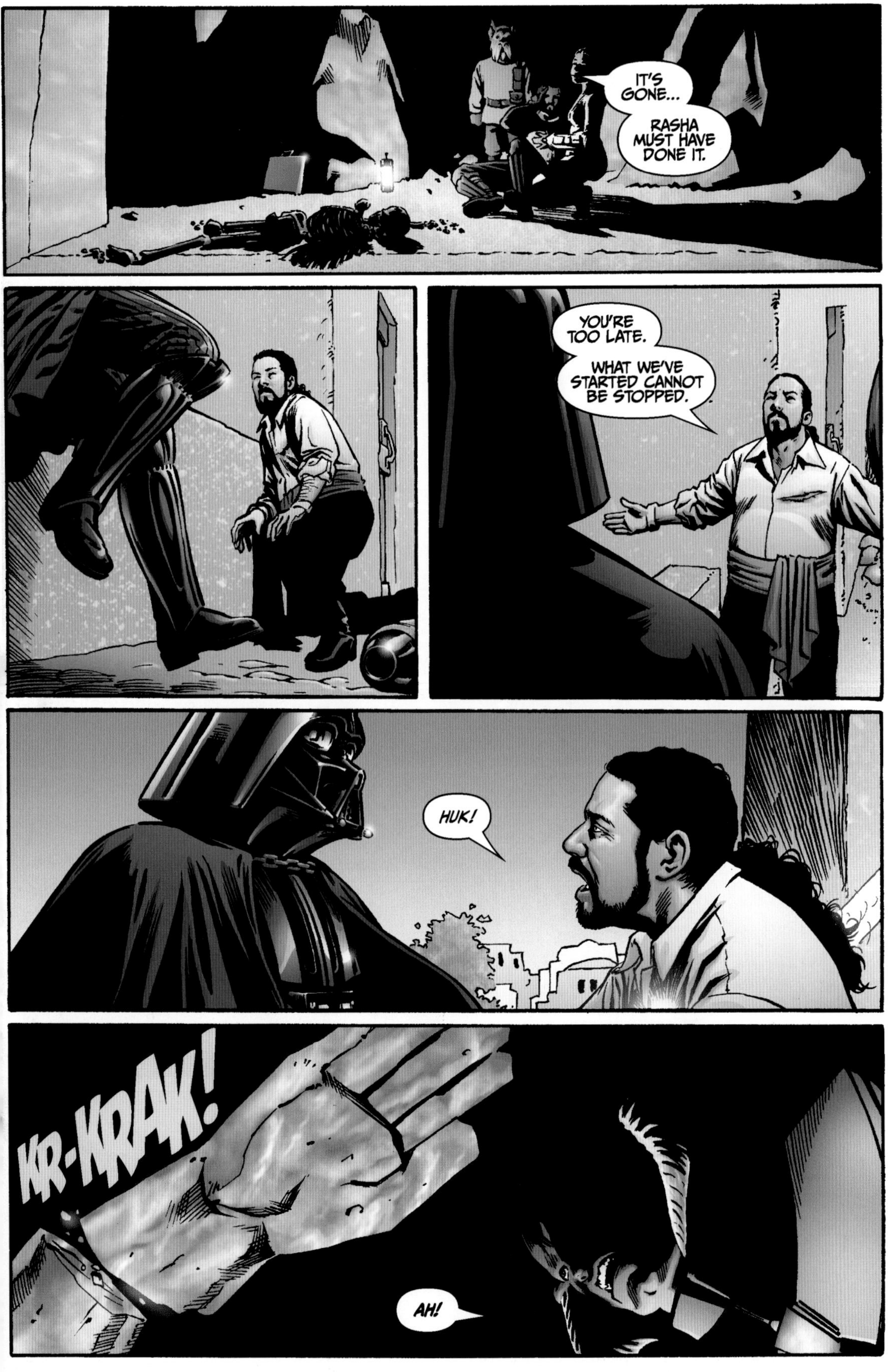
IT'S GONE...
RASHA MUST HAVE DONE IT.
YOU'RE TOO LATE.
WHAT WE'VE STARTED CANNOT BE STOPPED.
HUK!
KR-KRAK!
AH!

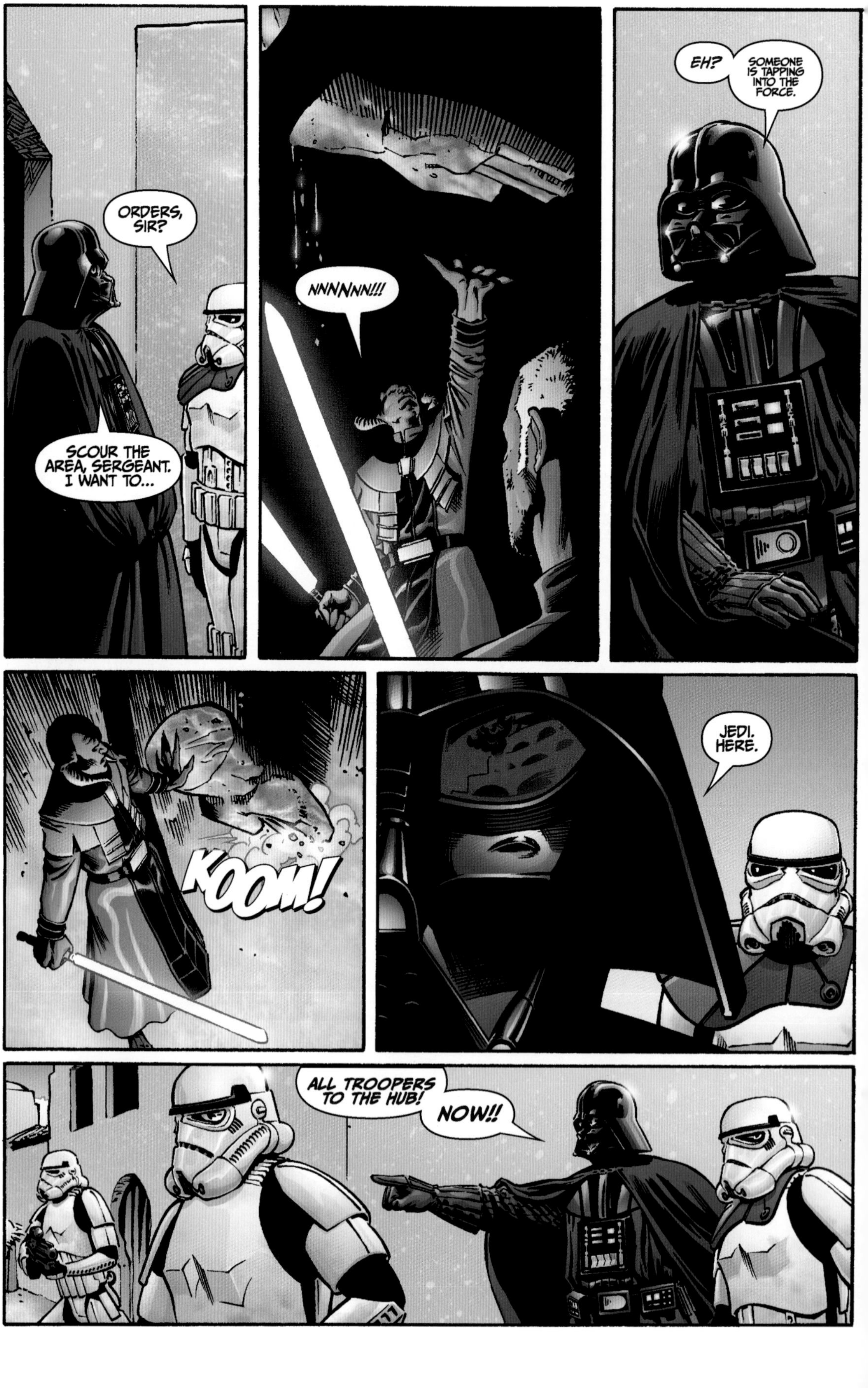
ORDERS, SIR?
SCOUR THE AREA, SERGEANT. I WANT TO...
NNNNNN!!!
EH?
SOMEONE IS TAPPING INTO THE FORCE.
KOOM!
JEDI. HERE.
ALL TROOPERS TO THE HUB!
NOW!!

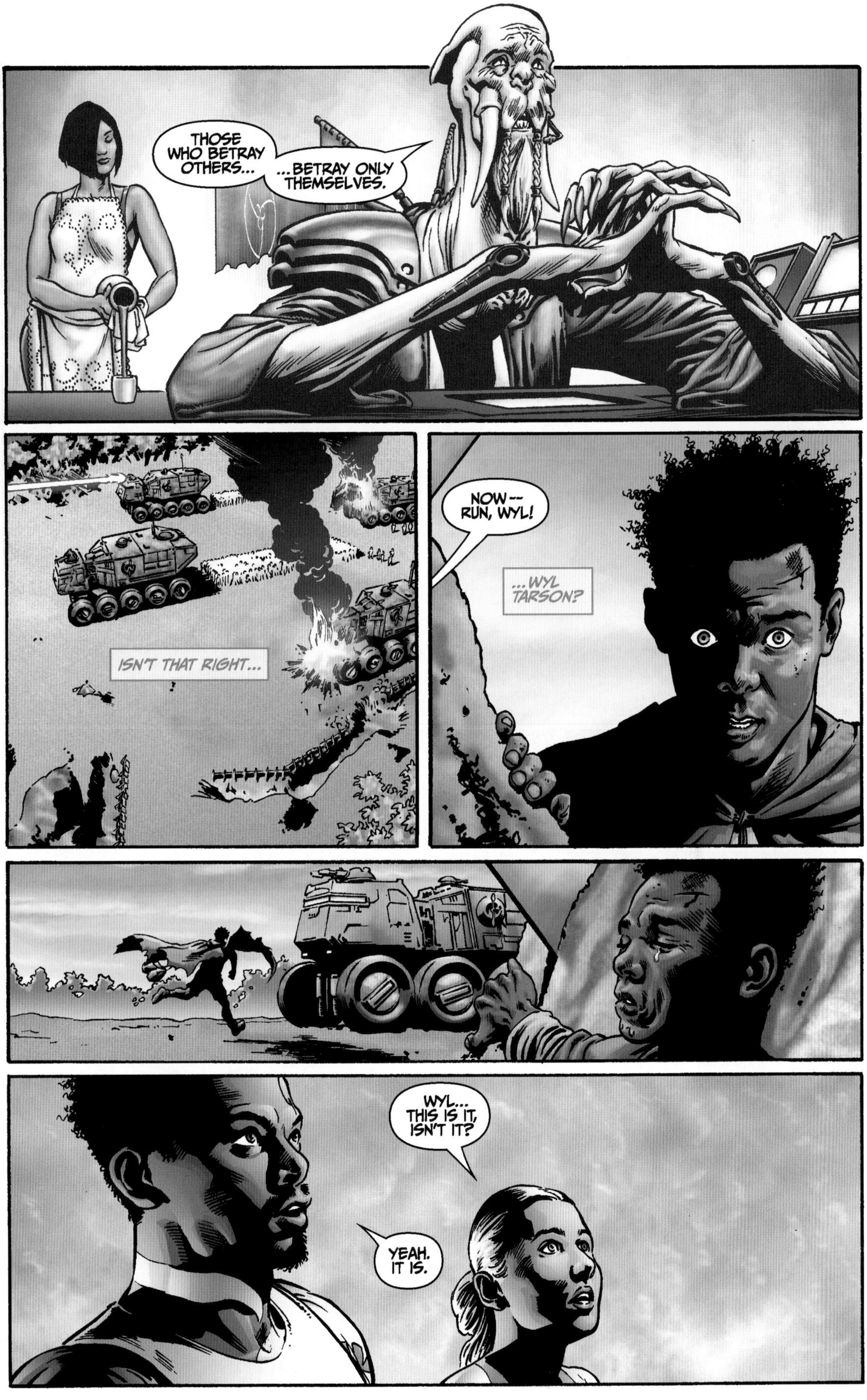
THOSE WHO BETRAY OTHERS...
...BETRAY ONLY THEMSELVES.
ISN'T THAT RIGHT...
NOW-- RUN, WYL!
...WYL TARSON?
WYL... THIS IS IT, ISN'T IT?
YEAH. IT IS.

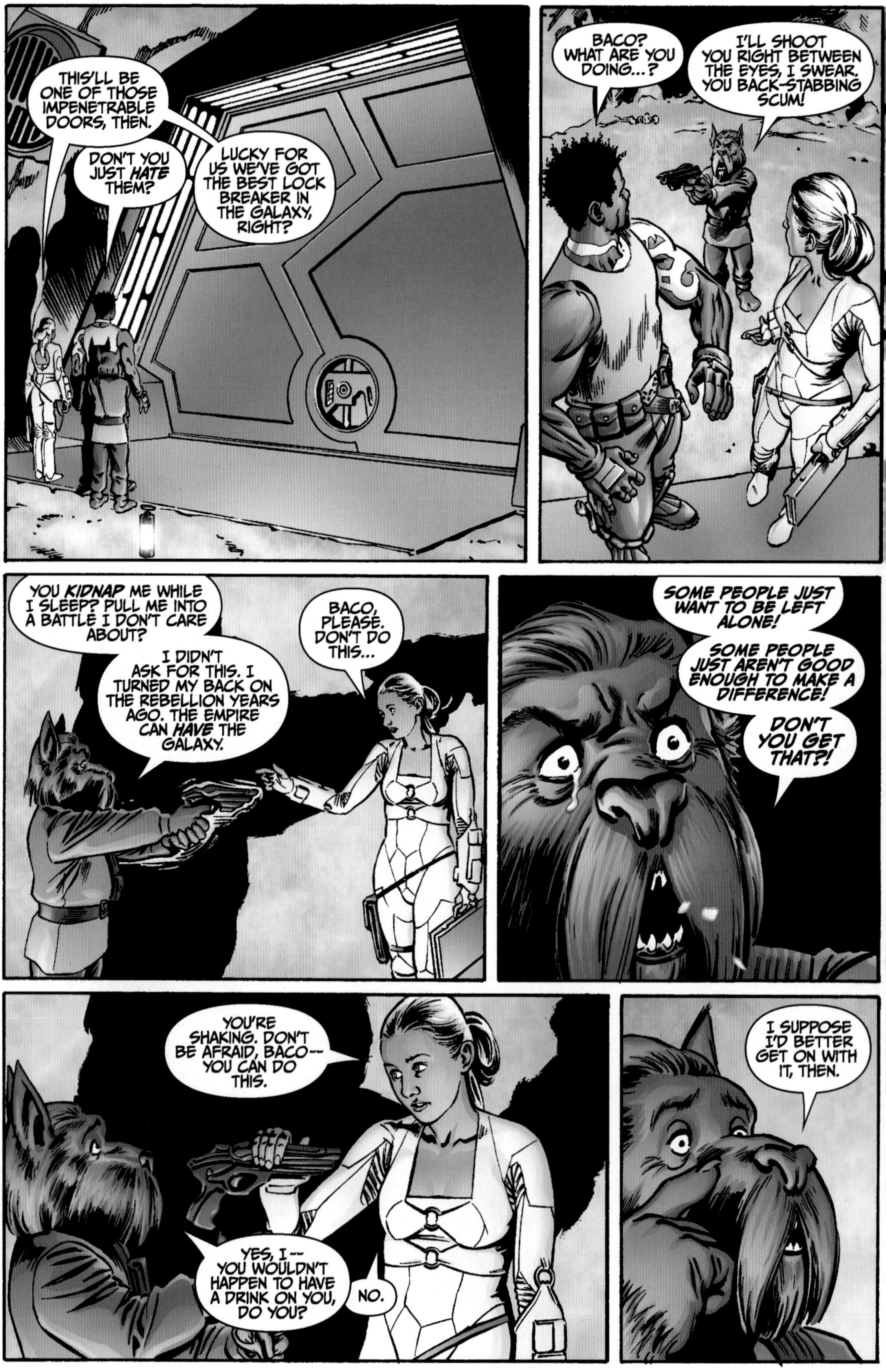
THIS'LL BE ONE OF THOSE IMPENETRABLE DOORS, THEN.
DON'T YOU JUST HATE THEM?
LUCKY FOR US WE'VE GOT THE BEST LOCK BREAKER IN THE GALAXY, RIGHT?
BACO? WHAT ARE YOU DOING...?
I'LL SHOOT YOU RIGHT BETWEEN THE EYES, I SWEAR. YOU BACK-STABBING SCUM!
YOU KIDNAP ME WHILE I SLEEP? PULL ME INTO A BATTLE I DON'T CARE ABOUT?
I DIDN'T ASK FOR THIS. I TURNED MY BACK ON THE REBELLION YEARS AGO. THE EMPIRE CAN HAVE THE GALAXY.
BACO, PLEASE. DON'T DO THIS...
SOME PEOPLE JUST WANT TO BE LEFT ALONE!
SOME PEOPLE JUST AREN'T GOOD ENOUGH TO MAKE A DIFFERENCE!
DON'T YOU GET THAT?!
YOU'RE SHAKING. DON'T BE AFRAID, BACO-- YOU CAN DO THIS.
YES, I-- YOU WOULDN'T HAPPEN TO HAVE A DRINK ON YOU, DO YOU?
NO.
I SUPPOSE I'D BETTER GET ON WITH IT, THEN.

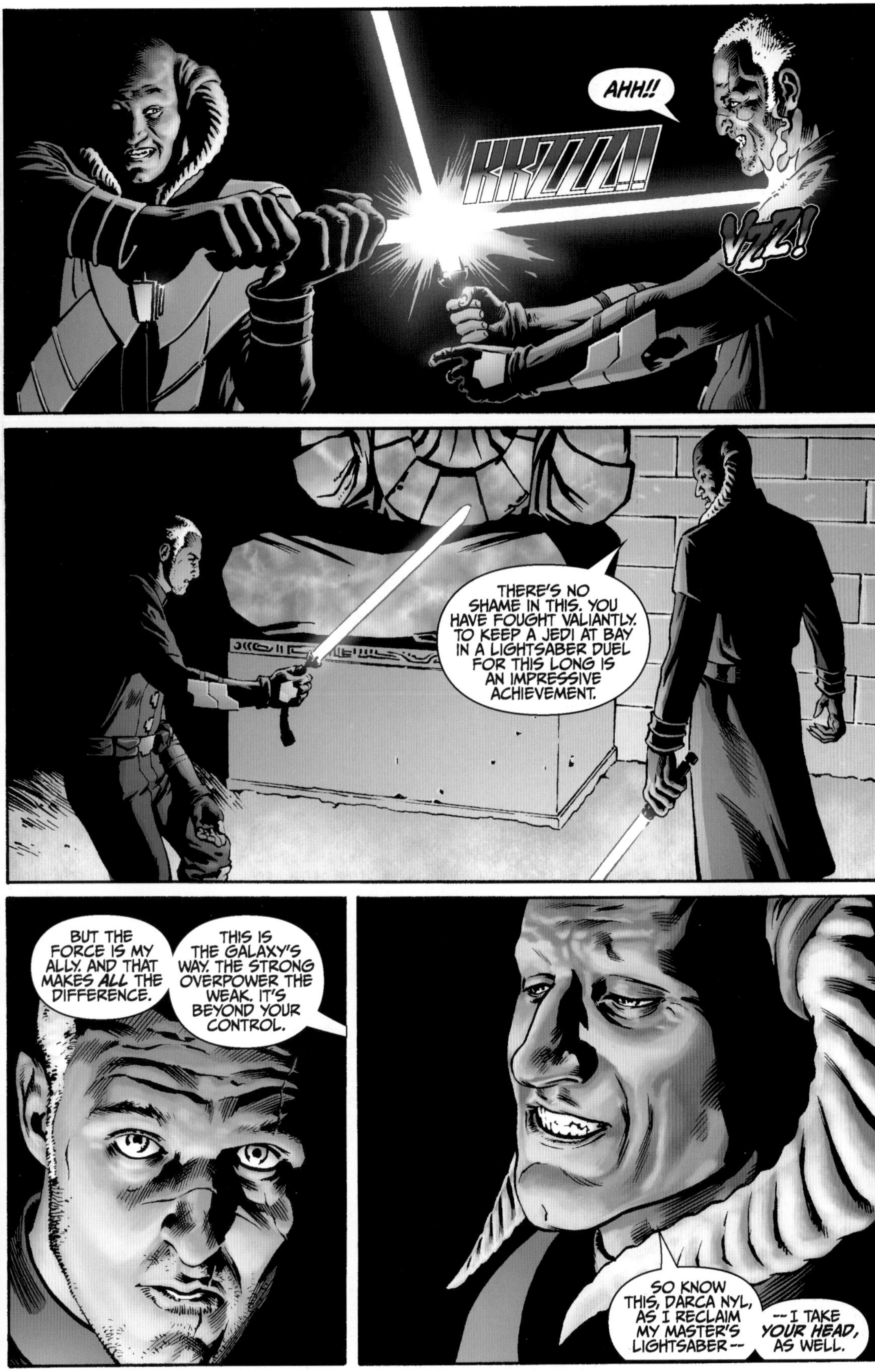
AHH!!
KKZZZZ!!
VZZ!
THERE'S NO SHAME IN THIS. YOU HAVE FOUGHT VALIANTLY. TO KEEP A JEDI AT BAY IN A LIGHTSABER DUEL FOR THIS LONG IS AN IMPRESSIVE ACHIEVEMENT.
BUT THE FORCE IS MY ALLY. AND THAT MAKES ALL THE DIFFERENCE.
THIS IS THE GALAXY'S WAY. THE STRONG OVERPOWER THE WEAK. IT'S BEYOND YOUR CONTROL.
SO KNOW THIS, DARCA NYL, AS I RECLAIM MY MASTER'S LIGHTSABER--
--I TAKE YOUR HEAD, AS WELL.

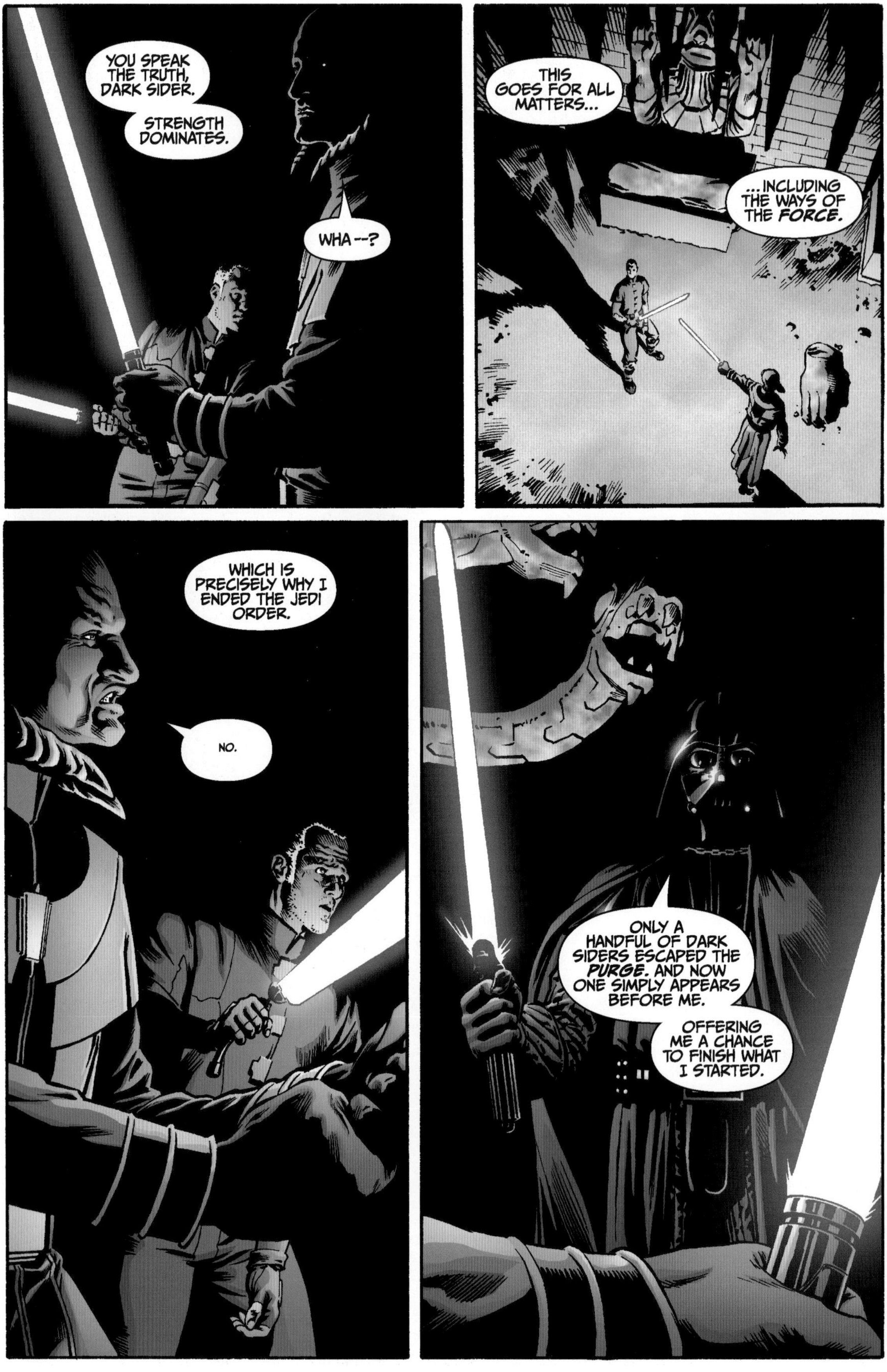
YOU SPEAK THE TRUTH, DARK SIDER.
STRENGTH DOMINATES.
WHA--?
THIS GOES FOR ALL MATTERS...
...INCLUDING THE WAYS OF THE *FORCE.*
WHICH IS PRECISELY WHY I ENDED THE JEDI ORDER.
NO.
ONLY A HANDFUL OF DARK SIDERS ESCAPED THE *PURGE.* AND NOW ONE SIMPLY APPEARS BEFORE ME.
OFFERING ME A CHANCE TO FINISH WHAT I STARTED.

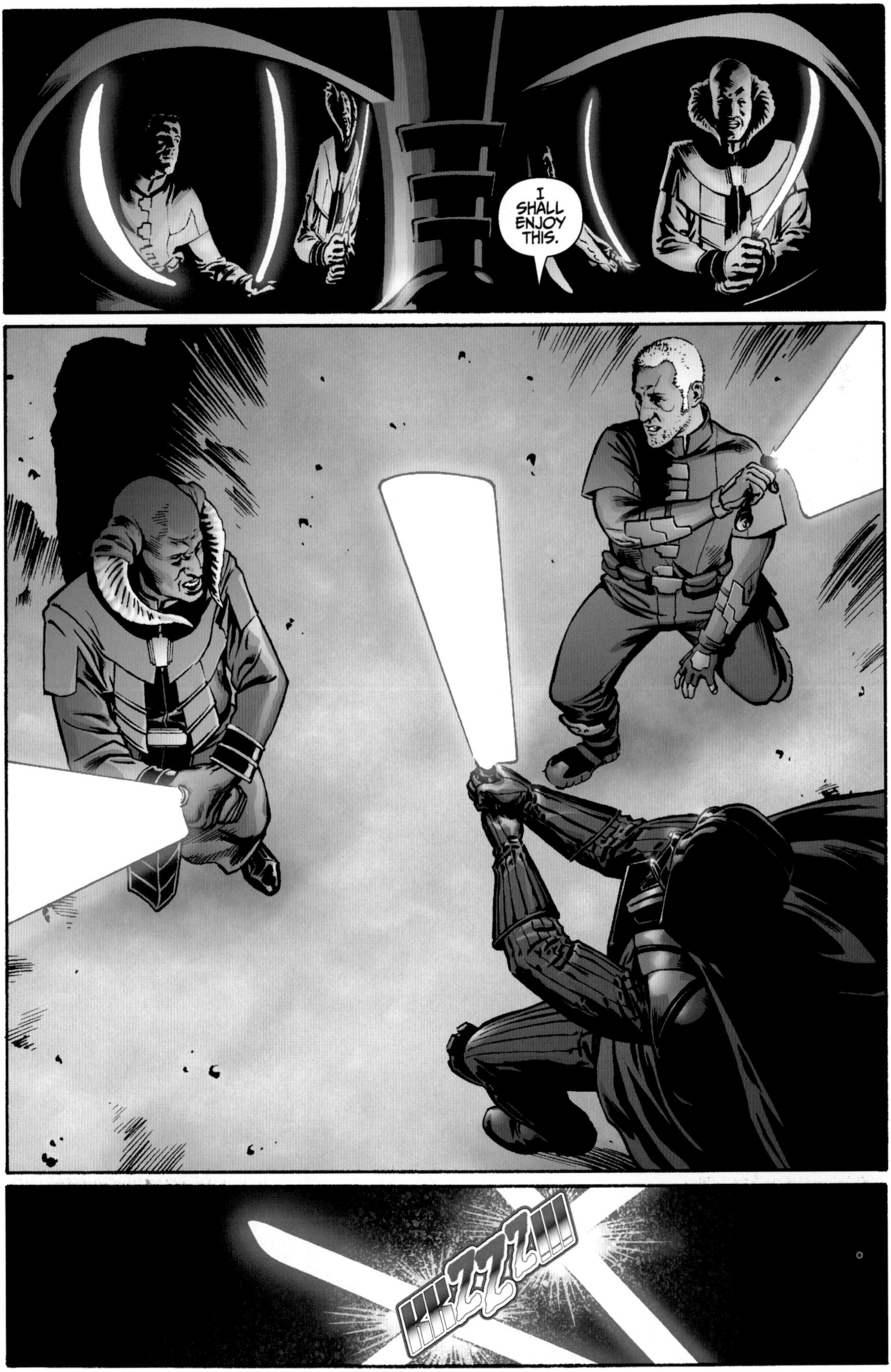
I SHALL ENJOY THIS.
KKZZZ!!!

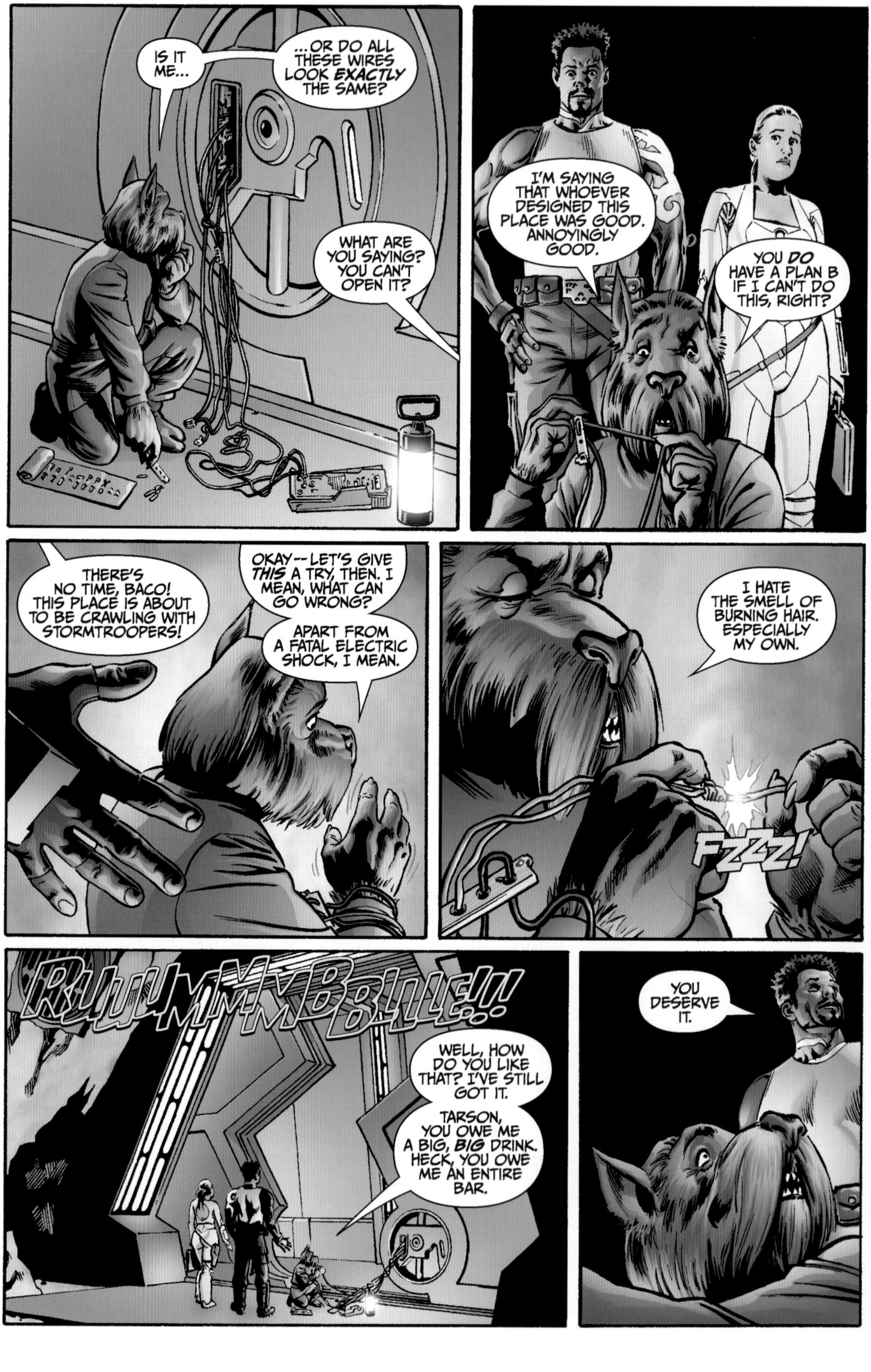
IS IT ME...
...OR DO ALL THESE WIRES LOOK EXACTLY THE SAME?
WHAT ARE YOU SAYING? YOU CAN'T OPEN IT?
I'M SAYING THAT WHOEVER DESIGNED THIS PLACE WAS GOOD. ANNOYINGLY GOOD.
YOU DO HAVE A PLAN B IF I CAN'T DO THIS, RIGHT?
THERE'S NO TIME, BACO! THIS PLACE IS ABOUT TO BE CRAWLING WITH STORMTROOPERS!
OKAY--LET'S GIVE THIS A TRY, THEN. I MEAN, WHAT CAN GO WRONG?
APART FROM A FATAL ELECTRIC SHOCK, I MEAN.
I HATE THE SMELL OF BURNING HAIR. ESPECIALLY MY OWN.
FZZZ!
RUUUMMMBBLLE!!
WELL, HOW DO YOU LIKE THAT? I'VE STILL GOT IT.
TARSON, YOU OWE ME A BIG, BIG DRINK. HECK, YOU OWE ME AN ENTIRE BAR.
YOU DESERVE IT.

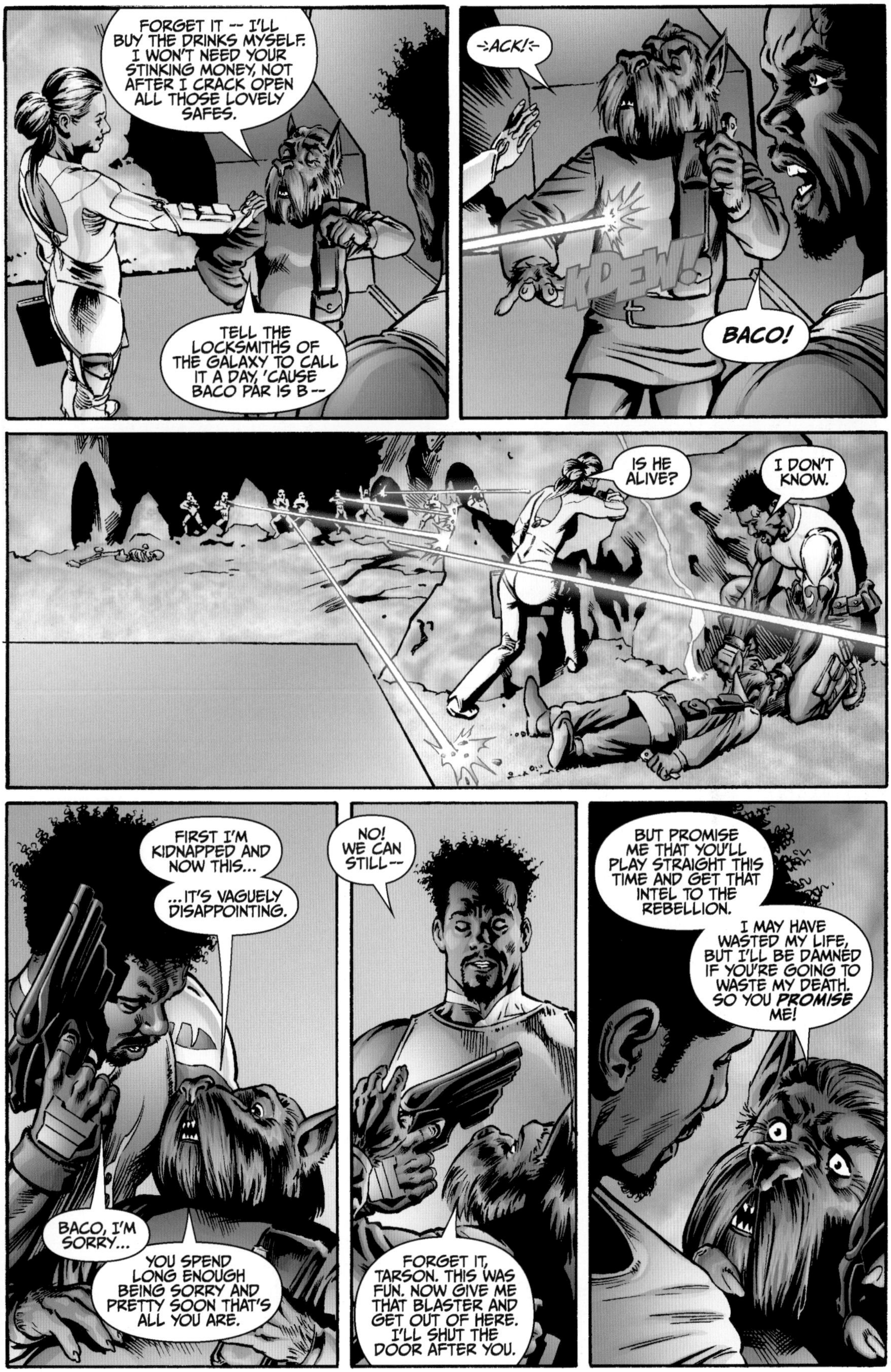
FORGET IT -- I'LL BUY THE DRINKS MYSELF. I WON'T NEED YOUR STINKING MONEY, NOT AFTER I CRACK OPEN ALL THOSE LOVELY SAFES.
TELL THE LOCKSMITHS OF THE GALAXY TO CALL IT A DAY, 'CAUSE BACO PAR IS B --
-ACK!-
KIDEW!
BACO!
IS HE ALIVE?
I DON'T KNOW.
FIRST I'M KIDNAPPED AND NOW THIS...
...IT'S VAGUELY DISAPPOINTING.
BACO, I'M SORRY...
YOU SPEND LONG ENOUGH BEING SORRY AND PRETTY SOON THAT'S ALL YOU ARE.
NO! WE CAN STILL--
FORGET IT, TARSON. THIS WAS FUN. NOW GIVE ME THAT BLASTER AND GET OUT OF HERE. I'LL SHUT THE DOOR AFTER YOU.
BUT PROMISE ME THAT YOU'LL PLAY STRAIGHT THIS TIME AND GET THAT INTEL TO THE REBELLION.
I MAY HAVE WASTED MY LIFE, BUT I'LL BE DAMNED IF YOU'RE GOING TO WASTE MY DEATH. SO YOU *PROMISE* ME!

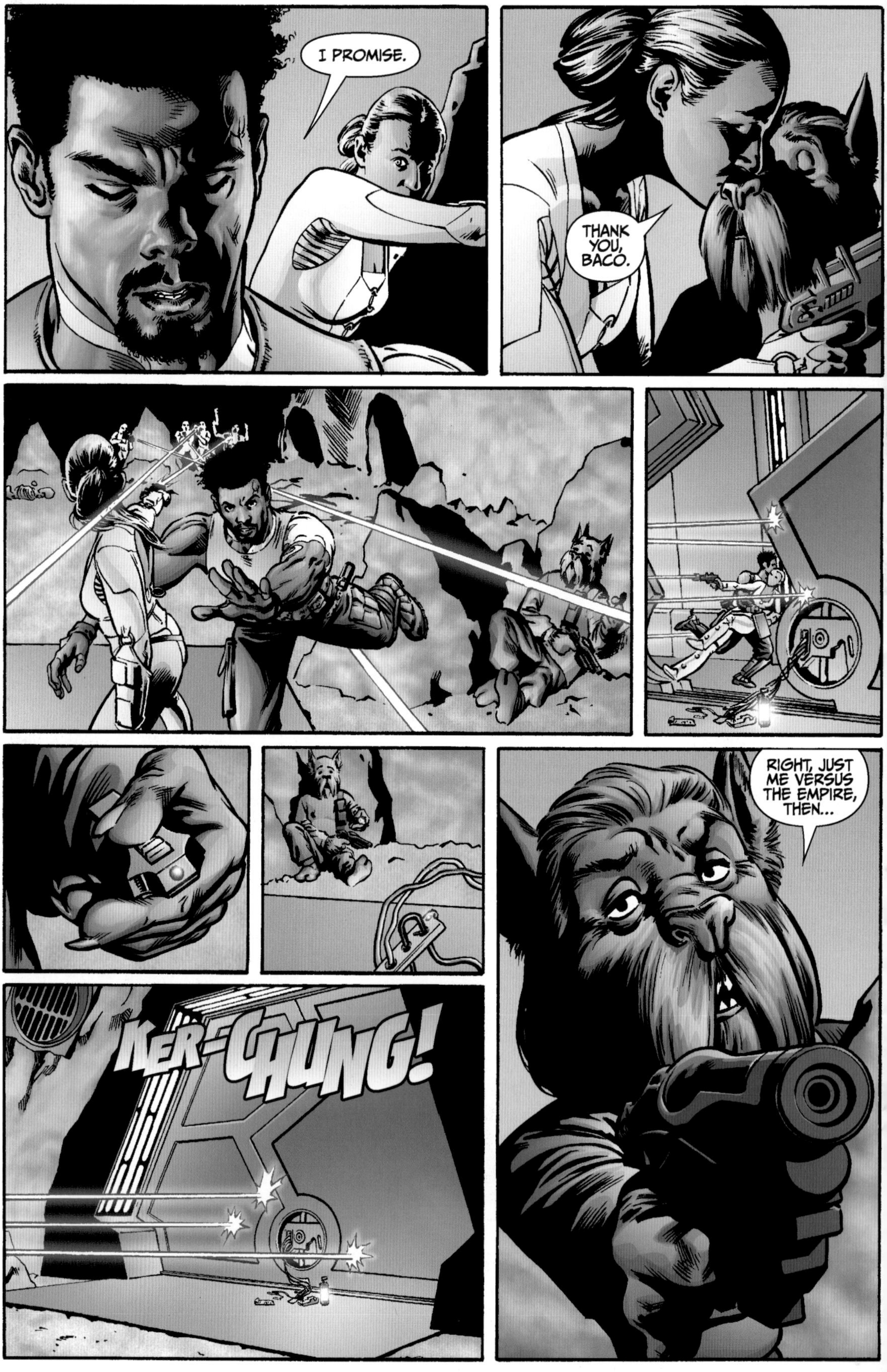
I PROMISE.
THANK YOU, BACO.
KER-CHUNG!
RIGHT, JUST ME VERSUS THE EMPIRE, THEN...

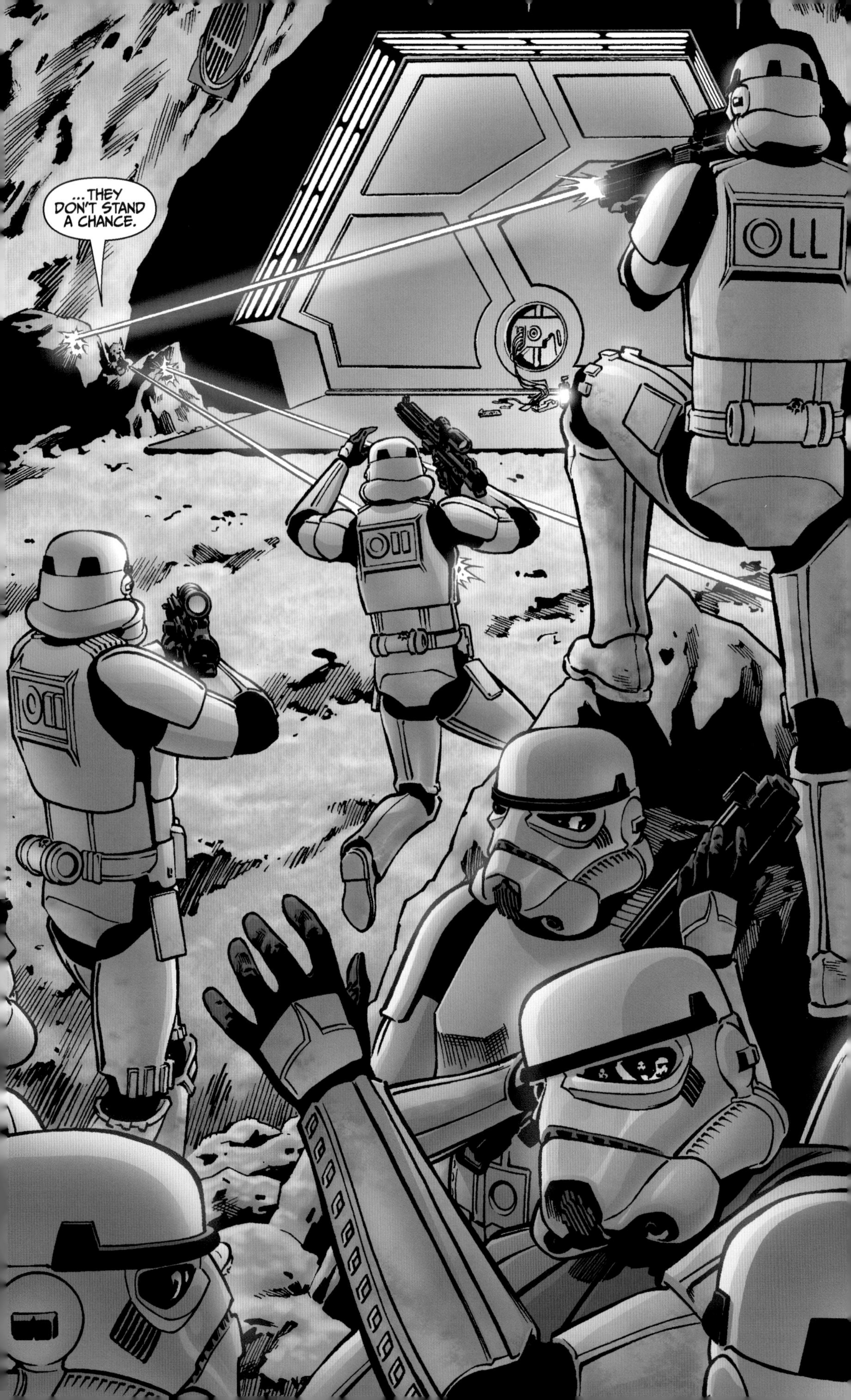
...THEY DON'T STAND A CHANCE.

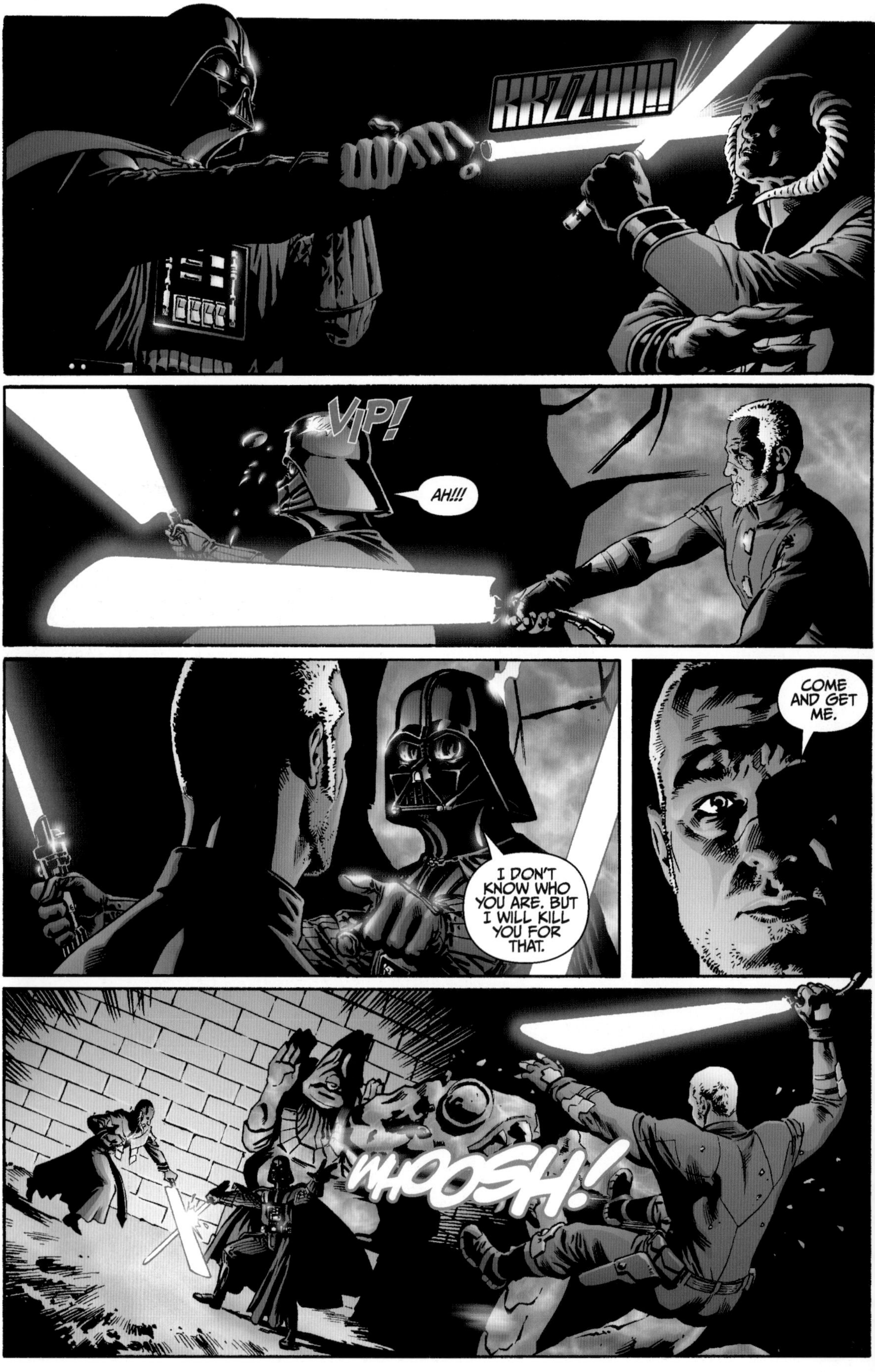
KKZZHH!!
VIP!
AH!!!
I DON'T KNOW WHO YOU ARE. BUT I WILL KILL YOU FOR THAT.
COME AND GET ME.
WHOOSH!

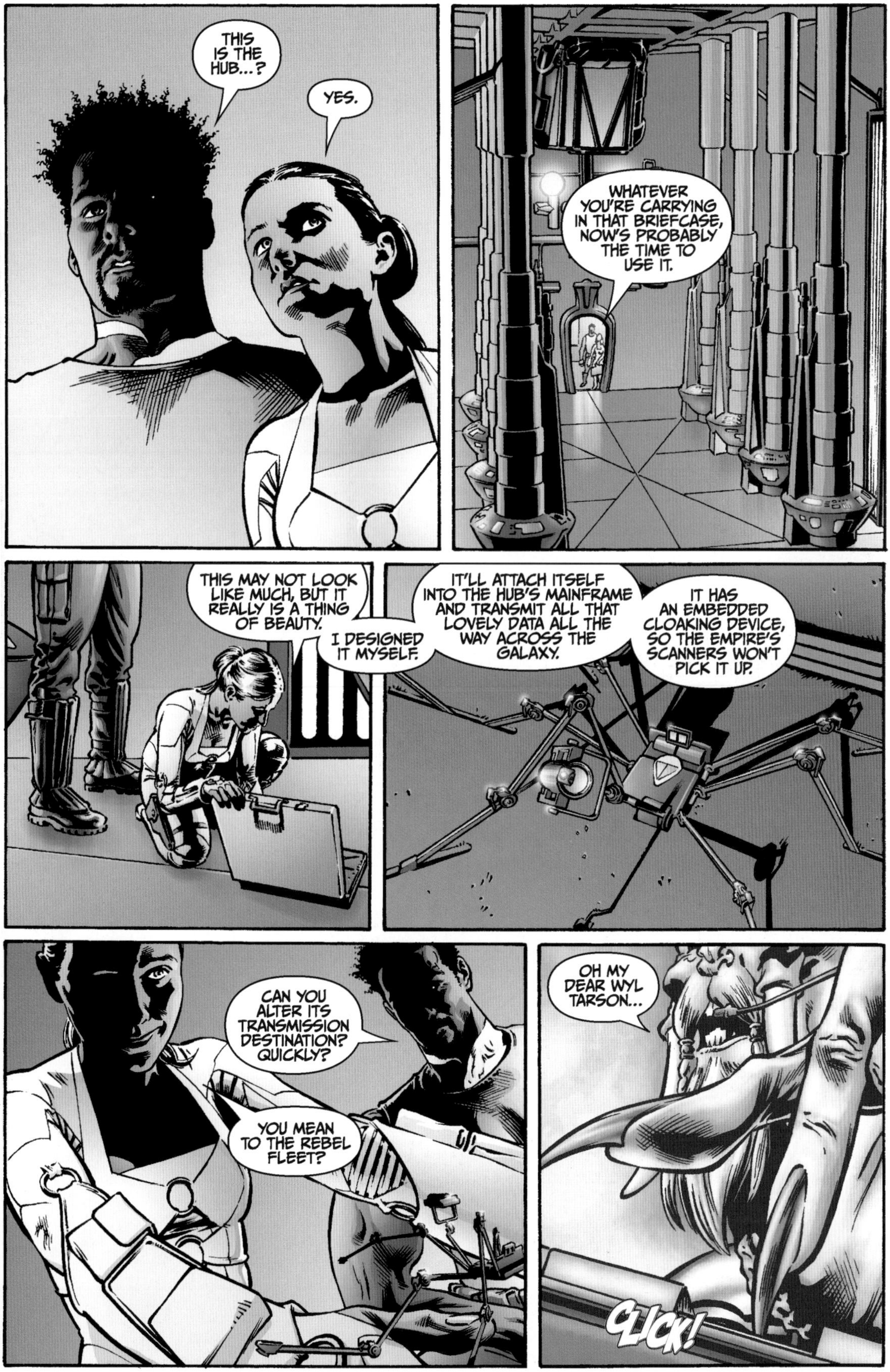
THIS IS THE HUB...?
YES.
WHATEVER YOU'RE CARRYING IN THAT BRIEFCASE, NOW'S PROBABLY THE TIME TO USE IT.
THIS MAY NOT LOOK LIKE MUCH, BUT IT REALLY IS A THING OF BEAUTY.
I DESIGNED IT MYSELF.
IT'LL ATTACH ITSELF INTO THE HUB'S MAINFRAME AND TRANSMIT ALL THAT LOVELY DATA ALL THE WAY ACROSS THE GALAXY.
IT HAS AN EMBEDDED CLOAKING DEVICE, SO THE EMPIRE'S SCANNERS WON'T PICK IT UP.
CAN YOU ALTER ITS TRANSMISSION DESTINATION? QUICKLY?
YOU MEAN TO THE REBEL FLEET?
OH MY DEAR WYL TARSON...
CLICK!

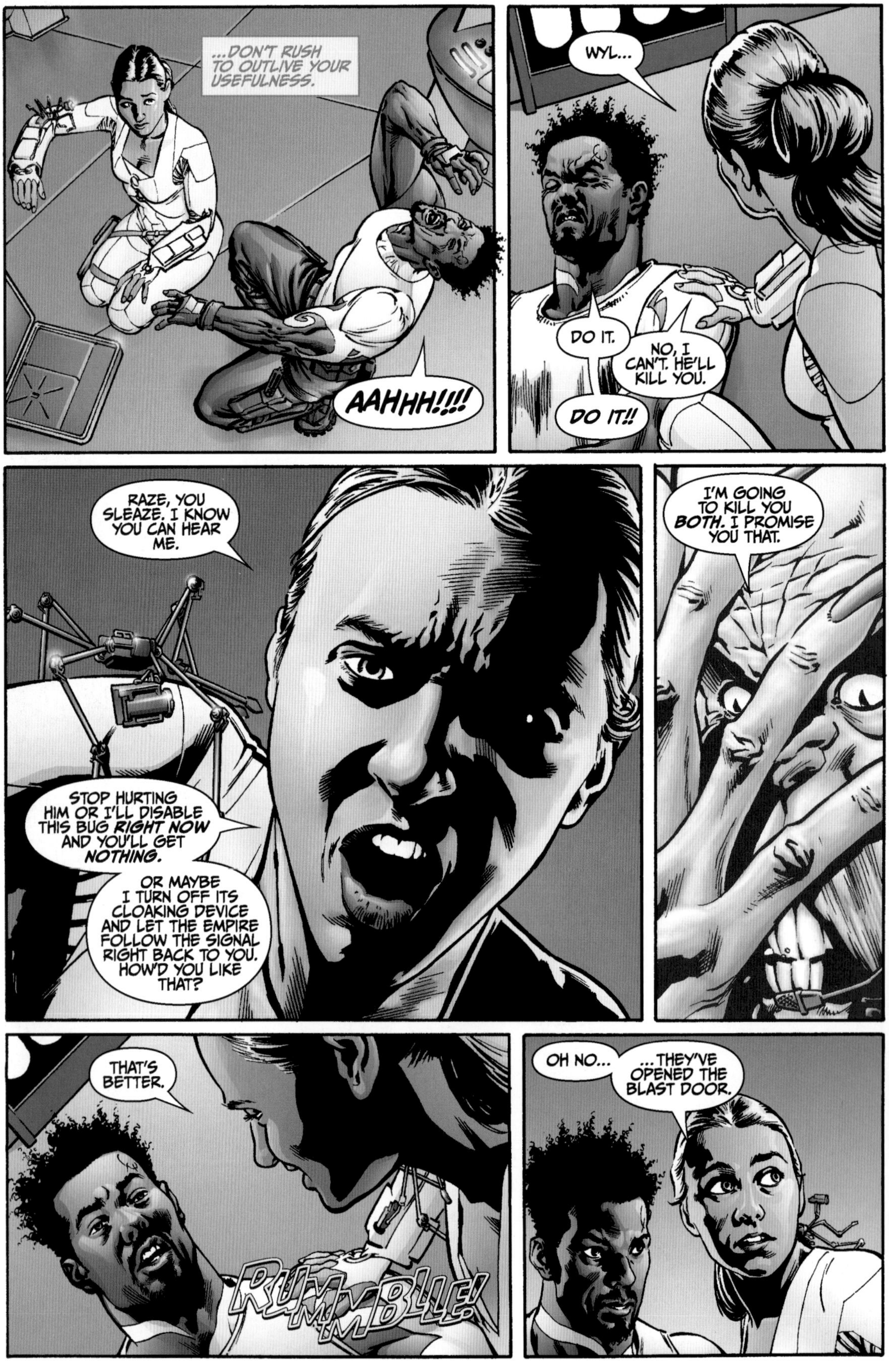
...DON'T RUSH TO OUTLIVE YOUR USEFULNESS.
AAHHH!!!!
WYL...
DO IT.
NO, I CAN'T. HE'LL KILL YOU.
DO IT!!
RAZE, YOU SLEAZE. I KNOW YOU CAN HEAR ME.
STOP HURTING HIM OR I'LL DISABLE THIS BUG RIGHT NOW AND YOU'LL GET NOTHING.
OR MAYBE I TURN OFF ITS CLOAKING DEVICE AND LET THE EMPIRE FOLLOW THE SIGNAL RIGHT BACK TO YOU. HOW'D YOU LIKE THAT?
I'M GOING TO KILL YOU BOTH. I PROMISE YOU THAT.
THAT'S BETTER.
RUMMMBLLE!
OH NO...
...THEY'VE OPENED THE BLAST DOOR.

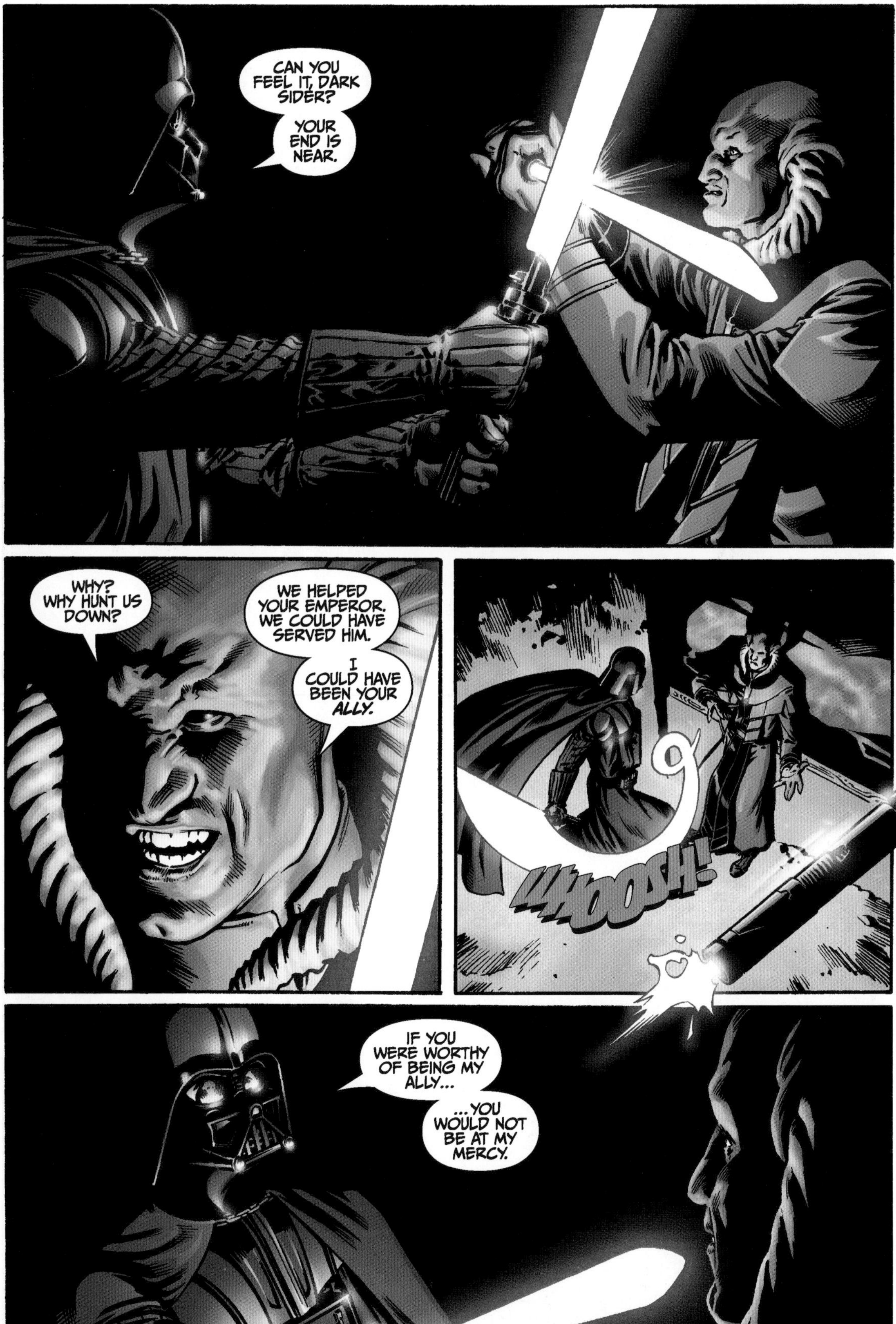
CAN YOU FEEL IT, DARK SIDER?
YOUR END IS NEAR.
WHY? WHY HUNT US DOWN?
WE HELPED YOUR EMPEROR. WE COULD HAVE SERVED HIM.
I COULD HAVE BEEN YOUR *ALLY.*
WHOOSH!
IF YOU WERE WORTHY OF BEING MY ALLY...
...YOU WOULD NOT BE AT MY MERCY.

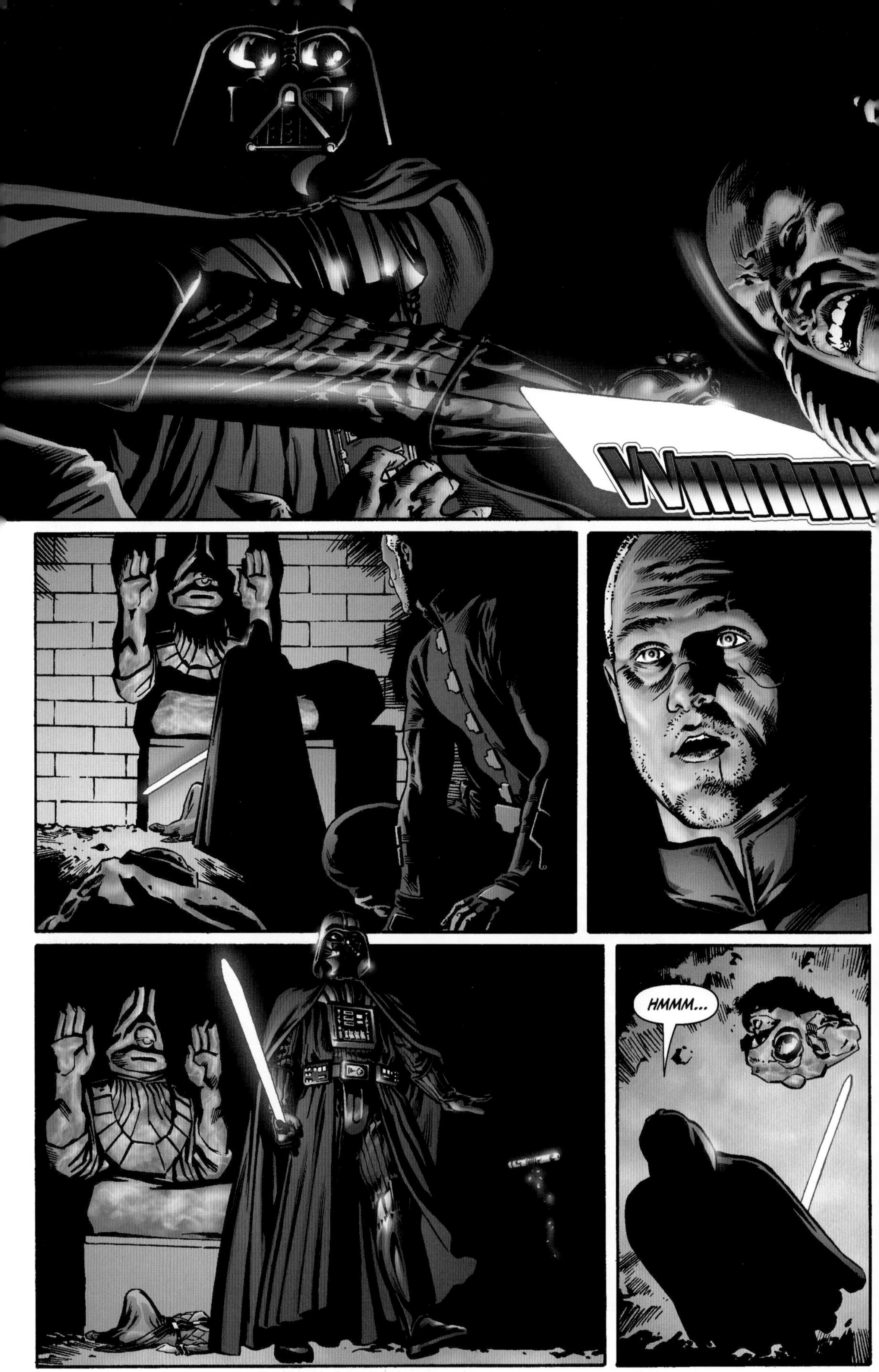
VVMMM
HMMM...

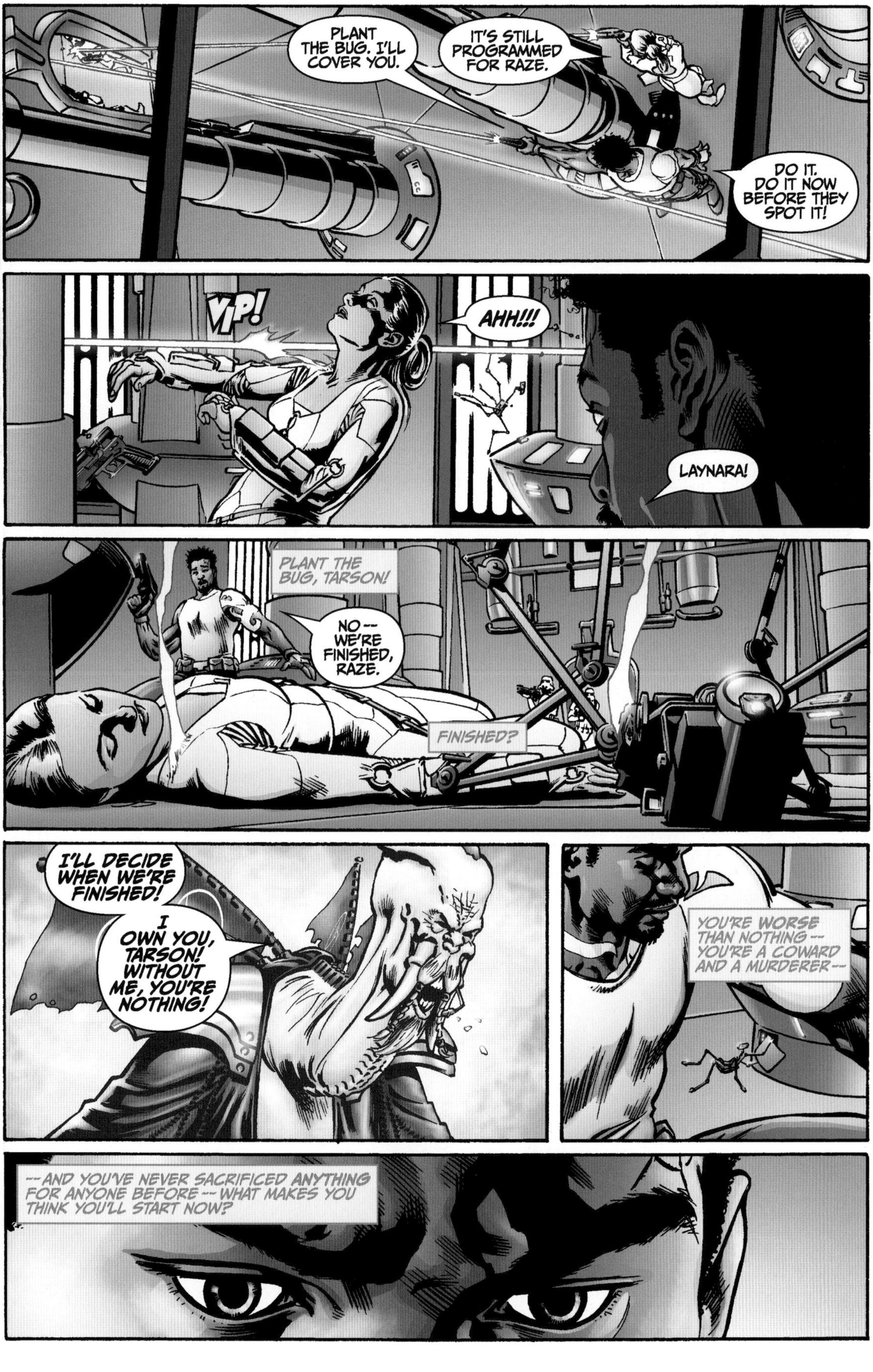
PLANT THE BUG. I'LL COVER YOU.
IT'S STILL PROGRAMMED FOR RAZE.
DO IT. DO IT NOW BEFORE THEY SPOT IT!
VIP!
AHH!!!
LAYNARA!
PLANT THE BUG, TARSON!
NO-- WE'RE FINISHED, RAZE.
FINISHED?
I'LL DECIDE WHEN WE'RE FINISHED!
I OWN YOU, TARSON! WITHOUT ME, YOU'RE NOTHING!
YOU'RE WORSE THAN NOTHING-- YOU'RE A COWARD AND A MURDERER--
--AND YOU'VE NEVER SACRIFICED ANYTHING FOR ANYONE BEFORE--WHAT MAKES YOU THINK YOU'LL START NOW?

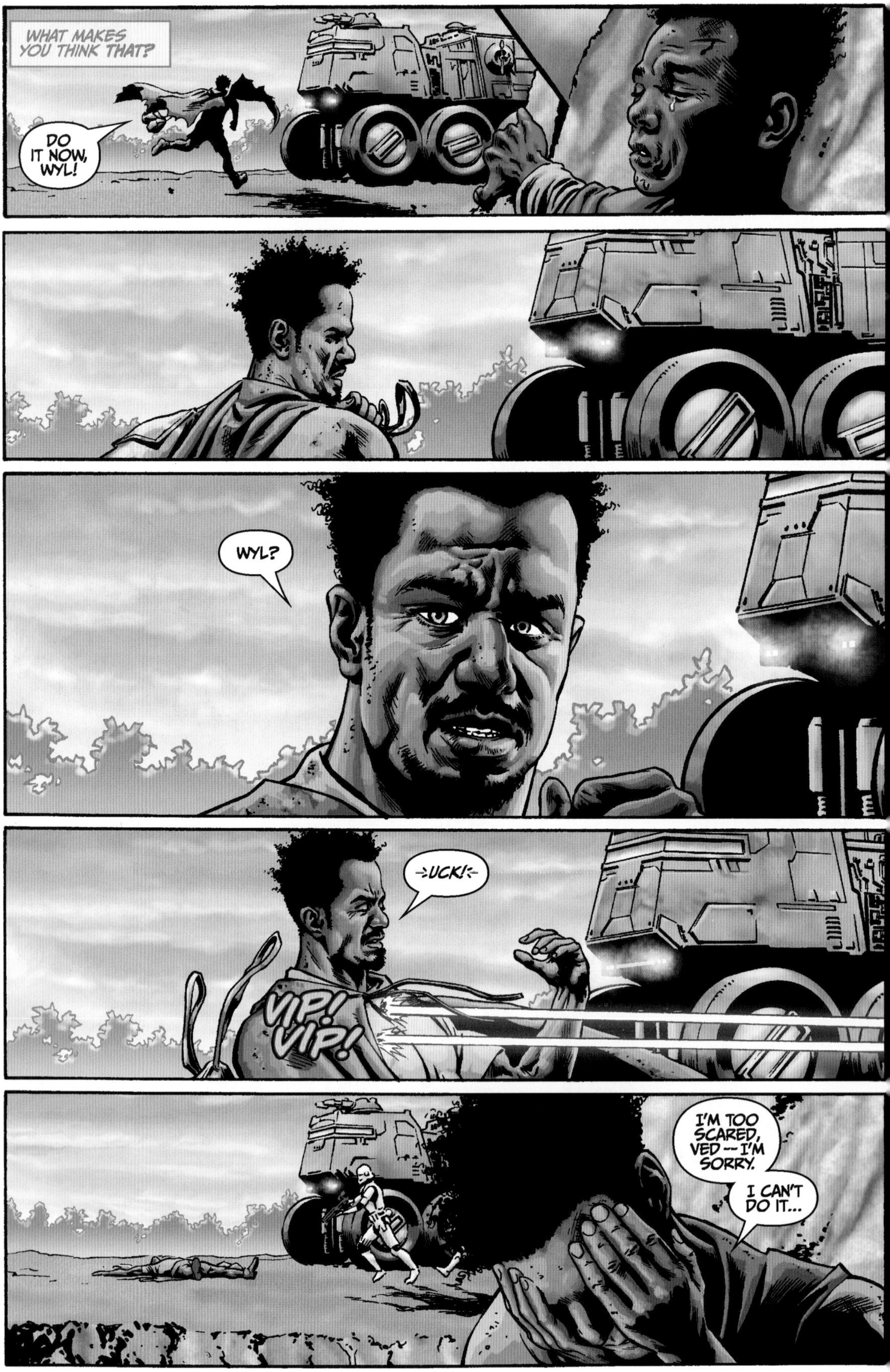
WHAT MAKES YOU THINK THAT?
DO IT NOW, WYL!
WYL?
-UCK!-
VIP! VIP!
I'M TOO SCARED, VED -- I'M SORRY.
I CAN'T DO IT...

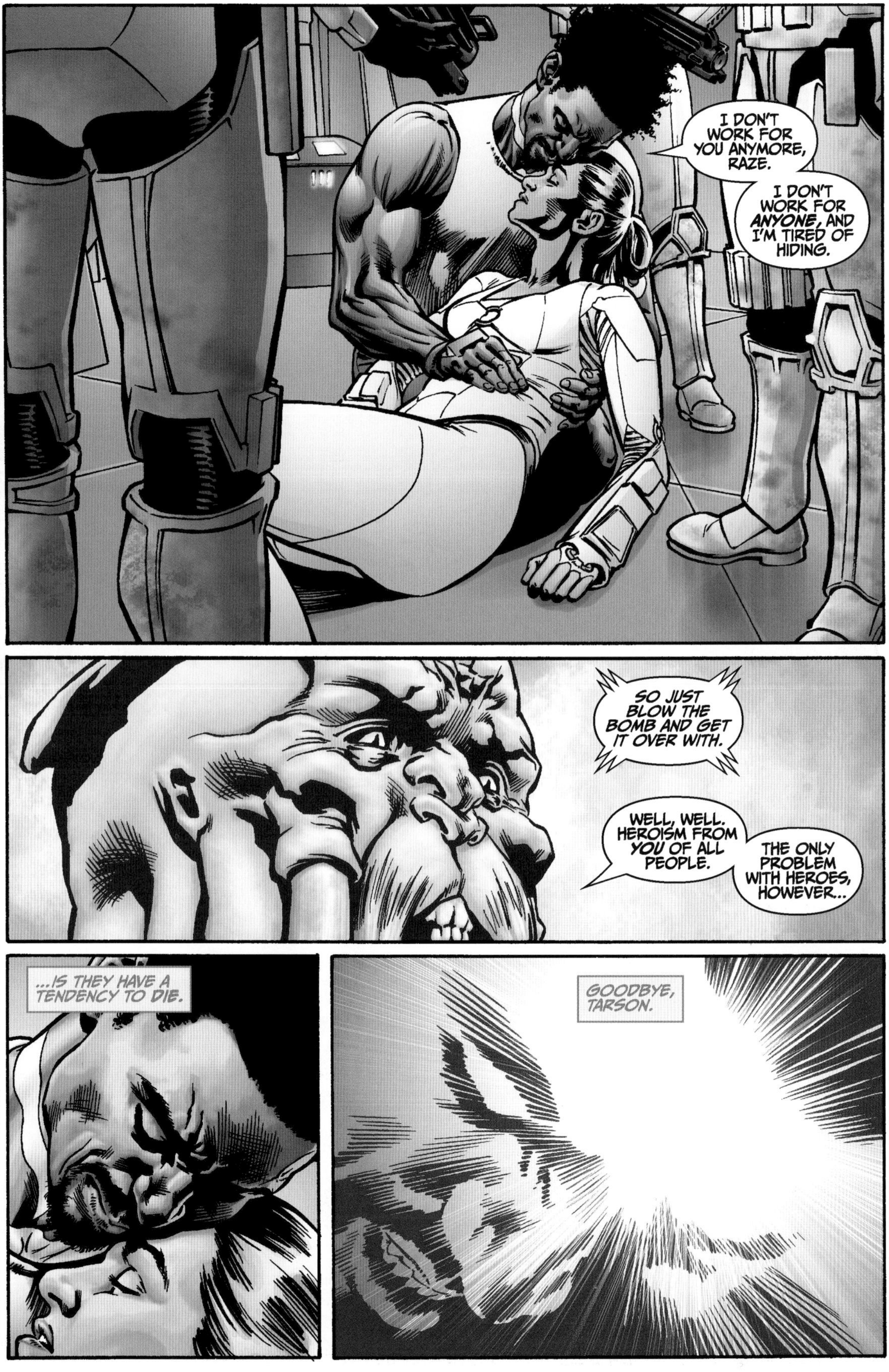
I DON'T WORK FOR YOU ANYMORE, RAZE.
I DON'T WORK FOR ANYONE, AND I'M TIRED OF HIDING.
SO JUST BLOW THE BOMB AND GET IT OVER WITH.
WELL, WELL. HEROISM FROM YOU OF ALL PEOPLE.
THE ONLY PROBLEM WITH HEROES, HOWEVER...
...IS THEY HAVE A TENDENCY TO DIE.
GOODBYE, TARSON.

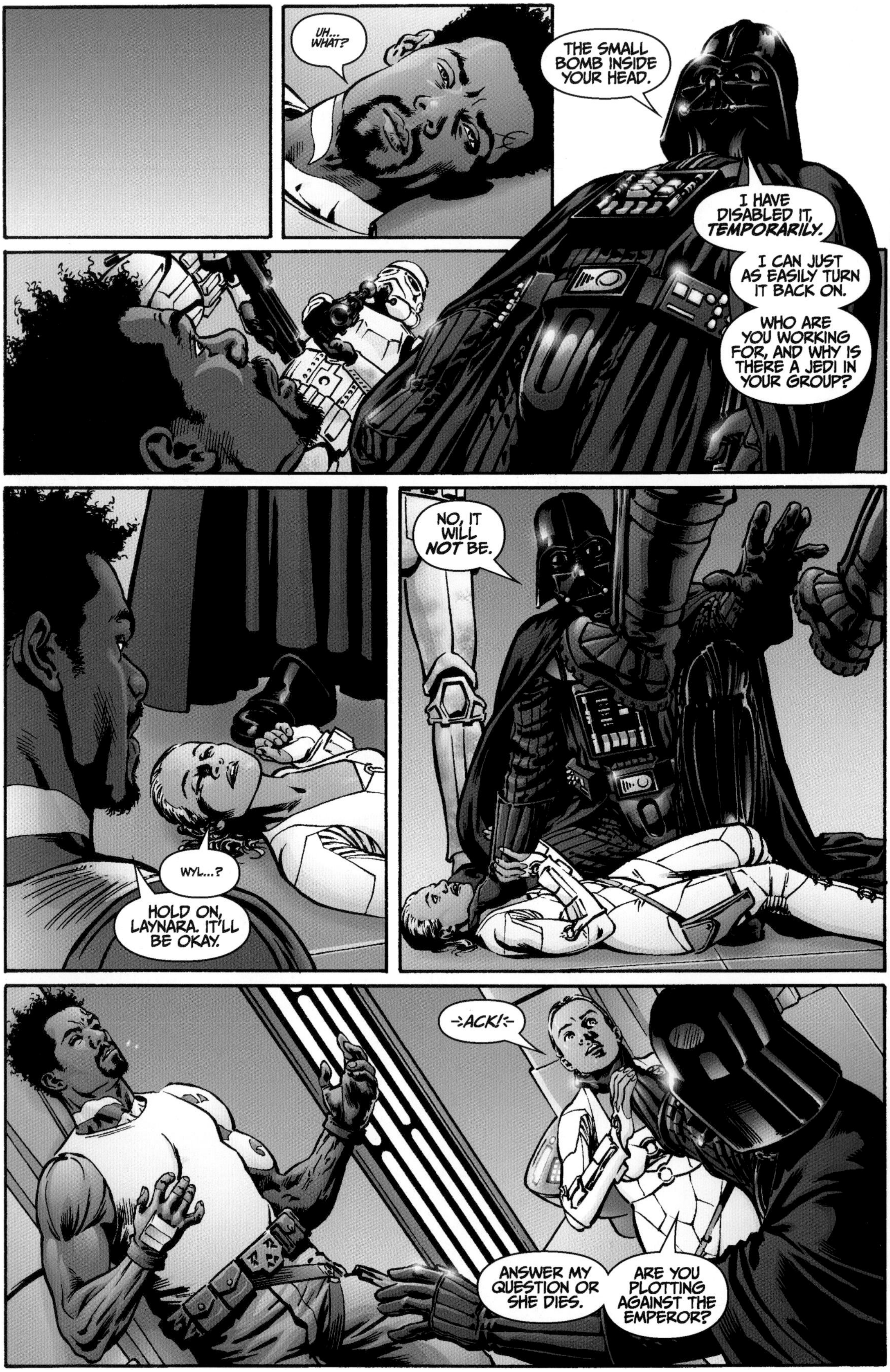
UH... WHAT?
THE SMALL BOMB INSIDE YOUR HEAD.
I HAVE DISABLED IT, *TEMPORARILY.*
I CAN JUST AS EASILY TURN IT BACK ON.
WHO ARE YOU WORKING FOR, AND WHY IS THERE A JEDI IN YOUR GROUP?
WYL...?
HOLD ON, LAYNARA. IT'LL BE OKAY.
NO, IT WILL *NOT* BE.
-ACK!-
ANSWER MY QUESTION OR SHE DIES.
ARE YOU PLOTTING AGAINST THE EMPEROR?

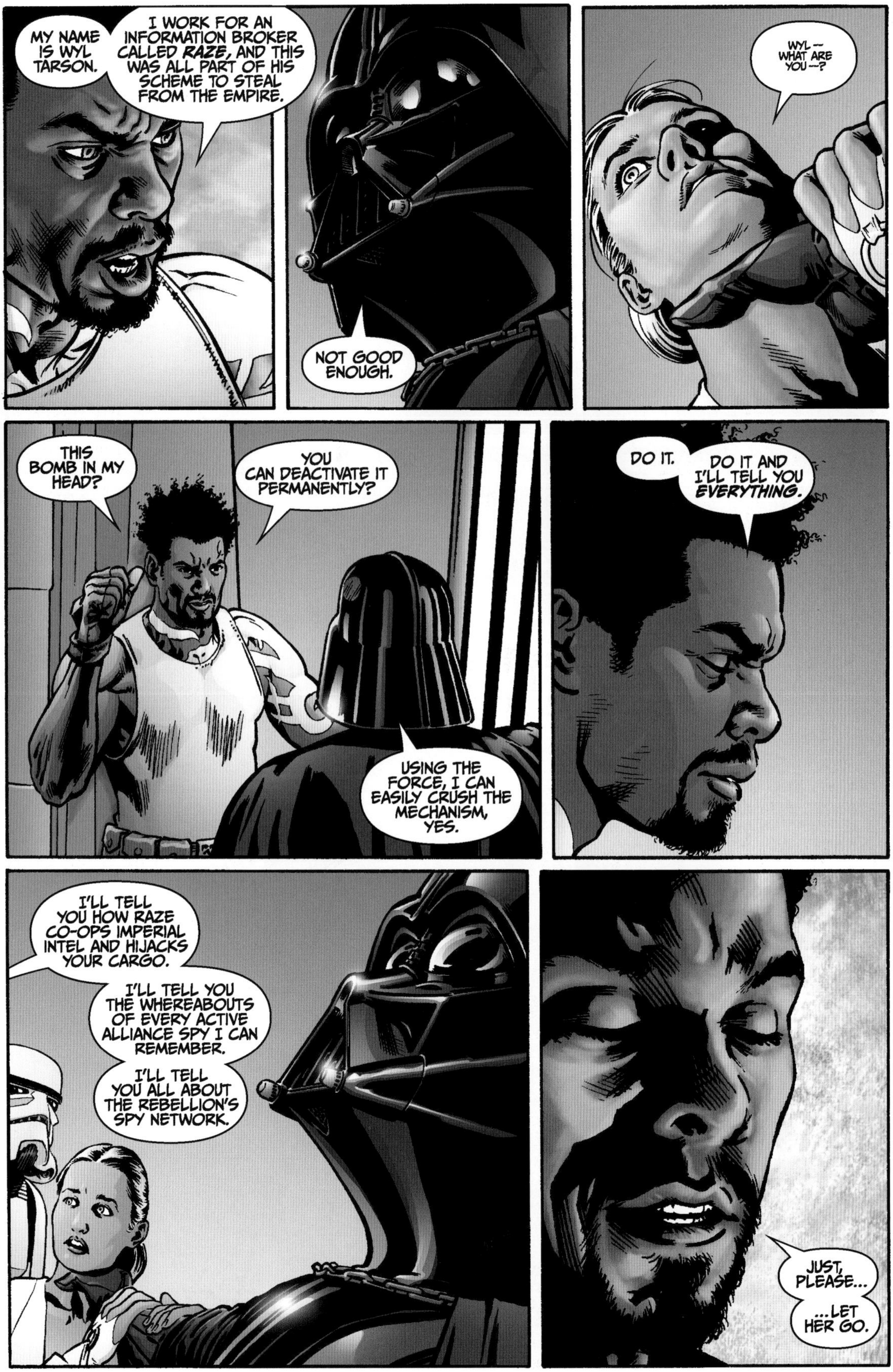
MY NAME IS WYL TARSON.
I WORK FOR AN INFORMATION BROKER CALLED RAZE, AND THIS WAS ALL PART OF HIS SCHEME TO STEAL FROM THE EMPIRE.
NOT GOOD ENOUGH.
WYL -- WHAT ARE YOU --?
THIS BOMB IN MY HEAD?
YOU CAN DEACTIVATE IT PERMANENTLY?
USING THE FORCE, I CAN EASILY CRUSH THE MECHANISM, YES.
DO IT.
DO IT AND I'LL TELL YOU EVERYTHING.
I'LL TELL YOU HOW RAZE CO-OPS IMPERIAL INTEL AND HIJACKS YOUR CARGO.
I'LL TELL YOU THE WHEREABOUTS OF EVERY ACTIVE ALLIANCE SPY I CAN REMEMBER.
I'LL TELL YOU ALL ABOUT THE REBELLION'S SPY NETWORK.
JUST, PLEASE...
...LET HER GO.

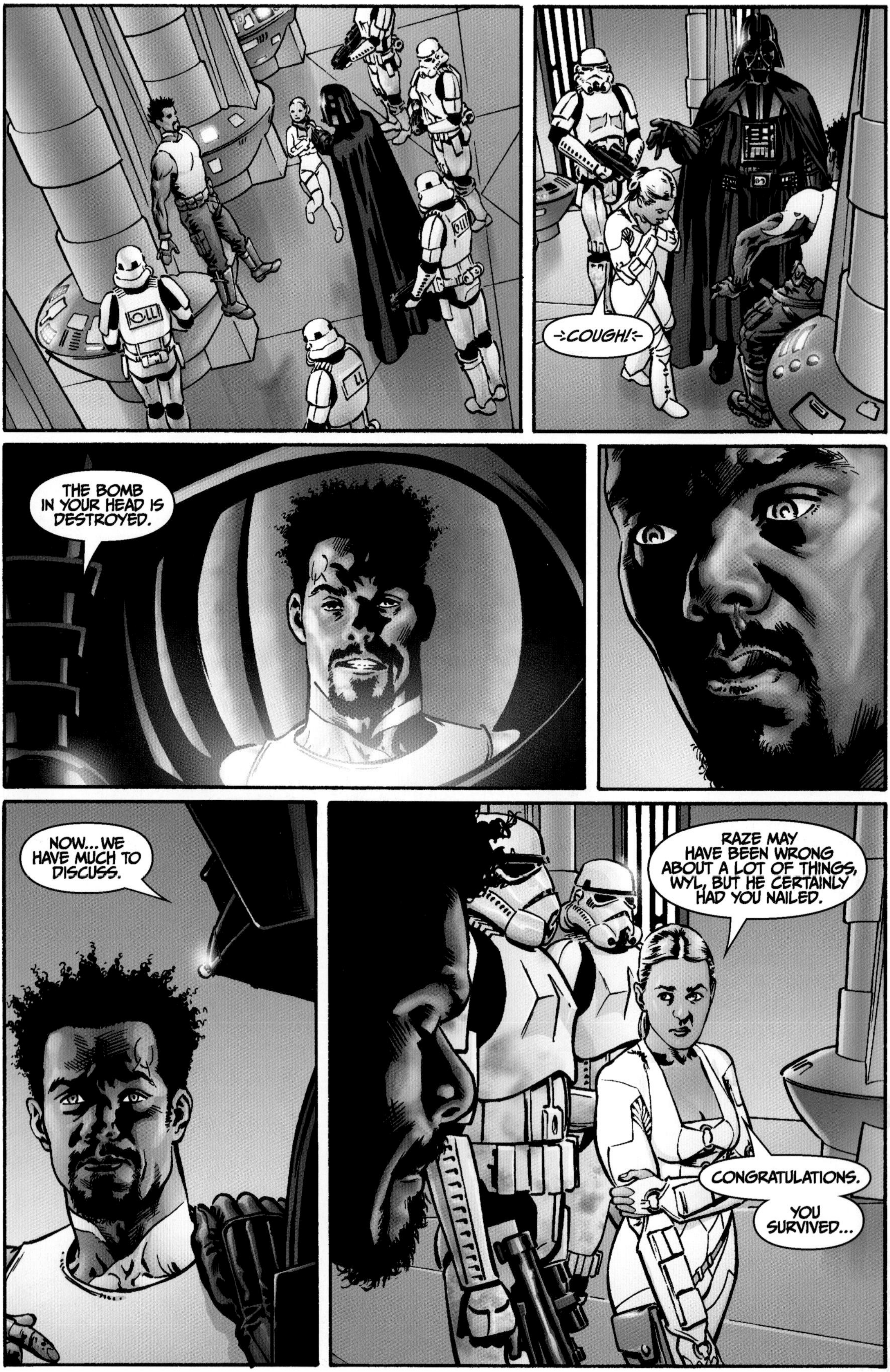
-COUGH!-
THE BOMB IN YOUR HEAD IS DESTROYED.
NOW... WE HAVE MUCH TO DISCUSS.
RAZE MAY HAVE BEEN WRONG ABOUT A LOT OF THINGS, WYL, BUT HE CERTAINLY HAD YOU NAILED.
CONGRATULATIONS.
YOU SURVIVED...

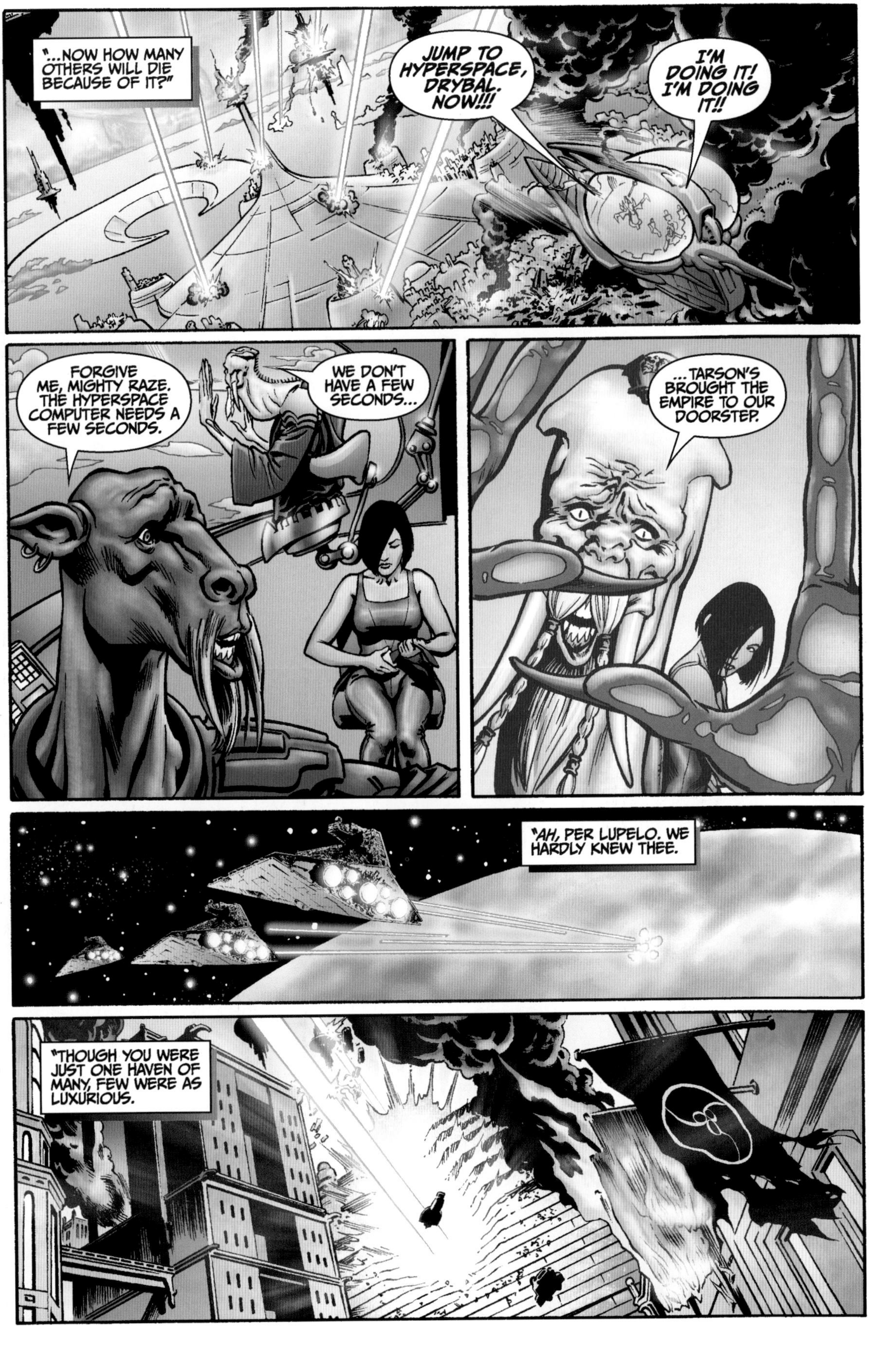
"...NOW HOW MANY OTHERS WILL DIE BECAUSE OF IT?"
JUMP TO HYPERSPACE, DRYBAL. NOW!!!
I'M DOING IT! I'M DOING IT!!
FORGIVE ME, MIGHTY RAZE. THE HYPERSPACE COMPUTER NEEDS A FEW SECONDS.
WE DON'T HAVE A FEW SECONDS...
...TARSON'S BROUGHT THE EMPIRE TO OUR DOORSTEP.
"AH, PER LUPELO. WE HARDLY KNEW THEE.
"THOUGH YOU WERE JUST ONE HAVEN OF MANY, FEW WERE AS LUXURIOUS.

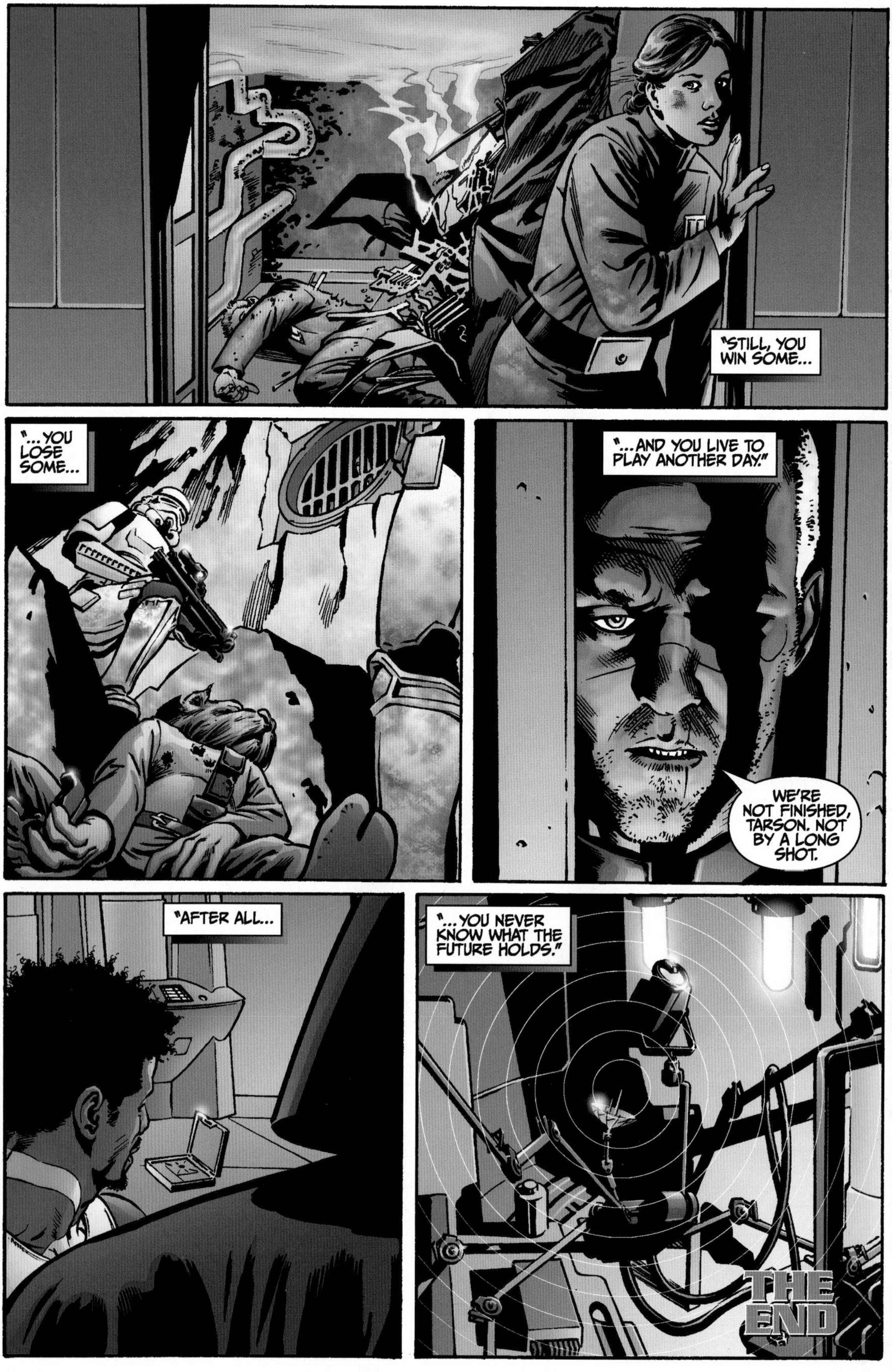
"STILL, YOU WIN SOME...
"...YOU LOSE SOME...
"...AND YOU LIVE TO PLAY ANOTHER DAY."
WE'RE NOT FINISHED, TARSON. NOT BY A LONG SHOT.
"AFTER ALL...
"...YOU NEVER KNOW WHAT THE FUTURE HOLDS."
THE END

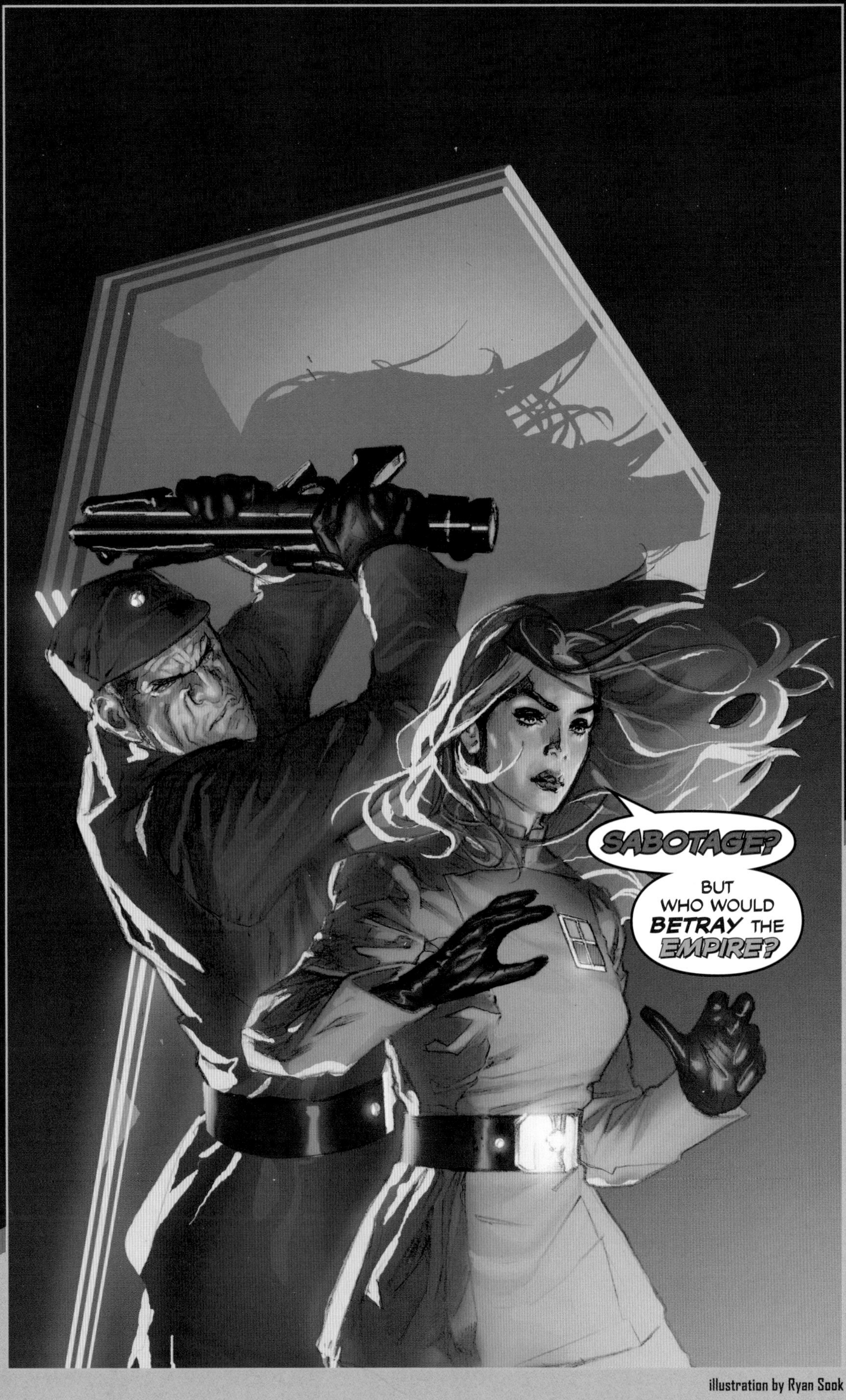
SABOTAGE?
BUT WHO WOULD BETRAY THE EMPIRE?

illustration by Ryan Sook

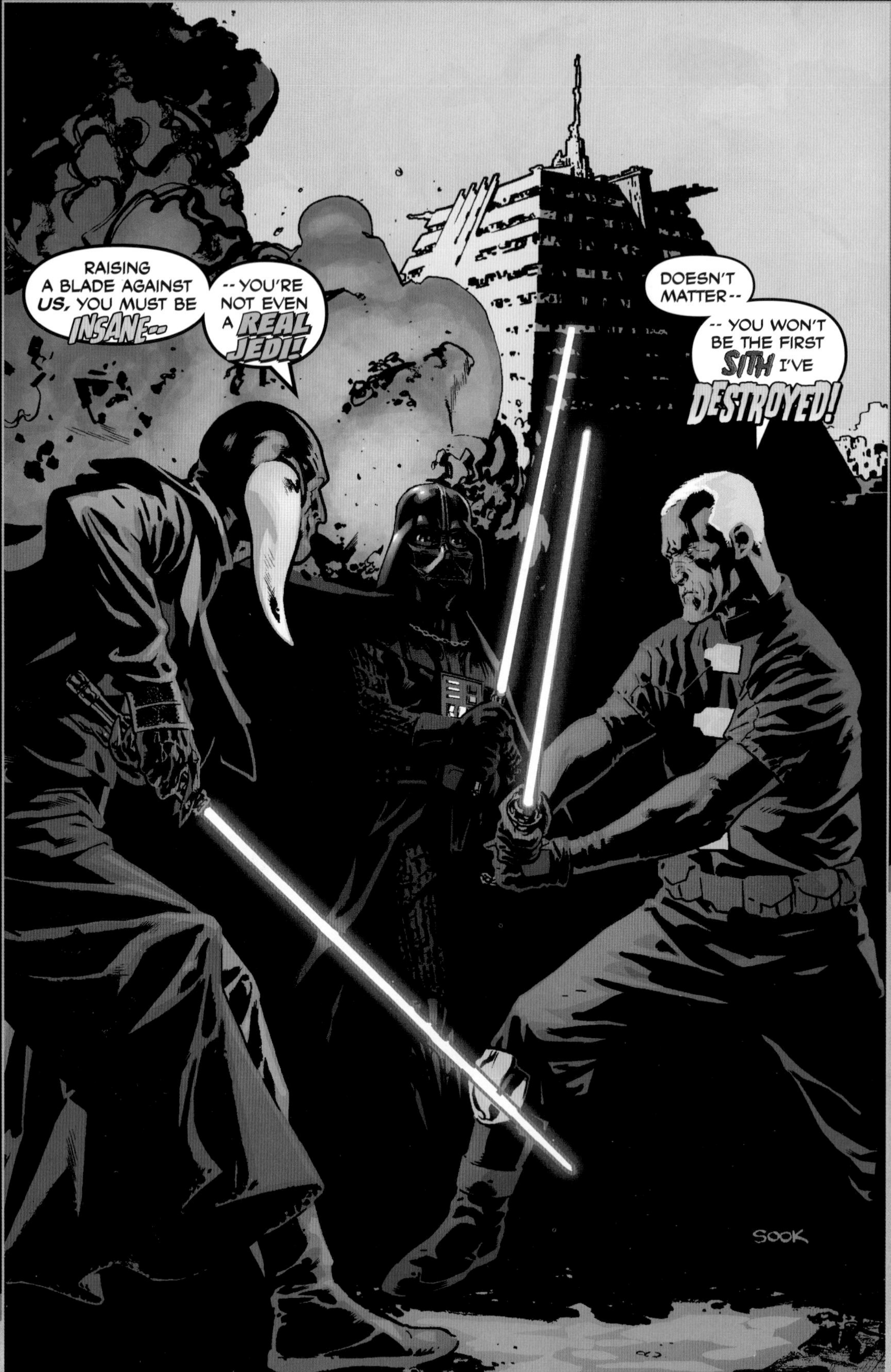
RAISING A BLADE AGAINST US, YOU MUST BE INSANE--
--YOU'RE NOT EVEN A REAL JEDI!
DOESN'T MATTER--
--YOU WON'T BE THE FIRST SITH I'VE DESTROYED!
SOOK

illustration by Ryan Sook and Dan Jackson